Caravan & Camping Holidays in Britain

2009

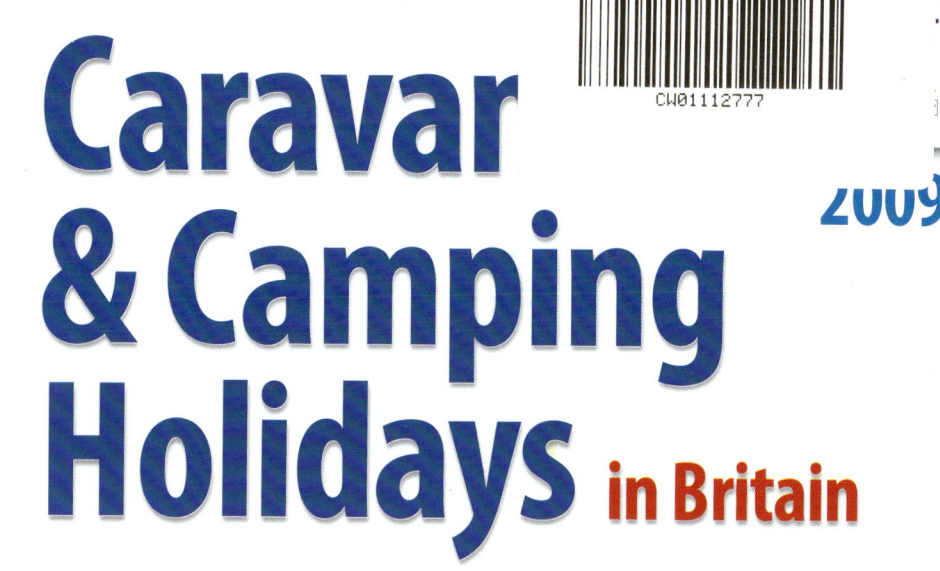

- Campsites and Caravan Parks
- Facilities fully listed

Cannich Caravan & Camping Park, Strathglass, Inverness-shire

© FHG Guides Ltd, 2009
ISBN 978-1-85055-415-8

Maps: ©MAPS IN MINUTES™ / Collins Bartholomew 2007

Typeset by FHG Guides Ltd, Paisley.
Printed and bound in China by Imago.

Distribution. Book Trade: ORCA Book Services, Stanley House,
3 Fleets Lane, Poole, Dorset BH15 3AJ
(Tel: 01202 665432; Fax: 01202 666219)
e-mail: mail@orcabookservices.co.uk
Published by FHG Guides Ltd., Abbey Mill Business Centre,
Seedhill, Paisley PA1 ITJ (Tel: 0141-887 0428 Fax: 0141-889 7204).
e-mail: admin@fhguides.co.uk

Guide to Caravan & Camping Holidays is published by FHG Guides Ltd,
part of Kuperard Group.

Cover design: FHG Guides
Cover Pictures: With thanks to
Woodlands Leisure Park, Dartmouth, Devon (see p 31)

Acknowledgements, Our thanks for pictures courtesy of:
Poole Tourism (p44), Eastbourne Borough Council (p70), Southend-on-Sea Borough Council (p79),
North East Lincolnshire Council, photo: Andy Tryner (p102), Shropshire Council (p105).

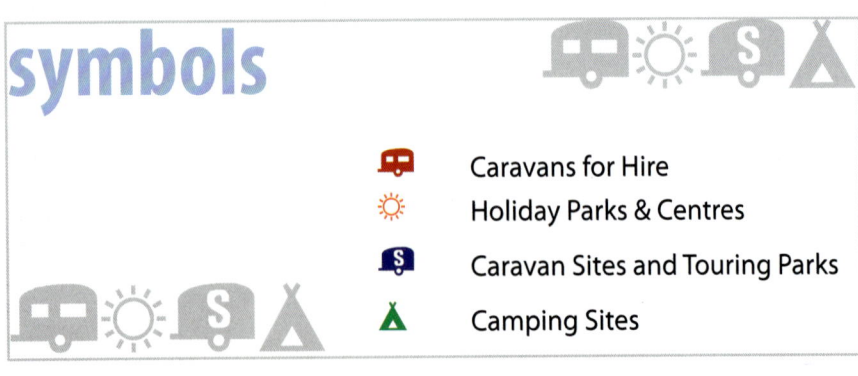

symbols

🚐	Caravans for Hire
☼	Holiday Parks & Centres
$	Caravan Sites and Touring Parks
▲	Camping Sites

Symbol	Meaning	Symbol	Meaning
	Electric hook-ups available		Facilities for disabled visitors
	Children's play area		Pets welcome
	Laundry facilities		Shop on site
	Licensed bar on site	W	Wifi access available

Contents

Editorial Section	2-10
Foreword	4
Tourist Board Ratings	180
Readers 'Offer Vouchers	205

SOUTH WEST ENGLAND
11

Cornwall and Isles of Scilly, Devon, Dorset, Gloucestershire, Somerset, Wiltshire

LONDON & SOUTH EAST ENGLAND
61

London, Berkshire, Buckinghamshire, Hampshire, Kent, East Sussex, West Sussex

EAST OF ENGLAND
75

Cambridgeshire, Essex, Hertfordshire, Norfolk, Suffolk

MIDLANDS
92

Derbyshire, Herefordshire, Leicestershire & Rutland, Lincolnshire, Nottinghamshire, Shropshire, Staffordshire, Warwickshire, Worcestershire, West Midlands

YORKSHIRE
114

East Yorkshire, North Yorkshire

NORTH EAST ENGLAND
124

Durham, Northumberland, Tyne & Wear

NORTH WEST ENGLAND
128

Cheshire, Cumbria, Lancashire,

SCOTLAND

Aberdeen, Banff & Moray	147
Angus & Dundee	149
Argyll & Bute	150
Ayrshire & Arran	155
Borders	158
Dumfries & Galloway	160
Edinburgh & Lothians	163
Highlands	166
Lanarkshire	173
Perth & Kinross	174
Stirling & The Trossachs	178
Scottish Islands	179

WALES

Anglesey & Gwynedd	182
North Wales	183
Carmarthenshire	192
Ceredigion	193
Pembrokeshire	194
Powys	196
South Wales	198

NORTHERN IRELAND
201

Antrim, Down, Fermanagh, Londonderry

REPUBLIC OF IRELAND
204

Kerry

Foreword

With the credit crunch beginning to bite we expect that many more people will opt to holiday at home in Britain rather than go to the expense of taking a trip abroad. Caravan and Camping holidays are often the first choice for those seeking an alternative and many of the Holiday Parks may have similar facilities to those foreign holiday venues, with swimming pools, beaches nearby, entertainment and shops, and eating facilities on site. As a long term holiday investment many people are opting for touring caravans, and find that the smaller sites and touring parks offer peace and tranquillity, variety and the opportunity to travel the length and breadth of the country.

The FHG Guide to Caravan & Camping Holidays 2009 also offers variety. Our selection covers England, Scotland, Wales and Ireland, and includes sites for tourers, static vans and holiday parks, which often cater for the camper as well.

ENQUIRIES AND BOOKINGS Give full details of dates (with an alternative), numbers and any special requirements. Ask about any points in the holiday description which are not clear and make sure that prices and conditions are clearly explained. You should receive confirmation in writing and a receipt for any deposit or advance payment.

CANCELLATIONS A holiday booking is a form of contract with obligations on both sides. If you have to cancel, give as much notice as possible. The longer the notice the better the chance that your host can replace your booking and therefore refund any payments. If the proprietor cancels in such a way that causes serious inconvenience, he may have obligations to you which have not been properly honoured. Take advice if necessary from such organisations as the Citizen's Advice Bureau, Consumer's Association, Trading Standards Office, Local Tourist Office, etc., or your own solicitor. It is possible to ensure against cancellation – brokers and insurance companies can advise you about this.

COMPLAINTS It's best if any problems can be sorted out at the start of your holiday. You should therefore try to raise any complaints on the spot. If you do not, or if the problem is not solved, you can contact the organisations mentioned above. You can also write to us. We will follow up the complaint with the advertiser – but we cannot act as intermediaries or accept responsibility for holiday arrangements.

FHG Guides Ltd. do not inspect accommodation and an entry in our guides does not imply a recommendation. However, our advertisers have signed their agreement to work for the holidaymaker's best interests and as their customer, you have the right to expect appropriate attention and service.

For popular locations, especially during the main holiday season, you should always book in advance. Please mention **The FHG Guide to Caravan and Camping Holidays** when you are making enquiries and bookings and don't forget to use our Readers' Offer Coupons (pages 205-234) if you're near any of the attractions which are kindly participating.

Anne Cuthbertson, **Editor**

A sign of excellence.
Just one of 200 superb Caravan Club Sites to choose from

Caravan Club Sites are renowned for their excellence. With most of those graded achieving 4 or 5 stars from VisitBritain, you can be sure of consistently high standards. From lakes or mountains to city or sea, there are some 200 quality Club Sites throughout Britain & Ireland to choose from.

With over 40 fabulous Club Sites open all year, why stay at home?

Whichever site you choose, you can be assured of excellent facilities and a friendly welcome from our Resident Wardens. Just look for the signs.

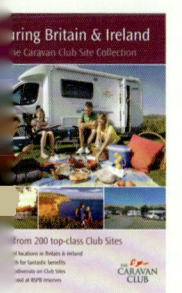

Broomfield Farm Caravan Club Site

Bunree Caravan Club Site

Burrs Country Park Caravan Club Site

Troutbeck Head Caravan Club Site

You don't have to be a member to stay on most Caravan Club Sites, but members save up to £7 per night on pitch fees!

Call today for your FREE Touring Britain & Ireland brochure on 0800 521 161 quoting FHG09 **or visit www.caravanclub.co.uk**

THE CARAVAN CLUB

The Caravan Club, East Grinstead House, East Grinstead, West Sussex RH19 1UA

Great Value Holiday Parks in Coast and Countryside Locations

Book online today for great value fun-filled family holidays from just £69 per family

TOURING BREAKS FROM £5 a night

WE WON'T BE BEATEN ON PRICE!

Park facilities can include:
- Heated pool
- Live family entertainment
- Family bar
- Kids' club
- Sky TV in club venue SKY SPORTS
- Wi-Fi internet access
- Restaurant/takeaway
- Children's play area

Facilities vary by park.

Looking for a touring park? - 8 of our parks also cater for you. Electric and non-electric pitches available.
Looking for quiet and relaxing or lively and fun?
Call the holiday hotline TODAY and choose a park to suit you.

SUFFOLK: Felixstowe Beach, Felixstowe
ESSEX: Clacton-on-Sea, St Osyth Beach, Seawick, Steeple Bay
KENT: Isle of Sheppey, Sheerness, Harts, Seaview, Alberta, Folkestone, New Beach, Marlie Farm
SUSSEX: Frenchman's Beach, Hastings, Winchelsea Sands
HAMPSHIRE: Solent Breezes, Chichester, Brighton
DORSET: Sandhills, Bournemouth, Lakeside, Coghurst Hall
DEVON: Peppermint, Exeter, Golden Sands, Torquay, Dawlish Sands, Waterside, Landscove, Riviera Bay, Plymouth

Also shown: Gloucester, Oxford, Swindon, Reading, LONDON, Bristol, Bath, Basingstoke, Salisbury

Go online and find out more about our fantastic holidays and touring.

CALL OUR HOLIDAY HOTLINE
0845 815 9797
or book online www.ParkHolidaysUK.com

PARK HOLIDAYS UK

Over 100 award-winning camp sites

The Camping and Caravanning Club
The Friendly Club

Hayfield Club Site

If you love camping as much as we do, you'll love staying on one of The Camping and Caravanning Club's 103 UK Club Sites. Each of our sites are in great locations and are an ideal base for exploring the UK.

There's just one thing: once you've discovered the friendly welcome, the excellent facilities and clean, safe surroundings, you'll probably want to join anyway!

To book your adventure or to join The Club call **0845 130 7633**
quoting code **2661** or visit
www.thefriendlyclub.co.uk

- More choice of highly maintained, regularly inspected sites
- Friendly sites that are clean and safe, so great for families
- Preferential rates – recoup your membership fee in just 6 nights' stay
- Reduced site fees for 55's and over and special deals for families
- Exclusive Member Services including specialist insurance and advice.

Hook-up to Haven for great value Caravan & Camping Breaks... Haven

Choose from 21 beautifully located Touring Parks throughout England, Scotland & Wales!

TOURING PITCHES SAVE UP TO 50%*

Facilities & fun to suit your needs...
- ✔ Well-maintained pitches
- ✔ Great on-site amenities
- ✔ 24-hour security
- ✔ Touring wardens
- ✔ Heated pools
- ✔ Kids' clubs
- ✔ Sports activities
- ✔ Round-the-clock family entertainment
- ✔ Much, much more

21 UK Parks

We Welcome: Motorhomes, Tourers, Tents, Trailer Tents

CALL OUR CENTRAL TOURING TEAM:
0871 230 1933 QUOTE TO_FHG

FOR MORE INFORMATION AND TO BOOK:
www.touringholidays.co.uk

caravan +camping

Terms & Conditions: Save up to 50% offer available during Spring/Autumn 2009 excluding School or Bank Holiday periods, subject to availability, please call for details. Only one offer per booking, offers cannot be combined with any other offer, discount or promotional voucher except for Freedom Trail discount. Please note that pitch types, activities, facilities and entertainment acts vary by Park and some are subject to a moderate extra charge, please check at time of booking. We reserve the right to withdraw this offer at any time. Pictures shown are for representational purposes only. Calls to the above number will cost no more than 10p per minute from a BT landline - calls from other networks may vary. Bourne Leisure Limited is registered in England, No. 04011660. 1 Park Lane, Hemel Hempstead, Hertfordshire, HP2 4YL.

GREEN WOOD PARKS

CONTACT US FOR FREE BROCHURE

HOLIDAY HOMES
Buy a home away from home, with space to grow your own garden, from a selection of new and used luxury holiday caravans.

IN THE COUNTRY
• Itchenor, Oxford, Thirsk, York •
Four superb parks dedicated to peace and quiet. Riverside, lakeside or just beautiful countryside. The choice is yours.
Hire Vans at all Parks.
Tourers and Tents also in North Yorkshire.
Head Office: Tel: 01243 514433 • Fax: 01243 513303
E-mail: greenwood.parks@virgin.net • www.greenwoodparks.com

Please note

All the information in this book is given in good faith in the belief that it is correct. However, the publishers cannot guarantee the facts given in these pages, neither are they responsible for changes in policy, ownership or terms that may take place after the date of going to press. Readers should always satisfy themselves that the facilities they require are available and that the terms, if quoted, still apply.

21 Great Holiday Parks

'21 fantastic locations throughout the UK for that perfect camping or caravanning break!'

All this is FREE ....
- Sparkling family entertainment
- Kid's clubs, shows & playgrounds
- Indoor & outdoor swimming pools
- Showers and washbasins
- Toilet facilities

Park Resorts

From only £5* per night

brochure line 08701 221 999 ~ bookings 0844 770 0326
www.park-resortstouring.com/fh Quote Ref: FH09

Park facilities may vary. Please see our website for further details.   *Based on a tent pitch Sun-Thurs in low season.

Looking for Holiday Accommodation?

FHG
KUPERARD

for details of hundreds of properties throughout the UK, visit our website

www.holidayguides.com

England and Wales • Counties

Counties shown on map:
NORTHUMBERLAND, TYNE & WEAR, DURHAM, CUMBRIA, ISLE OF MAN, NORTH YORKSHIRE, LANCASHIRE, WEST YORKSHIRE, EAST RIDING OF YORKSHIRE, GREATER MANCHESTER, S. YORKSHIRE, ISLE OF ANGLESEY, CONWY, CHESHIRE, DERBYSHIRE, NOTTINGHAMSHIRE, LINCOLNSHIRE, GWYNEDD, STAFFORDSHIRE, LEICESTERSHIRE, RUTLAND, NORFOLK, SHROPSHIRE, WEST MIDLANDS, CEREDIGION, POWYS, WORCESTERSHIRE, NORTHAMPTONSHIRE, CAMBRIDGESHIRE, SUFFOLK, HEREFORDSHIRE, WARWICKSHIRE, BEDFORDSHIRE, CARMARTHENSHIRE, PEMBROKESHIRE, GLOUCESTERSHIRE, BUCKINGHAMSHIRE, HERTFORDSHIRE, ESSEX, OXFORDSHIRE, GREATER LONDON, WILTSHIRE, SOMERSET, HAMPSHIRE, SURREY, KENT, DEVON, DORSET, WEST SUSSEX, EAST SUSSEX, CORNWALL, ISLE OF WIGHT

Unitary Authorities – England & Wales

1. Plymouth
2. Torbay
3. Poole
4. Bournemouth
5. Southampton
6. Portsmouth
7. Brighton & Hove
8. Medway
9. Thurrock
10. Southend
11. Slough
12. Windsor & Maidenhead
13. Bracknell Forest
14. Wokingham
15. Reading
16. West Berkshire
17. Swindon
18. Bath & Northeast Somerset
19. North Somerset
20. Bristol
21. South Gloucestershire
22. Luton
23. Milton Keynes
24. Peterborough
25. Leicester
26. Nottingham
27. Derby
28. Telford & Wrekin
29. Stoke-on-Trent
30. Warrington
31. Halton
32. Merseyside
33. Blackburn with Darwen
34. Blackpool
35. N.E. Lincolnshire
36. North Lincolnshire
37. Kingston-upon-Hull
38. York
39. Redcar & Cleveland
40. Middlesborough
41. Stockton-on-Tees
42. Darlington
43. Hartlepool

NORTH WALES
a. Denbighshire
b. Flintshire
c. Wrexham

SOUTH WALES
d. Swansea
e. Neath & Port Talbot
f. Bridgend
g. Rhondda Cynon Taff
h. Merthyr Tydfil
i. Vale of Glamorgan
j. Cardiff
k. Caerphilly
l. Blaenau Gwent
m. Torfaen
n. Newport
o. Monmouthshire

Cornwall

SOUTH WEST ENGLAND 11

HOLIDAY PARKS & CENTRES

CORNWALL. St Ives Bay Holiday Park, Upton Towans, Hayle TR27 5BH (0800 317713).
The park on the beach. St Ives Bay Holiday Park is set in sand dunes which run down to its own sandy beach. Many units have superb sea views. There is a large indoor pool and 2 clubs with FREE entertainment on the Park.
www.stivesbay.co.uk

symbols

- ☼ Holiday Parks & Centres
- 🚐 Caravans for Hire
- $ Caravan Sites and Touring Parks
- ▲ Camping Sites

12 SOUTH WEST ENGLAND

Cornwall
Bodmin, Bude

Lanarth

Touring Caravan Park (nine-and-a-half acres), country setting, in landscaped fields and gardens. Easy access on A39, at St Kew Highway, between Wadebridge four miles and Camelford six miles. On site, toilet block, swimming pool and hotel with licensed bar and restaurant. Dogs are welcome but must be on lead at all times (dog walking area). Caravan storage available. Some pitches have electricity, water and water disposal.
Terms £10 to £12, pitch with two adults.

**St Kew Highway
Bodmin, Cornwall PL30 3EE
Tel:01208 841215**

Hedley Wood Caravan & Camping Park
Bridgerule (Near Bude), Holsworthy, Devon EX22 7ED
Tel: 01288 381404 • Fax: 01288 382011

16 acre woodland family-run site with outstanding views, where you can enjoy a totally relaxing holiday with a laid-back atmosphere, sheltered and open camping areas. Just 10 minutes' drive from the beaches, golf courses, riding stables and shops.

On site facilities include: Children's Adventure Areas, Bar, Clubroom, Shop, Laundry, Meals and all amenities. Free Hot Showers/Water. **Nice dogs/pets are very welcome. Daily kennelling facility. Dog walks/nature trail.**
Static caravans for hire. Caravan storage available. **Open all year.**
Visit our website: www.hedleywood.co.uk or write or phone for comprehensive brochure

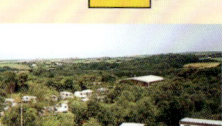

Budemeadows Touring Park

Widemouth Bay,
Bude, Cornwall. EX23 0NA
☎ 01288 361646 📠 08707 064825

A friendly family-run site in landscaped surroundings just 3 miles from Bude and a mile from Widemouth Bay.

✓ Heated Pool
✓ Children's Playgrounds
✓ Grumpy Pete's Bar
✓ Licensed Shop
✓ Laundrette
✓ Free Hot Water and Showers

Please ring or e-mail for a brochure.
Pool, bar and shop open mid and high season

Open all year
✉ holiday@budemeadows.com
🖱 www.budemeadows.com

Cornwall — SOUTH WEST ENGLAND 13
Bude, Coverack

Upper Lynstone
Caravan and Camping Park

Bude, Cornwall EX23 0LP
Tel: 01288 352017 • Fax: 01288 359034
e-mail: reception@upperlynstone.co.uk • www.upperlynstone.co.uk

Upper Lynstone is a quiet family-run park situated just three-quarters of a mile from Bude's town centre on the coastal road to Widemouth Bay. Bude's shops, beaches with outdoor pool, bars and restaurants are all within walking distance.

Enjoy the breathtaking beauty of the Cornish Coast from the footpath that leads from our park. The park has modern caravans for hire and spacious camping and touring fields with electric hook-ups. Facilities include a small but well equipped shop, free showers, laundry room, and children's play area. Calor and Camping Gas stockists. Well-behaved dogs welcome.

We have four and six berth caravans at Upper Lynstone. All have mains services, colour TV, fridge etc. The caravans are well spaced with plenty of room for you to park. They have splendid views to distant villages and moors. Enjoy our NEW 35ft, 3-bedroom static caravans with panoramic views, designed to sleep six in comfort.

WIDEMOUTH BAY

Overlooking beautiful Widemouth Bay, our 50 acre Park is only a few minutes from a safe sandy beach

★ Indoor Heated Pool ★ Children's Club ★ Safe Playground ★ Electric Hook-ups
★ Laundrette ★ Shop/Takeaway ★ Club Nightly ★ Entertainments
★ FREE Hot Showers ★ FREE Awning Space
★ FREE Entertainment ★ FREE Licensed Club

JOHN FOWLER HOLIDAY PARKS

TEL: 01271 866766
for bookings & details of our great deals, or visit
WWW.JOHNFOWLERHOLIDAYS.COM
DEPT AA, John Fowler Holidays, Marlborough Rd, Ilfracombe EX34 8PF

Little Trevothan • Coverack • Cornwall TR12 6SD

Set in the heart of the beautiful Lizard Peninsula, Little Trevothan provides the perfect location for a relaxing holiday. Near the picturesque fishing village of Coverack, this unspoilt corner of Cornwall offers glorious beaches and spectacular walks. A range of water sports is available locally. The beautiful Helford River, with its hidden villages and creeks (including Frenchman's Creek) and the renowned Seal Sanctuary, are within easy reach. This family site offers excellent facilities, including a shop and playground. Well behaved pets are accepted by prior arrangement. Fully equipped four/six berth caravans for hire. Tents and tourers welcome. Please contact Rachel & Sean Flynn. • **Tel: 01326 280260**
e-mail: sales@littletrevothan.co.uk
www.littletrevothan.co.uk

14 SOUTH WEST ENGLAND

Cornwall
Crackington Haven, Helston

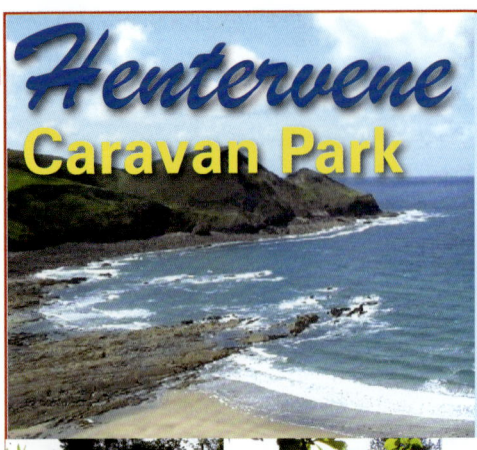

Hentervene Caravan Park

Peaceful family-run caravan park two miles from Crackington Haven beach and glorious coastal footpath. Positively no bar, disco or bingo; just beautiful countryside. Short drive from Bodmin Moor, fine surfing beaches like Widemouth Bay, the Camel Estuary for sailing, windsurfing, cycling and within easy reach of Padstow, Polzeath, Rock, etc. Many attractive country pubs locally, plenty of attractions for children.

Luxury caravans and pine lodge to let. Caravan sales. Pets welcome – dog walk on site and dog-friendly woods, beaches etc. within a 5 to 10 minute drive.

**Hentervene Caravan Park, Crackington Haven
Near Bude EX23 0LF • 01840 230365
e-mail: contact@hentervene.co.uk • www.hentervene.co.uk**

Franchis Holiday Park • Helston • Cornwall

A warm welcome awaits you at Franchis, centrally positioned on the Lizard Peninsula, where beaches, coves and cliff walks abound. Touring and camping or self-catering in our caravans or bungalows all surrounded by woodland and farmland. Four acres of closely mown grass. Electric hook-ups, hot showers, small shop. No entertainment or bar. Dogs welcome. Wreck and reef diving nearby.

**Cury Cross Lanes, Mullion, Helston TR12 7AZ
Tel: 01326 240301
e-mail: enquiries@franchis.co.uk
www.franchis.co.uk**

BOSCREGE
CARAVAN & CAMPING PARK

★ Special out of season offers
★ Award winning quiet family park close to local beaches and attractions with no bar or clubs
★ Static caravans available for holidays
★ Touring caravans ★ Tents & motor homes
★ Free showers ★ Microwave facilities ★ Games room
★ Child's play area ★ Laundry ★ Pets welcome

For Brochure Telephone:
01736 762231
www.caravanparkcornwall.com
enquiries@caravanparkcornwall.com

Cornwall

Helston, Looe

Lower Polladras Touring Park

Carleen, near Helston, Cornwall TR13 9NX

An attractive, peaceful and friendly, family run park.
Just 10 minutes from the nearest beach, Spotless facilities,
free showers. Dog exercising and wildlife walks.
All year caravan storage. Low season special deals.

Tel: 01736 762220
e-mail: lowerpolladras@btinternet.com
www.lower-polladras.co.uk

Trelay Farm Park

A small, peaceful, friendly, family-run site. It is quiet, uncommercialised and surrounded by farmland. The park lies on a gentle south-facing slope offering wide views of open countryside. Excellent new facilities include hot showers/launderette and disabled suite with wheelchair access. The three-acre camping field is licensed for 55 tourers/tents etc. Good access, generous pitches, hook ups. In adjoining area (1.5 acres) are 20 holiday caravans in a garden-like setting. The nearby village of Pelynt has shops, Post Office, restaurants, pub. Looe and Polperro are both just three miles away. The renowned Eden Project is 12 miles west. Luxury caravans for sale and rental. Pets welcome. New for 2008 – Child's Play Area.

Pelynt, Looe PL13 2JX
Tel: 01503 220 900
e-mail: stay@trelay.co.uk
www.trelay.co.uk

Looking for holiday accommodation?

for details of hundreds of properties
throughout the UK including
comprehensive coverage of all areas of Scotland try:

www.holidayguides.com

Tregoad Park

A unique Cornish 4 star holiday experience

Set in 55 acres of rolling countryside well away from the road and with stunning views of Looe Island and the sea beyond Tregoad Park offers the ideal location for both fun filled family holidays and quiet relaxing out of season breaks. Close to the pretty fishing town of Looe and beaches we can guarantee you a beautiful location, all the facilities and a very warm and friendly welcome.

We have 190 large flat & terraced pitches of which 60 are hardstanding ideal for touring caravans, motorhomes and tents. Most are southerly facing and all pitches have electric hook-up.

There are ample water and waste points around the park and access roads are tarmac so getting on and off your pitch is easy.

The toilet and shower facilities are modern, clean and free of charge and there is a launderette at the lower block. The reception building contains a well stocked shop and visitor information centre together with internet access point and post box.

- Well stocked shop • Boules Area • Table Tennis
- Crazy Golf Course • Secure Kids play park
- Heated outdoor swimming pool (May-September)
- Pool Tables • Air Hockey • Video Games
- Disco and live entertainment (July-August only)
- Modern toilets buildings with free showers
- Family bathrooms • Wash up Sinks
- Disabled wet room. • Launderette
- Ball Sports and Kite Field • Dog Walk Area
- Licenced conservatory bar open in mid and high season. • Kids future space adventure play structure.
- Fast food takeaway open in mid season.
- Restaurant open in high season only, local pubs and restaurants available.
- Dolby Widescreen Cinema
- 55 acres of park to explore • Carp fishing lakes

Tregoad Park, St Martin, Near Looe, Cornwall PL13 1PB
Tel: 01503 262718 • Fax: 01503 264477 • e-mail: info@tregoadpark.co.uk
www.tregoadpark.co.uk

Cornwall

SOUTH WEST ENGLAND

Mawgan Porth, Newquay

Marver Holiday Park
Mawgan Porth, Near Newquay TR8 4BB

Small, quiet family-run site. Offering beautiful views of the Lanherne valley. Approximately 150 yards from the beach, which is excellent for children, surfers and fishing. Only five miles from Newquay and eight miles from the historic fishing port of Padstow. The site offers chalets and static caravans for hire and a level campsite suitable for caravans, motor homes and tents. On site there is a toilet and shower block, sauna and launderette, in which there is a payphone, washing up facilities and a freezer for the use of our guests. Nearby fishing, surfing, horse riding, golf and shops, also good public houses, surf board and wet suit hire.

Tel: 01637 860493
e-mail: familyholidays@aol.com

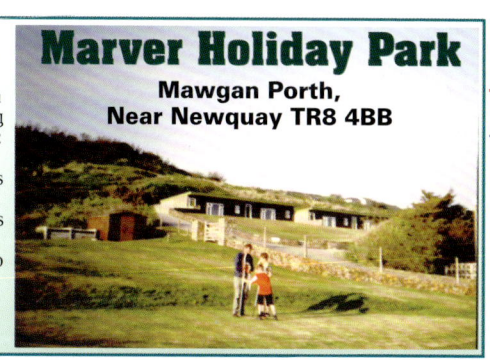

WATERGATE BAY TOURING PARK

- HEATED OUTDOOR POOL
- CAFETERIA · LAUNDERETTE
- INDIVIDUAL PITCHES
- NO OVERCROWDING
- LEVEL SITE · ELECTRIC HOOKUPS
- FULLY LICENSED CLUBHOUSE
- AMUSEMENT ARCADE
- KIDS PLAY AREA
- SELF SERVICE SHOP
- FREE EVENING ENTERTAINMENT
- FREE COURTESY MINIBUS TO THE BEACH (DURING PEAK SEASON)

www.watergatebaytouringpark.co.uk
email@watergatebaytouringpark.co.uk

TELEPHONE 01637 860387
FAX 0871 661 7549

Treloy Touring Park

A friendly family site for touring caravans, tents and motor homes, just off the A3059 Newquay Road. A central location for touring the whole of Cornwall. Facilities include heated swimming pool, licensed bar/family room, entertainment, cafe/takeaway, shop, laundry, FREE showers, private washing cubicles, baby bathrooms, indoor dishwashing sinks, TV and games rooms, adventure playground. Facilities for the disabled. Electric hook-ups.

Coarse fishing nearby. Own superb 9-hole Par 32 golf course with concessionary green fees for our guests. Terms £8 to £15 per night for two adults, car and caravan. Please write or telephone for free colour brochure.

Treloy Touring Park • Newquay TR8 4JN
Tel: 01637 872063/876279
www.treloy.co.uk

18 SOUTH WEST ENGLAND — **Cornwall**
Newquay

Quarryfield
Holiday Park

quarryfield@crantockcaravans.orangehome.co.uk
www.quarryfield.co.uk

Superbly situated overlooking beautiful Crantock Bay and the River Gannel estuary, park with fully equipped modern caravans for hire, and separate level camping field.

Contact: **MRS WINN, TRETHERRAS, NEWQUAY, CORNWALL TR7 2RE**
Tel & Fax: **01637 872792**

Bar • Pool • Children's Play Area

Trevarrian
HOLIDAY PARK

Tel: **01637 860381**
e-mail: holidays@trevarrian.co.uk
www.trevarrian.co.uk

Mawgan Porth, Newquay, Cornwall TR8 4AQ

Situated in quiet countryside close to fabulous beaches on the North coast of Cornwall between the bays of Mawgan Porth and Watergate Bay, Trevarrian Holiday Park has been owned and run by the Phillips family for over 35 years. Superb facilities include heated pool, self-service shop, launderette, TV/video and games room, children's play area, tennis court and pitch and putt. Free evening entertainment during peak season. "Stimbles" with club licence, bar snacks. Individual pitches, electric hook-ups available, modern toilets and hot showers.

No overcrowding, even at the busiest time of year, spacious pitches allow more privacy and comfort. Three fields are linked by well illuminated roads.

Cornwall's vast number of attractions are also within easy reach. Trevarrian Holiday Park caters exclusively for families and couples.

Write or phone for free colour brochure.

Cornwall
Padstow

Trevean Farm
St Merryn, Padstow PL28 8PR

Small, pleasant site close to several sandy beaches with good surfing and lovely, golden sands. Splendid sea views. Riding school and golf club within 2 miles. Village shops one mile. Sea and river fishing nearby. Three static six-berth luxury caravans with cooker, fridge, mains water supply, flush toilet, shower and digital TV. Modern toilet/shower block with free showers. New family room with disabled facilities. Electric hook-ups. Pay phone, children's play area and small shop(Whitsun to September) on-site. Pets permitted in tents and tourers but not in static caravans. Weekly rates for static vans from £175 to £475 according to season. Touring caravans and tents welcome from £8 to £12 per night. Open Easter to October.

Tel: 01841 520772 • e-mail: trevean.info@virgin.net

Harlyn Sands HOLIDAY PARK
Family owned, family run for families

★ **STRICTLY FAMILIES ONLY** ★

Enjoy a good old family Bucket and Spade Holiday on this golden sandy beach. Miles of coastal walks and award-winning waters. Top class family entertainment*, immaculate luxurious accommodation.
Fish and Chippy, Arcade. Children's Play Park, Kids' Club mornings, afternoons and evenings.
On-site Shop, Launderette, Shower Block, Electric Hook-Ups.

SUPER SPLASH FUN POOL
with toddlers' pool, flume and rapids**

Situated right on Trevose Head, 3 miles from Padstow, 12 miles from Newquay, only 30 minutes from the Eden Project.

Lighthouse Road, Trevose Head, Padstow, Cornwall PL28 8SQ
e-mail: harlyn@freenet.co.uk
www.harlynsands.co.uk

RING OUR BROCHURE HOTLINE: 01841 520720

*main season; during quiet times limited services available.** small charges apply; restrictions apply for non-swimmers.

The Padstow to Rock ferry

SOUTH WEST ENGLAND

Cornwall

Penzance, Perranporth

Bone Valley Holiday Park

Situated in a pretty valley, ideal for exploring the countryside and coast of West Cornwall, this small, family-run park is surrounded by mature hedges and trees. There is also a pretty stream running along the park. We are located approx. ¾ mile from the centre of Penzance, in the village of Heamoor which has shops, a pub and a regular bus service.

17 pitches (some hardstanding) • Pitches for tents • Electric hook-ups available • Static Caravans, fully equipped • Budget Caravans
On-site facilities include: showers, baby changing facility, kitchen/laundry room (microwave, electric kettle etc), shop, campers' lounge with colour TV, public telephone, free ice pack service, chemical disposal, gas and Camping Gaz, BBQ loan.

Please contact Mr & Mrs Ward • Tel & Fax: 01736 360313

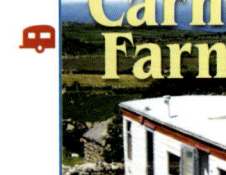

Bone Valley Holiday Park
Heamoor, Penzance TR20 8UJ
www.bonevalleyholidaypark.co.uk

Carne Farm

is situated on the North Cornish Coast, one mile from the nearest beach at Portherras Cove. It is excellent for walking, close to coastal footpath and with climbing nearby. Visitors are only six miles from Penzance, eight miles from St Ives and two miles from the nearest village shop, pubs and restaurants at Pendeen. The spacious eight-berth caravan is located in the field above the farmhouse, with fenced lawn and garden furniture, and has lovely views of fields, moorland and sea. It has a double bedroom, twin bedroom/cot, shower and toilet. It is equipped with electricity, fridge, full sized cooker, fire and hot and cold water, duvets, pillows and kitchen equipment. Television. Linen provided. Visitors welcome on the farm • Babysitting available • Basic Camping available. *Ring for details* • *Rates: from £120 to £220.*

C. Hichens, Carne Cottage, Morvah, Pendeen, Penzance TR19 7TT
Tel: 01736 788529 • Mobile: 07733 486347
• e-mail: andrewvlh@btopenworld.com

HOLIDAY PARKS & CENTRES

PERRANPORTH. Perran Sands Holiday Park, Perranporth.
Famous for its top surfing action, Perran Sands is situated near the ever-popular resort of Newquay and plays host to a wide variety of sports activities and entertainment facilities for the whole family to enjoy. From heated indoor and outdoor FunPools to archery, fencing and judo, there's something for everyone. If these sound too much like hard work, why not visit the awesome Eden Project or explore the enchanting Tintagel Castle – they're within easy driving distance. Kick back and relax in the knowledge of first rate Touring facilities and on-site amenities and let Perran Sands become your Touring holiday hot-spot. **See also Colour Advertisement.**
Call our UK Central Team: 0871 230 1933 (open 7 days, 9am-9pm) or book on-line (quote: TO_FHG) www.touringholidays.co.uk
• Great for Groups! Just book 5 or more holiday homes for extra benefits and savings.
Visit www.havengroups.co.uk or call 0871 230 1911.

---

symbols

- ☼ Holiday Parks & Centres
- 🚐 Caravans for Hire
- $ Caravan Sites and Touring Parks
- ⛺ Camping Sites

Cornwall
Polzeath

SOUTH WEST ENGLAND 21

www.polzeath camping.co.uk

North Cornwall camping at its best

Two Great Campsites in One Great Location

Tristram caravan & campsite

Tristram is one of the closest campsites to the beach in the whole of Cornwall. It caters for both camping and caravans and has stunning views of Polzeath and has brilliant modern facilities.

For more details call:
01208 862215
or email:
info@tristramcampsite.co.uk

for photos and information on the campsites visit www.polzeathcamping.co.uk

SouthWinds caravan & campsite

Many families love Southwinds because it is so quiet and peaceful. It has beautiful panoramic sea and rural views and is only half a mile from the beach.

for more details call: 01208 863267
or email: info@southwindscamping.co.uk
or visit our web site at: www.polzeathcamping.co.uk

AA

MEMBER 2009
Visit Cornwall southwesttourism

SOUTH WEST ENGLAND

Cornwall
Redruth

Lanyon Caravan & Camping Park

For those wanting a memorable holiday look no further. We have lots to offer you.
Superb central location surrounded by beautiful countryside.
A range of caravans to suit all pockets. Indoor heated pool. All day games room.
Bar/ Restaurant/Takeaway/Free entertainment in high season. Play area.
Three upgraded toilet/bath/shower blocks. Launderette/dish washing facility/free hot water.
Spacious level pitches and short grass.
Best of all, you will be looked after by caring resident family. Pets welcome.
A real gem of a park.

**Mr & Mrs J Reilly, Lanyon Caravan and Camping Park,
Four Lanes, Redruth TR16 6LP**

Tel: 01209 313474 • Fax: 01209 313422
www.lanyonholidaypark.co.uk

Globe Vale Holiday Park
Radnor, Redruth, Cornwall TR16 4BH

Globe Vale is a quiet countryside park situated close to the town of Redruth and the main A30. There are panoramic views across green fields to the coast; 10 minutes' drive to the nearest beach. Campers/tourers; static caravans for hire, and also plots available if you wish to buy your own new static holiday home. Facilities on site include fully serviced pitches, electric hook-ups, modern shower/toilet block, launderette and chemical disposal. Licensed bar with games room. Breakfast/evening meals served. There is also a children's play area, and open spaces for ball games. We are happy to accept pets on site at extra charge. Caravan storage available.

Contact Paul and Louise Owen on 01209 891183
e-mail: info@globevale.co.uk • www.globevale.co.uk

symbols

- ☀ Holiday Parks & Centres
- 🚐 Caravans for Hire
- $ Caravan Sites and Touring Parks
- ⛺ Camping Sites

Wheal Rose
Caravan & Camping Park

A secluded, 6-acre family-run touring park, central for all West Cornwall. Adjacent to the park is Mineral Tramway popular with walkers and cyclists. The park consists of 50 level, grassed pitches with electrical hook-ups. Spotlessly clean, purpose-built shower/toilet block, shop, children's play area, TV/games room, laundry and disabled facilities.

HEATED OPEN AIR SWIMMING POOL

Prices from £9.00 per night. Open March to December.

Scorrier, Redruth TR16 5DD
Tel/Fax: 01209 891496

e-mail: les@whealrosecaravanpark.co.uk
www.whealrosecaravanpark.co.uk

PLEASE CONTACT FOR SPECIAL OFFERS

24 SOUTH WEST ENGLAND

Cornwall
Redruth, St Agnes

TEHIDY HOLIDAY PARK

Harris Mill, Illogan, Redruth, Cornwall TR16 4JQ

Welcome to one of Cornwall's finest small, family-owned 4 Star Parks

Clean, modern, well equipped facilities. Free showers, laundry, dish washing room, play area, games room and shop. Nestled in the heart of a wooded valley and a natural haven for wildlife. Near broad sandy beaches, hidden coves and the crystal clear ocean. An ideal base for exploring both the rugged North coast or the gentle South. Walks and buses from site. Something for everyone - beaches, surfing, cycling, walking, gardens, picturesque fishing villages, easy access to all the major attractions.

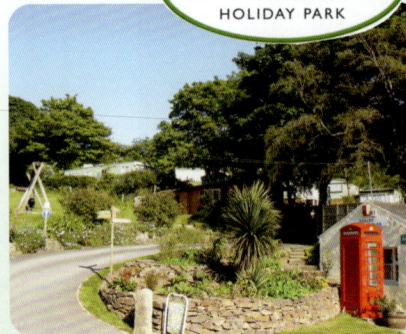

TEHIDY HOLIDAY PARK

2007 David Bellamy Conservation Award SILVER

Holiday Park of the Year Award 2008

Telephone: 01209 216489
www.tehidy.co.uk

Chiverton Park

- Caravan Holiday Homes
- Touring & Camping
- Families & Couples
- Pets Welcome
- Exclusive leisure facility:
- Gym, Sauna & Steamroom
- Shop • Laundry room
- Games room
- Children's play area
- Multi-service hook-ups
- Satellite TV in all units
- No club, bar or disco

Set in the heart of Cornish countryside, yet only a short distance from superb beaches, this spacious, well-run park offers peace and relaxation in a delightful rural setting. Holiday homes are fully equipped (except linen, which may be hired).

Chiverton Park, Blackwater, Truro TR4 8HS • 01872 560667
info@chivertonpark.co.uk • www.chivertonpark.co.uk

---

4 very different parks in Devon & Cornwall

"Own or Hire a Caravan or Luxury Lodge..."

Motorhome, Tourer and Tent pitches also available.

Tel: 01837 680100
FREE colour brochure with **Special Offers**

Award winning coast & country parks

SURF BAY LEISURE
QUALITY HOLIDAY PARKS

www.surfbayholidays.co.uk

ROSE AWARD GOLD

...on one of our parks"

Cornwall
St Austell, St Ives

SOUTH WEST ENGLAND 25

Court Farm

Set in 30 acres of peaceful pasture land, with 4 acres designated for touring caravans and tents, to a limit of 20 pitches (between 50 and 100 pitches in August), with 16 EHUs.

The shower block has free hot showers, flush toilets, laundry facility, freezer, and dishwashing area. There is a chemical disposal point.

We have a small coarse fishing lake, and an astronomical telescope for star-gazing, lectures by arrangement.

Centrally based for beaches and all of Cornwall's attractions; the Eden Project and the Lost Gardens of Heligan are each 6 miles away.

Court Farm Caravan and Camping
St Stephen, St Austell PL26 7LE

e-mail: truscott@ctfarm.freeserve.co.uk • www.courtfarmcornwall.co.uk

Tel & Fax: 01726 823684

Bill & Anne Truscott and Simon & Lisa Palmer

From £9.50 to £22.50 per night based on unit size.

Small and welcoming, Hellesveor is an approved farm site situated just one mile from the sweeping beaches and town centre of St Ives. Located on the Land's End road and only five minutes from the bus route for touring the dramatic landscape of West Cornwall and taking spectacular countryside walks.

Hellesveor Caravan and Camping Site
Hellesveor Farm, St Ives TR26 3AD

Laundry facilities on site. Special terms for early and late season.
Campers and touring caravans welcome. Static Caravans for hire. Electrical hook-ups.
Dogs allowed under strict control.
Shop, pub, restaurant, indoor heated pool, tennis courts, fishing, horse riding, pony trekking, golf course, bowling greens and leisure centre all nearby.

SAE for further details.

• SHORT BREAKS - TELEPHONE FOR AVAILABILITY •

Contact G & H Rogers Tel: 01736 795738
www.caravancampingsites.co.uk/cornwall/hellesveor

26 SOUTH WEST ENGLAND

Cornwall

Truro

Summer Valley Touring Park
Shortlanesend, Truro TR4 9DW

Situated just two miles from Truro, Cornwall's cathedral city, and ideally placed as a centre for touring all parts of Cornwall. This quiet, small, secluded site is only one-and-a-half miles from the main A30 and its central situation is advantageous for North Cornwall's beautiful surfing beaches and rugged Atlantic coast or Falmouth's quieter and placid fishing coves. Horse riding, fishing and golf are all available within easy distance. This compact site is personally supervised by the owners. Facilities include a toilet block with free hot water, washing cubicles, showers, shaving points, launderette, iron, hairdryer, etc; caravan electric hook-ups; children's play area. Shop with dairy products, groceries, bread, confectionery, toys, Calor/Camping gas.

Mr and Mrs C.R. Simpkins • Tel: 01872 277878 • www.summervalley.co.uk

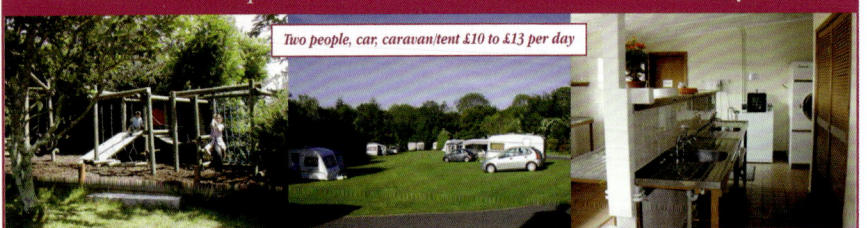

Two people, car, caravan/tent £10 to £13 per day

TREVARTH HOLIDAY PARK

Trevarth is a small, well-kept family-run park excellently situated for north and south coast resorts. All our luxury caravan holiday homes are modern with all main services. Tourers and campers are well catered for with level pitches, some sheltered, with ample hook-ups.

Blackwater, Truro TR4 8FR
e-mail: trevarth@lineone.net
www.trevarth.co.uk
Tel: 01872 560266
Fax: 01872 560379

ROSE AWARD CARAVAN HOLIDAY PARK 2008

Cornwall
Wadebridge

Gunvenna Holiday Park

Gunvenna Holiday Park is a well-drained site of level grassland on 10 acres commanding uninterrupted views of the countryside within five minutes' drive of safe golden sandy beaches. It makes the ideal holiday park for families and couples.

There are large spacious pitches some of which are fully serviced; mains water, gray waste, and electric. If you are looking to spend your holiday in a relaxing part of the south west of England this area will not disappoint.

Local activities include golf, fishing, tennis and cycle hire. Visit the Eden Centre or go karting at St Eval Kart Circuit.

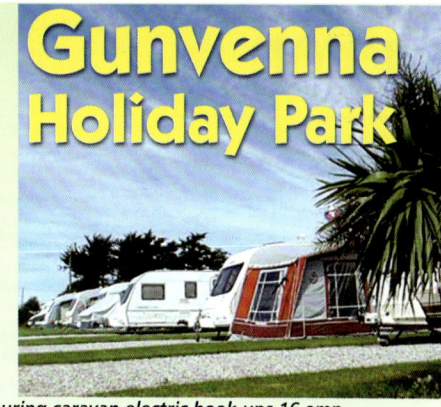

- Touring caravan electric hook-ups 16 amp.
- A modern toilet and shower block with FREE hot and cold water shaving points and hairdryers.
- Guests disabled toilet. • Launderette. • Post box.
- Ample mains water points. • Chemical disposal units.
- Waste water drains. • Children's play area on sand.
- Games room. • Telephone kiosk (outgoing only).
- Dog exercise area and shower. • On site shop.
- Indoor heated swimming pool.

St Minver, Wadebridge PL27 6QN
Tel: 01208 862405

Other specialised holiday guides from FHG

PUBS & INNS OF BRITAIN

COUNTRY HOTELS OF BRITAIN

WEEKEND & SHORT BREAKS IN BRITAIN & IRELAND

THE GOLF GUIDE WHERE TO PLAY, WHERE TO STAY

500 GREAT PLACES TO STAY

SELF-CATERING HOLIDAYS IN BRITAIN

BED & BREAKFAST STOPS IN BRITAIN

PETS WELCOME!

FAMILY BREAKS IN BRITAIN

Published annually: available in all good bookshops or direct from the publisher:
FHG Guides, Abbey Mill Business Centre, Seedhill, Paisley PA1 1TJ
Tel: 0141 887 0428 • Fax: 0141 889 7204
e-mail: admin@fhguides.co.uk • www.holidayguides.com

Devon

Devon is unique, with two different coastlines: bare rugged cliffs, white pebble beaches, stretches of golden sands, and the Jurassic Coast, England's first natural World Heritage Site. Glorious countryside: green rolling hills, bustling market towns and villages, thatched, white-washed cottages and traditional Devon longhouses. Wild and wonderful moorland: Dartmoor, in the south, embraces wild landscapes and picture-postcard villages; Exmoor in the north combines breathtaking, rugged coastline with wild heather moorland. Step back in time and discover historic cities, myths and legends, seafaring characters like Drake and Raleigh, and settings for novels by Agatha Christie and Conan Doyle.

Devon is home to an amazing and diverse range of birds. Enjoy special organised birdwatching trips, perhaps on board a RSPB Avocet Cruise or a vintage tram. Devon is the walking county of the South West – imagine drifts of bluebells lit by dappled sunlight, the smell of new mown hay, the sound of the sea, crisp country walks followed by a roaring fire and hot 'toddies'! If pedal power is your choice, you will discover exciting off-road cycling, leisurely afternoon rides, and challenging long distance routes such as the Granite Way along Dartmoor, the Grand Western Canal and the coastal Exmouth to Budleigh Circuit.

Devon

SOUTH WEST ENGLAND

Branscombe, Brixham, Chudleigh, Colyton, Crediton

CARAVANS FOR HIRE

BRANSCOMBE. Mrs A.E. White, Berry Barton, Branscombe, Near Seaton EX12 3BD (01297 680208; Fax: 01297 680108).
Our park stands above the picturesque old village of Branscombe with thatched cottages, bakery museum and smithy. There are two freehouses in the village, the nearest within easy walking distance. We offer a quiet, peaceful holiday for both retired people and families; there is a large area for children to play. The site is on our 300 acre dairy and mixed farm, with one mile of coastline. Riding available nearby. There are many lovely walks with golf and fishing within easy reach, as are Seaton and Sidmouth (5 miles), the fishing village of Beer (3 miles) and the motorway (17 miles). Mains water; flush toilets; mains electricity; colour TV; fridge. All caravans have toilets, showers and hot water. All are 12ft wide and from 30-35ft long. Three touring caravan pitches available, camper vans and campers welcome.
- Six-berth caravans available from March to November.

BRIXHAM. Galmpton Touring Park, Greenway Road, Galmpton, Brixham TQ5 0EP
Tel 01803 842166 • Fax 01803 844358 • www.galmptontouringpark.co.uk
On the edge of a village between Brixham and Paignton, this friendly park offer a tranquil base for families and couples to explore the many attractions of this popular area. Tourers, motorhomes and tents welcome. Open Easter to September.

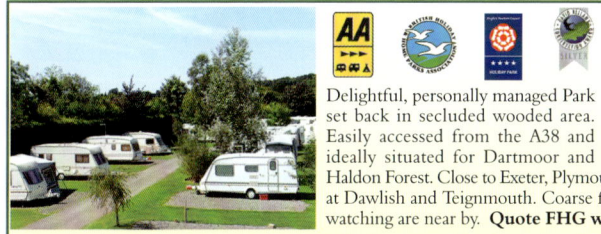

Holmans Wood Holiday Park

Delightful, personally managed Park set back in secluded wooded area. Easily accessed from the A38 and ideally situated for Dartmoor and Haldon Forest. Close to Exeter, Plymouth and Torquay, and sandy beaches at Dawlish and Teignmouth. Coarse fishing, golf, horse riding and bird watching are near by. **Quote FHG when booking.**

Our facilities: • Deluxe all-weather pitches • Electric hook-ups • Excellent toilets/showers • Meadow for camping
Seasonal pitches • Storage available • Holiday homes for sale • Credit card facility for telephone bookings

Chudleigh, Devon TQ13 0DZ • Tel: 01626 853785
e-mail: enquiries@holmanswood.co.uk • www.holmanswood.co.uk

BONEHAYNE FARM
COLYTON, DEVON EX24 6SG

COTTAGE: CARAVAN: BOARD

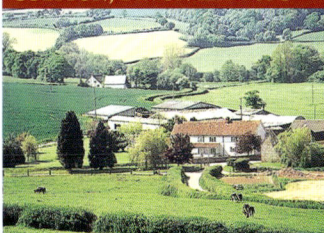

- Family 250 acre working farm • Competitive prices
- Spectacular views • South facing 6-berth luxury caravan
- Cottage with four-poster and central heating
- Four miles to the beach • Five minutes from Colyton
- Spacious lawns/gardens • Laundry room, BBQ, picnic tables
- Good trout fishing, woods to roam, walks

**Contact: Mrs S. Gould • 01404 871416
or Mrs R. Gould • 01404 871396**

www.bonehayne.co.uk • e-mail: gould@bonehayne.co.uk

CREDITON. Beare Mill Caravan Site, Crediton EX17 3QP
Tel 01363 772973 • Fax 01363 772973
Secluded site, within easy reach of both north and south coasts of this popular holiday county. The level, lawned site has a river running through it and is just one mile from the historic market town of Crediton. Tourers welcome. Open May to October.

Stowford Country Holidays
Stowford Farm Meadows

Stowford Country Holidays is an award winning touring caravan and camping site close to Combe Martin in the beautiful surroundings of the North Devon countryside

- Indoor Heated Swimming Pool
- Shop for food & supplies
- Take-Away Cafe & 'The Pantry'
- Old Stable & Old Barn Bars
- Family Orientated Entertainment
- Horse Riding Centre & Cycle Hire
- Kiddies' Cars
- 'PETORAMA' Undercover Mini-Zoo
- 18 Hole Fun Golf
- 9 Hole Crazy Golf
- Sports Field & Play Areas
- Extensive Woodland Walks

Country Lodges

An exclusive new development on the fringe of Exmoor National Park. Your very own luxury timber countryside retreat for all year holiday use. Call for more information or visit our website.

your natural choice

Combe Martin, Devon, EX34 0PW
℡ 01271 882476
www.stowford.co.uk

Graded ★★★★

MANLEIGH HOLIDAY PARK

Manleigh HOLIDAY PARK

COMBE MARTIN EX34 0NS
Tel: 01271 883353

Quiet, family-run site set in beautiful countryside near village, beaches, rocky coves and Exmoor. Chalets, caravans and log cabins tastefully sited on side of Combe Martin valley. Children's play area, laundry. Dog walk. Wine Bar serving delicious home-made food.

Colour Brochure:
Lynne & Craig Davey
www.manleighpark.co.uk

Devon
SOUTH WEST ENGLAND 31
Cullompton, Dartmouth, Dawlish, Dawlish Warren

FOREST GLADE Caravan & Camping Park

A small country estate surrounded by forest in which deer roam. Situated in an area of outstanding natural beauty.

FREE Indoor Heated Pool

Large, flat, sheltered camping/touring pitches Central facilities building, luxury 6-berth full service holiday homes, also self contained flat for 2 persons. Forest walks with dog.

CULLOMPTON DEVON EX15 2DT

COLOUR BROCHURE ON REQUEST
Tel: (01404) 841381 (Evgs to 8pm)
Fax: (01404) 841593 • www.forest-glade.co.uk • email: enquiries@forest-glade.co.uk

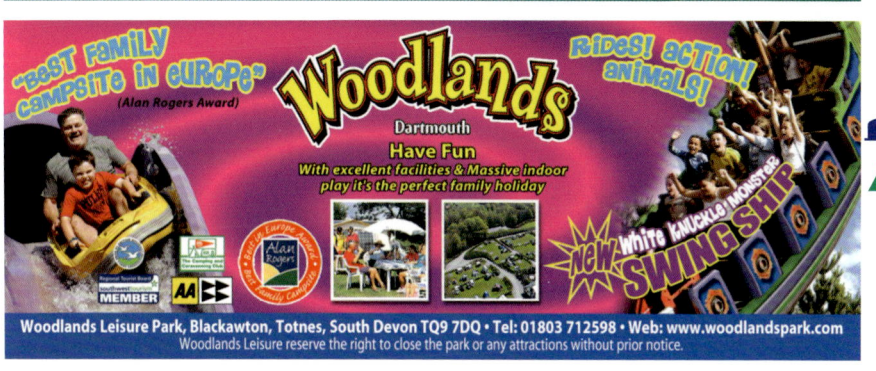

Woodlands — Dartmouth
"Best Family Campsite in Europe" (Alan Rogers Award)
Rides! Action! Animals!
Have Fun
With excellent facilities & Massive indoor play it's the perfect family holiday
NEW White Knuckle Monster SWING SHIP

Woodlands Leisure Park, Blackawton, Totnes, South Devon TQ9 7DQ • Tel: 01803 712598 • Web: www.woodlandspark.com
Woodlands Leisure reserve the right to close the park or any attractions without prior notice.

Cofton Country HOLIDAYS
Superb family-run four star holiday park in a Glorious Corner of Devon

- swimming pools · Swan pub · play areas · fishing lakes
- blue flag beach five minutes · take-away · park shop · WiFi
- holiday homes · touring · camping · cottages · apartments

0800 085 8649   www.coftonholidays.co.uk

DAWLISH WARREN. Peppermint Holiday Park, Warren Road, Dawlish Warren EX7 0PQ
Tel 0845 815 9775 • www.ParkHolidaysUK.com
A well laid out site with some of the best facilities in the area and easy access from the M5. Regular family entertainment throughout the season. plus indoor and outdoor swimming pools. 250 tourer/motorhome pitches and 100 tent pitches. Tourers, motorhomes and tents welcome.

Electric hook-ups available		Facilities for disabled visitors
Children's play area		Pets welcome
Laundry facilities		Shop on site
Licensed bar on site		Wifi access available

SOUTH WEST ENGLAND

Devon
Exmouth, Ilfracombe

HOLIDAY PARKS & CENTRES

EXMOUTH. Devon Cliffs Holiday Park, Sandy Bay, Exmouth.
Devon Cliffs is simply spectacular. For things that make you go 'oooh' nothing quite matches our flagship Park. Devon Cliffs feels like a top resort due to its recent £12m makeover. With its very own Spa, fantastic pools and wonderful sea views, Devon Cliffs is the place to be for relaxation and pampering. As well as all this, Devon Cliffs plays host to a wide range of activities for the whole family to enjoy. P.S. don't forget the first class Touring facilities and on-site amenities to cater for all your Touring needs. **See also Colour Advertisement.**
Call our UK Central Team: 0871 230 1933 (open 7 days, 9am-9pm) or book on-line (quote: TO_FHG) www.touringholidays.co.uk

• Great for Groups! Just book 5 or more holiday homes for extra benefits and savings.
Visit www.havengroups.co.uk Or call 0871 230 1911.

St John's Farm
Caravan & Camping Park
St Johns Road
Withycombe,
Exmouth EX8 5EG

Our unique situation away from the hustle and bustle of the main town of Exmouth is ideal for those seeking a little peace and quiet, yet is ideally situated as a base to explore all the things that Devon is famous for, including Orcombe Point, the start of the East Devon Heritage Coast. The caravan park and camp site is situated in pleasant pasture land with rural views, yet only 10 minutes away from two miles of glorious sandy beaches or unspoilt heathland.

Stop overnight, spend a weekend with us, or stay for a month!
Whatever you choose you will be assured of a warm Devonshire welcome at this family-run site.

Facilities include: farm/site shop, electric hook-ups, toilets/disabled facilities, showers, hairdryers, water points, children's playground and pets corner. Dogs welcome - exercise area available.

Tel: 01395 263170
e-mail: stjohns.farm@virgin.net
www.stjohnscampsite.co.uk

Looking to take a break somewhere special?
Luxurious Touring & Camping Park

FOR A FREE INFORMATION PACK
Call 01271 813837

Hidden Valley

www.hiddenvalleypark.com

Devon
Kingsbridge

SOUTH WEST ENGLAND 33

Mounts Farm Touring Park
The Mounts, Near East Allington, Kingsbridge TQ9 7QJ
01548 521591 • www.mountsfarm.co.uk

MOUNTS FARM is a family-run site in the heart of South Devon. On-site facilities include **FREE** hot showers, flush toilets, **FREE** hot water in washing-up room, razor points, laundry and information room, electric hook-ups and site shop. We welcome tents, touring caravans and motor caravans.

- Large pitches in level, sheltered fields. • No charges for awnings.
- Children and pets welcome.

Situated three miles north of Kingsbridge, Mounts Farm is an ideal base for exploring Dartmouth, Salcombe, Totnes, Dartmoor and the many safe, sandy beaches nearby.

Self-catering cottage also available.

Alston Farm Camping & Caravan Site
Malborough, Kingsbridge TQ7 3BJ

The family-run site is set in a quiet secluded, sheltered valley adjoining the Salcombe Estuary in amongst Devon's loveliest countryside. Level pitches, ample space and conveniences.

Dish washing and clothes washing facilities. Electric hook-ups, Calor and Gaz stockists. Shop, (high season only), payphone on site. Children and pets welcome.

From £8 per night for two adults and caravan.

Please phone for brochure:
Phil Shepherd.

Tel: 01548 561260

e-mail:
info@alstoncampsite.co.uk

www.alstoncampsite.co.uk

34 SOUTH WEST ENGLAND
Devon
Modbury, Newton Abbot

Pennymoor
Caravan & Camping Park
Modbury, Devon PL21 0SB

Welcome to the leisurely, relaxed atmosphere of Pennymoor, a delightful and spacious rural camping and caravanning site with panoramic views of Dartmoor and Devon countryside...

Immaculately maintained, well-drained, peaceful rural site with panoramic views, Midway between Plymouth and Kingsbridge (A379). An ideal centre for touring moors, towns and beaches, only five miles from Bigbury-on-Sea and nine miles from Salcombe. Golf courses at Bigbury and Thurlestone and boating at Salcombe, Newton Ferrers and Kingsbridge. Large, superb toilet/shower block with fully tiled walls and floors, and hairdryers. Facilities for the disabled holidaymaker. Dishwashing room - FREE hot water. Laundry room. Children's play area. Shop. Gas. Public telephone on site. Luxury caravans for hire, all services, fully equipped including colour TV. Ideal for touring caravans and tents.

Write, phone or e-mail quoting FHG for free colour brochure.

Tel & Fax: 01548 830542 • Tel: 01548 830020
e-mail: enquiries@pennymoor-camping.co.uk
www.pennymoor-camping.co.uk

Twelve Oaks Caravan Park
Twelve Oaks Farm, Teigngrace, Newton Abbot TQ12 6QT
Mrs M. A. Gale • Tel & Fax: 01626 352769 • www.twelveoaksfarm.co.uk

A unique experience - set in quiet countryside - a working farm and its animals!
• Serviced pitches with electric hook-up points • TV hook-up
• On site shop • Luxury showers/toilets • Free hot water
• Dish wash area • Laundry facilities • Pets welcome at no extra charge • Calor gas stockist • Heated swimming pool, ideal for all the family to relax and have fun • Coarse fishing on site.
Open all year. Find us off the A38 Expressway.

ALSO: Two carefully converted cottages, each with one double and one twin room, bathroom and shower room. Heating, TV, fridge, microwave and laundry facilities. Parking.

symbols

- ☼ Holiday Parks & Centres
- 🚐 Caravans for Hire
- $ Caravan Sites and Touring Parks
- ▲ Camping Sites

Devon — SOUTH WEST ENGLAND 35
Paignton

• Hoburne Torbay •

Grange Court Holiday Centre

Grange Road,
Goodrington
Paignton TQ4 7JP

Two and three-bedroom modern holiday caravans on this popular site. Some have sun decking with garden furniture. They are fully equipped with microwaves, electric cookers and heating. The site offers a licensed clubhouse with entertainments and children's play area, restaurant and indoor pool. Other facilities include an outdoor pool, launderette, shop for papers and groceries and a café. Goodrington Beach is 15 minutes' walk or there are two car parks. Sorry, no pets. Brochure available.

For further information & reservations contact:
W.& M. Gould, 3 Pulteney Terrace, Bath BA2 4HJ • Tel:01225 316578

Beverley HOLIDAYS

holidays to remember

Escape to the perfect seaside resort and rediscover the things that really matter.

- Family run 5 star holidays
- Playground & children's room
- Indoor & outdoor pools
- Great nightly entertainment
- Crazy golf, tennis & snooker tables
- On site bars, restaurants & takeaway

HOLIDAY CARAVANS   TOURING   LODGES

Call for a brochure 01803 661955

Award winning holidays on The English Riviera

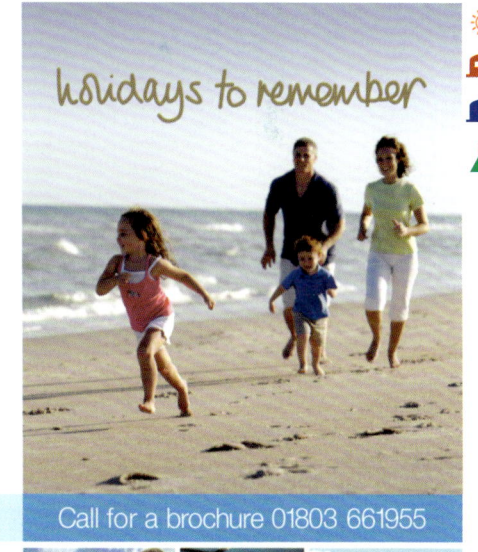

www.beverley-holidays.co.uk

Salcombe Regis

Camping & Caravan park
Sidmouth, Devon EX10 0JH
Tel: 01395 514303
Fax: 01395 514314
contact@salcombe-regis.co.uk
www.salcombe-regis.co.uk

Large Amenities Block
- FREE hot water to all Showers and Basins
- Shaver Points • Dishwashing Area
- Laundrette • Ironing facilities
- Hairdryers • Family Bathroom
- Baby Changing facilities

Shop and Reception
- Information Area • Payphone
- Calor Gas and Camping Gaz sales/refills
- Battery charging service • Basic camping supplies
- Basic General Stores • Freezer Pack Service
- Daily Newspapers (to order only) • Park Post Box

On Site
- Electric Hook-ups
- Chemical and Grey water Disposal Points
- Children's Playground • Putting Green
- Badminton Net • Large Dog Exercise Field
- Barbeques permitted (NOT disposables)
- Parking on Departure Day (off pitch, small charge)
- Caravan storage subject to availability

The Hook Family Welcomes You

Adjoining our family home and covering 16 acres, Salcombe Regis Camping and Caravan Park offers unrivalled space and tranquillity.
Beautiful views of the combe, with the sea beyond, can be seen from our camping field where young and old may enjoy open expanses of grass ideal for picnics, ball games, flying a kite or just quiet reflection.
Paths lead to the world heritage coast, where Salcombe Mouth boasts a delightful pebble beach, forming part of the Jurassic Coastline, which at low tide gives access to Weston and Sidmouth beaches. **FREE COLOUR BROCHURE**

Devon
Seaton

SOUTH WEST ENGLAND 37

AXEVALE CARAVAN PARK

Beautiful views, first class facilities, and just a short walk from both the town and the beach, Axevale is the perfect choice for an easy going, relaxing holiday in Devon.

A quiet, family-run park with 70 modern and luxury caravans for hire.
The park overlooks the delightful River Axe Valley, and is just a 10 minute walk from the town with its wonderfully long, award-winning beach.

Ideal for children and families
The park is fenced and safe for children, who will love our extensive play area, with its sand pit, paddling pool, swings and slide. A reliable babysitting service is available so you can enjoy an evening out on your own

Quiet and peaceful
With no clubhouse, a relaxing atmosphere is ensured.
All of our caravans have a shower, toilet, fridge and TV.
Sited on hard standing which connect dry pathways and tarmac roads. Axevale is the perfect choice in spring and autumn too.

Shopping and Laundry
Laundry facilities are provided and there is a wide selection of goods on sale in the park shop which is open every day.

Prices from £90 per week; reductions for three or fewer persons early/late season.

Axevale Caravan Park, Colyford Road, Seaton, Devon EX12 2DF
Tel: 0800 0688816
e-mail: info@axevale.co.uk   www.axevale.co.uk

38 SOUTH WEST ENGLAND   Devon
Seaton, South Molton, Tavistock

SEATON. Couchill Farm Caravan Site, Beer, Seaton EX12 3AL
Tel 01297 20704 • Fax 01297 20704
Nestling in a valley, only 10 minutes' walk from nearest beach and ideal for exploring Jurassic Coast. Lots of good walks over the farmland, and sports/leisure facilities in the area. Tourers and motorhomes welcome. Open all year.

Riverside Caravan Park
Marsh Lane, North Molton Road, South Molton EX36 3HQ

A beautiful, family-owned caravan and camping park in 40 acres of flat meadow and woodland near the market town of South Molton, an ideal base for exploring Exmoor. 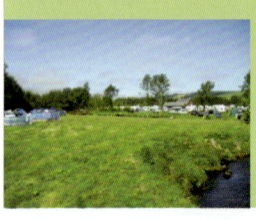
- Luxurious heated shower and toilet block with free hot showers.
- Laundry facilities and baby changing area.
- Children and pets welcome. • Barbecue and picnic tables.

hard standing, level Europitches • electrical hook-up • TV aerial sockets
Tel: 01769 579269/574853
e-mail: relax@exmoorriverside.co.uk
www.exmoorriverside.co.uk

HARFORD BRIDGE
HOLIDAY PARK
1985 — 20 — 2005

Beautiful, award-winning family-run park set in Dartmoor National Park with delightful views of the moor. Beside the River Tavy, offering riverside camping and other level pitches.
Luxury self-catering caravan holiday homes open all year.
(Off the A386 Okehampton Road, two miles from Tavistock. Take Peter Tavy turning).

A lovely, peaceful camping facility where you can be assured of warm personal care and attention.
120 pitches available for any mix of touring caravans, motor homes, trailer tents and tents.

Included in our charges is free hot water and showers, use of a hard tennis court, children's enclosed
play area, table tennis and games room (no slot machines),
a quiet room with television and comprehensive library,
a large recreation green for leisure facilities,
a plentiful supply of picnic tables and 2 permanent barbecue facilities.
All pitches are on a level plain with parking alongside for one car.

Harford Bridge Holiday Park
Peter Tavy, Tavistock, Devon PL19 9LS
Tel: 01822 810349 • Fax: 01822 810028
e-mail: enquiry@harfordbridge.co.uk
www.harfordbridge.co.uk

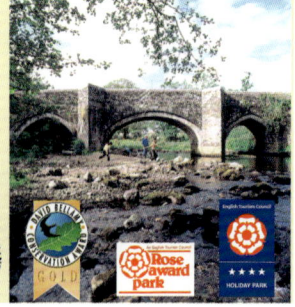

Electric hook-ups available		Facilities for disabled visitors	
Children's play area		Pets welcome	
Laundry facilities		Shop on site	
Licensed bar on site		Wifi access available	

Devon — SOUTH WEST ENGLAND

Thornbury, Woolacombe

Woodacott Holiday Park
Woodacott, Thornbury, Devon EX22 7BT

Peaceful, rural Devon

A small site taking touring caravans and letting self-catering bungalows. Plenty of hard standing pitches, all with electric points. Toilets and shower rooms are available together with water taps and waste disposal.

We have two lakes for coarse fishing, and an indoor heated swimming pool together with jacuzzi and sauna.

Please telephone for further details:
01409 261 162

e-mail: stewartwoodacott@yahoo.co.uk

www.woodacottholidaypark.co.uk

Welcome to the surf
EUROPA PARK
WOOLACOMBE NORTH DEVON
SEE OUR WEBSITE

WWW.EUROPAPARK.CO.UK

CAMPING & TOURING GET 2 DAYS FREE!!!
(TERMS APPLY)

- CLUB
- SAUNA
- INDOOR POOL
- HAPPY HOUR
- RESTAURANT
- SPAR SHOP
- LAUNDERETTE
- GAMES ROOM

SURFERS PARADISE

EUROPA PARK IS A LIVELY HOLIDAY PARK IN AN IDEAL LOCATION **ONLY 1 MILE FROM WOOLACOMBE BEACH.** WE CAN OFFER CAMPING AND TOURING FACILITIES AS WELL AS A VAST CHOICE OF SURF ACCOMMODATION FROM OUR FAMOUS SURF CABINS SLEEPING FROM 4 - 6 PEOPLE AND OUR SURF MOTEL WITH EN-SUITE FACILITIES - IDEAL FOR LARGE GROUPS UP TO 40 PEOPLE! WE CAN ALSO OFFER BUNGALOWS, STATIC CARAVANS AND OUR EXCELLENT SURF LODGES.

TEL 01271 871425 - EMAIL HOLIDAYS@EUROPAPARK.CO.UK

SOUTH WEST ENGLAND — Devon — Woolacombe

fun filled holidays

Seaview Camping and Touring plus Luxury Lodges & Holiday Homes

Four award winning Holiday Parks set in Devon's breathtaking countryside next to Woolacombe's 3 miles of golden Blue Flag sandy beach!

- 10 PIN Bowling • Waves Ceramic Studio
- 17th Century Inn • Restaurants & Bars
- Affiliated Golf Club • Amusement Arcade
- Super Site Pitches • Electric Hook-ups
- Laundry Facilities • On-site Shop

All this is FREE!!
- 10 Heated Pools • Nightly Entertainment
- Cinema • Health Suite • Crazy Golf
- Tennis • Kid's Clubs ... Plus so much more!

REGISTER ONLINE FOR LATEST OFFERS
woolacombe.com/fcc

WOOLACOMBE BAY — **01271 870 343**

North Morte Farm Caravan & Camping
Dept. FHG, Mortehoe, Woolacombe EX34 7EG
(01271 870381)

The nearest camping and caravan park to the sea, in perfectly secluded beautiful coastal country.

Our family-run park, adjoining National Trust land, is only 500 yards from Rockham Beach, yet only five minutes' walk from the village of Mortehoe with a Post Office, shops, cafes and pubs – one of which has a children's room.

Four to six berth holiday caravans for hire and pitches for tents, dormobiles and touring caravans, electric hook-ups available. We have hot showers and flush toilets, laundry room, shop and off-licence; Calor gas and Camping Gaz available; children's play area. Dogs accepted but must be kept on lead. Open April to end September. Brochure available.

Dorset

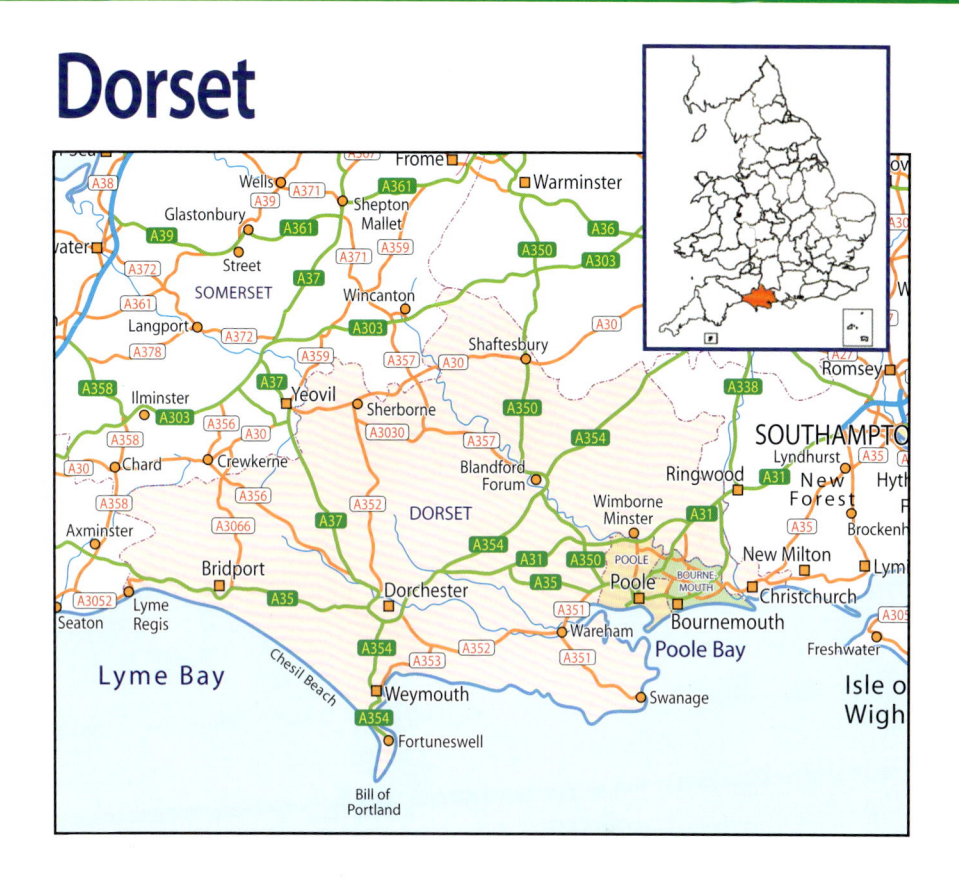

SOUTH WEST ENGLAND 41

Other specialised holiday guides from FHG

PUBS & INNS OF BRITAIN • **COUNTRY HOTELS** OF BRITAIN
WEEKEND & SHORT BREAK HOLIDAYS IN BRITAIN
THE GOLF GUIDE WHERE TO PLAY, WHERE TO STAY
500 GREAT PLACES TO STAY • **SELF-CATERING HOLIDAYS** IN BRITAIN
BED & BREAKFAST STOPS • **PETS WELCOME!**
FAMILY BREAKS IN BRITAIN

Published annually: available in all good bookshops or direct from the publisher:
FHG Guides, Abbey Mill Business Centre, Seedhill, Paisley PA1 1TJ
Tel: 0141 887 0428 • Fax: 0141 889 7204
e-mail: admin@fhguides.co.uk • www.holidayguides.com

THE INSIDE PARK

Touring Park, Blandford, Dorset

Dorset — Blandford

So Relaxing You Won't Want To Leave!

- ✪ Extra Large Pitches
- ✪ All modern Facilities
- ✪ Free Hot Water
- ✪ Shop
- ✪ Ideal Family Site
- ✪ Quiet & Secluded
- ✪ Children's Play Area
- ✪ Country Walks & Wildlife
- ✪ Farm Tours
- ✪ Caravan Storage

BROCHURE / BOOKINGS - 01258 453719
WEB SEARCH - THE INSIDE PARK

Dorset

SOUTH WEST ENGLAND 43

Dorchester, Highcliffe-on-Sea

CAMPING SITES

DORCHESTER near. Home Farm, Rectory Lane, Puncknowle, Near Dorchester DT2 9BW (01308 897258). Small secluded site in beautiful area, one-and-a-half-miles from West Bexington, four miles from Abbotsbury and Burton Bradstock. We can accommodate tents, touring caravans, and motor caravans. Facilities include mains water, washbasins, toilets, washing-up sinks, showers, razor points, disposal point for chemical toilets, electric hook-ups; gas. Sea fishing available locally. Good food served at the village inn. Must pre-book at all times. Further information on request.
- Well behaved children and dogs welcome.

Giant's Head

Caravan & Camping Park • Tel: 01300 341242
Old Sherbourne Road, Cerne Abbas, Dorchester DT2 7TR

A quiet site with wonderful views of Dorset Downs and the Blackmoor Vale. Two miles north-east of Cerne Abbas. We are in an ideal position for a motoring, cycling or walking holiday. Places to visit include Cheddar Caves, Longleat House and Lion Reserve, Thomas Hardy's birthplace and various wildlife parks. Fishing, boating and bathing at Weymouth and Portland. Site facilities include toilets, water supply, showers. Electric hook-ups available. Laundry room. Hot water. Good approach road. Site holds 60 caravans and tents; campers and camper vans also welcome. Terms on request.
- Children welcome. • Pets accepted on lead.
- Self Catering also available

e-mail: holidays@giantshead.co.uk
www.giantshead.co.uk

Cobbs Holiday Park

Sorry No Tents / Tourers / Motorcaravans

Welcome to freedom...

We have a fully licensed social club, Music, dancing, fancy dress competition, Bingo & lots more. An ideal place to spend time with your family.

All accommodation includes gas, electricity and is fully equipped (except for linen). Approx. 400 metres from the beach & 150 metres from the town. On-site launderette with ironing facilities & tumble dryers. All caravans fitted with TV, shower, wash hand basin, microwave, fridge, hot & cold water & WC. safe children's play area. Christchurch in Bloom Award Winner.

**COBBS HOLIDAY PARK, 32 Gordon Road,
Highcliffe-on-Sea, Christchurch, Dorset BH23 5HN
Tel: 01425 273301 or 275313, Fax: 01425 276090**

e-mail: enquiries@cobbsholidaypark.co.uk • www.cobbsholidaypark.co.uk

44 SOUTH WEST ENGLAND

Dorset
Poole

HOLIDAY PARKS & CENTRES

POOLE. Rockley Park Holiday Park, Hamworthy, Poole.
With its own boat Park and gorgeous views over Poole Harbour, this is a great choice for beach buddies and watersports wizards alike. If you also love to live it up a little, that's all plain sailing too. Just make the most of the great pools, bars and entertainment venues. Set in wonderful surroundings, Rockley Park plays host to a whole range of activities, sports and entertainment facilities. With superb Touring facilities and on-site amenities to cater for all your Touring needs, Rockley Park is the place to be for a fun-packed family holiday. **See also Colour Advertisement.**
Call our UK Central Team: 0871 230 1933 (open 7 days, 9am-9pm) or book on-line (quote: TO_FHG) www.touringholidays.co.uk
• Great for Groups! Just book 5 or more holiday homes for extra benefits and savings.
Visit www.havengroups.co.uk Or call 0871 230 1911.

Beacon Hill Touring Park enjoys the beauty of 30 acres of partly wooded heathland, together with a wide selection of wildlife. We are a Conservation Award winning park, three miles west of Poole town centre, and just five miles from some of the best beaches Britain has to offer.

Beacon Hill Touring Park
Blandford Road North
Poole · Dorset · BH16 6AB
01202 631631
www.beaconhilltouringpark.co.uk
bookings@beaconhilltouringpark.co.uk

- Heated swimming pool
- Games rooms
- Children's adventure play areas
- All-weather tennis court
- Fishing, with horse riding nearby
- Take-Away/Coffee Shop
- Fully licensed bar
- Well stocked shop
- Showers with free hot water
- Baby changing unit
- Laundry rooms with adjacent dishwashing facilities
- Electric hook-ups
- Ample water, waste and chemical disposal points
- Wireless internet

Sandbanks beach, Poole

Dorset SOUTH WEST ENGLAND 45
Poole

SOUTH LYTCHETT MANOR CARAVAN & CAMPING PARK

A family-run park in 20 acres of stunning parkland. Dog walking area around our pond and woods.
Luxurious brand new amenity blocks. including disabled and family bathrooms.
Electric hook-ups, TV connection and hard standings.
Two village pubs within walking distance.
Excellent bus service outside our gates.
Just three miles from Poole.

3rd Place – Practical Caravan's Top 100 Sites 2008
Voted Best Park in Dorset by Practical Caravan Readers 2008

South Lytchett Manor Caravan & Camping Park
Dorchester Road, Lytchett Minster, Poole Dorset BH16 6JB
T: 01202 622577 or 01202 622620
e-mail: info@southlytchettmanor.co.uk
www.southlytchettmanor.co.uk

Dorset
Wareham

Wareham Forest
Tourist Park

Resident Proprietors: Tony and Sarah Birch

Enjoy the peace and tranquillity of Wareham Forest, together with the luxury of our park. We offer a choice of fully serviced electric or standard pitches, grass/hard standing

- Heated outdoor swimming pool and children's paddling pool open all day free (high season)
- Children's adventure playground • Self-service shop/off licence • Launderette
- Washing up room • Heated toilet block during winter period • Unisex disabled room
- Dogs permitted strictly on leads in designated areas
- OPEN ALL YEAR • Midway between Wareham and Bere Regis, off A35
- Credit cards accepted • Wifi available

Wareham Forest Tourist Park, North Trigon, Wareham BH20 7NZ

Please see our detailed website or call for a brochure on:

Tel/Fax: 01929 551393

e-mail: holiday@warehamforest.co.uk

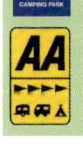

www.warehamforest.co.uk

Manor Farm Caravan Park

We look forward to welcoming you at our quiet and clean Park in the Frome Valley. Situated just off the A352, in the village of East Stoke, mid-way between Wareham and Wool in an Area of Outstanding Natural Beauty. An ideal base from which to explore the beautiful Dorset countryside and the Jurassic coast.

60 units – seasonal pitches – storage.
Shower and toilet block, children's play area.
Calor Gas/Camping gaz exchange.
Site supervised 24 hours a day and the toilet block is lit all night. Three quarters of pitches are electrical 240V – 16amp. Although we allow dogs on site (1 per pitch), they have to be leashed at all times, exercised and toiletted off the site.

David and Gillian Topp
Manor Farm Caravan Park
East Stoke, Wareham, Dorset BH20 6AW
Tel : 01929 462870
e- mail info@manorfarmcp.co.uk
www.manorfarmcp.co.uk

Dorset

West Bexington, Weymouth

SOUTH WEST ENGLAND 47

GORSELANDS CARAVAN PARK
West Bexington-on-Sea · Dorset

Peace and Tranquillity
Small select park with stunning views over Jurassic Coastline

- Excellent beach fishing
- Pets Welcome • Caravans & Apartments
- Camping nearby mid July-August • Shop and Launderette
- Village Pub 100 yards • Beach and car park one mile

Tel: 01308 897232 • Fax: 01308 897239
www.gorselands.co.uk
e-mail: info@gorselands.co.uk
**West Bexington-on Sea,
Near Bridport, Dorset DT2 9DJ**

HOLIDAY PARKS & CENTRES

WEYMOUTH. Littlesea Holiday Park, Lynch Lane, Weymouth.
A firm favourite with families looking for variety and choice, Littlesea Holiday Park offers the opportunity to stay put for the excellent all-weather pools and fantastic sports, leisure and entertainment facilities it has to offer, or you can take advantage of its great location near Weymouth and explore the enchanting Dorset coastline. Why not soak up the buzzing holiday village atmosphere at this family-friendly Park, take an adventure with the family to see the coastal and rural delights of Dorset, then enjoy knockout evening entertainment. With superb Touring facilities and on-site amenities, you can't go wrong at Littlesea. **See also Colour Advertisement.**
Call our UK Central Team: 0871 230 1933 (open 7 days, 9am-9pm) or book on-line (quote: TO_FHG) www.touringholidays.co.uk
• Great for Groups! Just book 5 or more holiday homes for extra benefits and savings.
Visit www.havengroups.co.uk Or call 0871 230 1911.

Pebble Bank Caravan Park
Camp Road, Wyke Regis, Weymouth DT4 9HF

Pebble Bank Caravan Park is situated 1½ miles from Weymouth town centre. The Park is broadly divided into two sections, one for touring vans/campers and recreational space, the other for privately owned static holiday vans, some of which are let for holiday bookings.

Facilities include numerous water points and electric hook-ups, first class toilet and shower facilities and chemical disposal points, laundry room, children's play area, etc. Dogs allowed provided they are well behaved and kept on leads.

Our aim is to give the discerning visitor the most relaxed, comfortable and enjoyable holiday possible. Brochure available.

e-mail: info@pebblebank.co.uk
www.pebblebank.co.uk
Tel & Fax: 01305 774844

48 SOUTH WEST ENGLAND — Dorset

Weymouth, Wimborne, Wool

HOLIDAY PARKS & CENTRES

WEYMOUTH. Seaview Holiday Park, Preston, Weymouth.
Set in a picturesque spot overlooking Weymouth Bay, Seaview has a relaxed yet happening atmosphere. Days are a total mix of water fun, sports action or leisurely activities and, if you can fit it in, exploring the beautiful Dorset coastline. Seaview offers plenty to keep the whole family entertained both day and night or you can simply take the weight off your feet and relax. With great Touring facilities and on-site amenities, all your holiday needs will be taken care of, leaving you to enjoy your holiday in style. **See also Colour Advertisement.**
Call our UK Central Team: **0871 230 1933 (open 7 days, 9am-9pm)** or book on-line (quote: TO_FHG) www.touringholidays.co.uk
• Great for Groups! Just book 5 or more holiday homes for extra benefits and savings.
Visit www.havengroups.co.uk Or call 0871 230 1911.

Woolsbridge Manor Farm caravan park

Three Legged Cross, Wimborne, Dorset BH21 6RA
Telephone: 01202 826369

Your base for exploring Dorset and the New Forest

Situated approximately three-and-a-half-miles from the New Forest market town of Ringwood – easy access to the south coast. Seven acres level, semi-sheltered, well-drained spacious pitches. Quiet country location on a working farm, ideal and safe for families. Showers, mother/baby area, laundry room, washing up area, chemical disposal, payphone, electric hook-ups, battery charging. Children's play area on site. Site shop. Dogs welcome on leads. Fishing adjacent.
Moors Valley Country Park golf course one mile. Pub and restaurant 10 minutes' walk.

e-mail: woolsbridge@btconnect.com • www.woolsbridgemanorcaravanpark.co.uk

---

Whitemead Caravan Park

East Burton Road, Wool Dorset BH20 6HG

Peaceful, family-run site set in mature woodland. New toilet block with excellent facilities for 2005/6 with free showers and hot water. We have two children's play areas, a games room. Our shop is open daily selling groceries, sweets, gas, newspapers and accessories. Takeaway food on site. Monkey World is within walking distance, as are the village pubs, restaurants and shops. The Tank Museum is also close with Lulworth Cove only five miles away. Excellent walking and cycling all round. The perfect base to explore the beautiful county of Dorset. Dogs welcome.

Tel & Fax: 01929 462241
e-mail: whitemeadcp@aol.com • www.whitemeadcaravanpark.co.uk

Gloucestershire
Cirencester

Gloucestershire

Gloucestershire, in an enviable position west of London between Bath, Oxford and Stratford-on-Avon, has style, elegance, charm.....and cheese rolling. The funkiest Farmers' Markets, happening hotels and, once a year, a mad scramble down the steepest slope to catch a cheese or two.

The county is best known for the Cotswolds, but the area includes The Royal Forest of Dean, Cheltenham, Tewkesbury and Gloucester.

In recent years the Cotswolds area has reinvented itself. Forget twee B&Bs and chintzy hotels, the Cotswolds is now a hotspot of chic hotels, award-winning designer farm shops and entertaining farmers' markets. Liz Hurley, Hugh Grant, Kate Moss, Kate Winslet and Sam Mendes have recently moved to the area and it's easy to see why. The Cotswolds offer space and escape in a beautiful environment and that's exactly what's on offer to visitors too.

Nearby, the Royal Forest of Dean is the last great English broadleaf forest, formerly a hunting ground for the kings of England. Nowadays it's emerging as a great destination for adrenaline sports and activity breaks, all against the backdrop of acres of woodland and nature reserves. It's one of the most colourful corners of England - daffodils, green shoots and bluebells in spring, and gold in Autumn.

CIRENCESTER. Hoburne Cotswold, Broadway Lane, South Cerney, Cirencester GL7 5UQ
Tel: 01285 860216 • www.hoburne.com/cotswold_main.asp
For those who love an aquatic adventure, Hoburne Cotswold is an ideal centre for water-based sports, with four lakes, indoor & outdoor pools, fishing, canoes and pedalos. No pets allowed. 302 touring pitches available. Caravans, motorhomes and tents welcome. Open all year round.

CIRENCESTER. Mayfield Park, Cheltenham Road, Cirencester GL7 7BH
Tel: 01285 831301 • www.mayfieldpark.co.uk
A warm welcome is given to everyone at this friendly site. Modern facilities including hot showers are provided, but no on-site entertainment. There are wildlife parks and stately homes to visit nearby, as well as bridlepaths and various eateries. Open all year round. 36 touring pitches available. Tents and caravans welcome.

Electric hook-ups available		Facilities for disabled visitors	
Children's play area		Pets welcome	
Laundry facilities		Shop on site	
Licensed bar on site		Wifi access available	

50 SOUTH WEST ENGLAND   Gloucestershire
Coleford, Cotswolds, Lower Wick

COLEFORD. Christchurch Camping and Caravan Site, Bracelands Drive, Coleford GL16 7NN
Tel: 01594 833376
Come to Coleford for long woodland walks down to the river and visits to the Clearwell Caves and Ancient Iron Mines, just some of the attractions of the beautiful Wye Valley area. Open from March to January. 280 touring pitches available. Caravans, motorhomes and tents welcome.

COLEFORD. Braceland Camping & Caravan Park, Bracelands Drive, Coleford GL16 7NN
Tel: 01594 833376
This site provides spacious touring pitches with panoramic views of Highmeadow Woods and the Wye Valley. 530 touring pitches available. Caravans, motorhomes and tents welcome.

COLEFORD. Woodland Caravan and Camping Site, Coleford GL1 7NN
Tel: 01594 833376
Secluded pitches in a woodland setting, perfect for a peaceful holiday. No toilet/shower facilities. Open from March to November. Tents not permitted. 90 touring pitches available. Caravans and motorhomes welcome.

The Red Lion Camping and Caravan Park
Wainlode Hill, Norton, Near Gloucester GL2 9LW
Tel & Fax: 01452 730251 • www.redlioninn-caravancampingpark.co.uk

Set in an idyllic riverside location in glorious countryside, the park provides an ideal base for exploring the surrounding countryside, and nearby historic towns of Gloucester, Tewkesbury and Cheltenham. Full facilities are available including electric hookups, toilets and showers, well-stocked shop on-site and launderette, with a wide range of food available at the neighbouring Red Lion Inn. Seasonal tourer pitches and static caravans available for sale.

'A warm and friendly welcome at all times of the season'

AA LISTED.

English Tourism Council
BRITISH HOLIDAY PARKS ASSOCIATION
CAMPING PARK

This site is set between the Cotswold Escarpment and Severn Vale, in open rural countryside. Many local amenities including swimming, golf, riding, fishing. Tourist attractions include Westonbirt Arboretum, Berkeley Castle, Slimbridge Wild Fowl Trust, Jenner Museum and Cotswold Way. Ideal for touring the many picturesque towns and villages on hills and vales and as a stopover for north/south journeys. Inn within walking distance and many inns and hotels within close proximity.

• Gas and electric hook-ups available • Elsan disposal
• Toilets and shower • washing-up facilities • Laundry
• Children's play area • Storage available all year.

Pets welcome under control. Terms from £8 to £10 tents, £9.50 caravans and motor homes.

Hogsdown Farm Camp Site, Dursley, Lower Wick GL11 6DB • 01453 810224

FREE or REDUCED RATE entry to Holiday Visits and Attractions – see our READERS' OFFER VOUCHERS on pages 205-234

Gloucestershire

SOUTH WEST ENGLAND 51

Moreton-in-Marsh, Slimbridge, Tewkesbury

MORETON-IN-MARSH. Moreton-in-Marsh Caravan Club Site, Bourton Road, Moreton-in-Marsh GL56 0BT
Tel: 01608 650519 • Fax: 01608 652515
Moreton-in-Marsh is a quaint little market town situated in the Cotswold countryside. The caravan park offers facilities for all the family, including crazy golf, 5-a-side football, volleyball, boules and a climbing frame. Open all year. 182 touring pitches available.

Quiet country site next to the Sharpness/Gloucester Canal, 800 yards from the world famous Wildfowl Trust. A David Bellamy Conservation Gold Award Winner since 2000. Tudor Arms pub & restaurant next door. Ideal base for cycling or touring the Cotswolds. Under the personal supervision of resident owners. Electric hook-ups, hardstandings, toilets, showers, Elsan disposal, separate area for adults only. Visit Berkeley Castle, Gloucester Docks, Bristol, Westonbirt Arboretum, etc. Children and pets welcome. Terms from £10 per night.

Tudor Caravan Park
Shepherds Patch, Slimbridge GL2 7BP • Tel: 01453 890483
e-mail: fhg@tudorcaravanpark.co.uk • www.tudorcaravanpark.com

---

TEWKESBURY. Winchcombe Camping & Caravanning, Brooklands Farm, Near Tewkesbury GL20 8NX
Tel: 01242 620259.
Winchombe is situated near Tewkesbury, a quaint little town with antique shops and tea rooms. The site is a perfect base for touring the surrounding area with its lakes and rolling countryside. 90 touring pitches available. Caravans and tents welcome. Open March to January.

TEWKESBURY. Croft Farm Leisure & Waterpark, Bredons Hardwick, Tewkesbury GL20 7EE
Tel: 01684 772321 • Fax: 01684 773379 • www.croftfarmleisure.co.uk
Croft Farm is ideal for all the family, with facilities and activities to suit all ages. These include a fully equipped gym, sauna and sunbed, as well as a varieity of watersports. The caravan pitches are situated on two sides of the waterpark's lake. Open from March to January. Caravans, motorhomes and trailer tents welcome.

TEWKESBURY. Tewkesbury Abbey Caravan Club Site, Gander Lane, Tewkesbury GL20 5PG
Tel: 01684 294 035
This excellently positioned site is ideal for families. It offers great opportunities to walk to the old town for day trips to museums, markets or even for a cruise on the river. 160 touring pitches available. Caravans, motorhomes and tents welcome. Open from March to November.

🚐 Electric hook-ups available		♿ Facilities for disabled visitors	
🛝 Children's play area		🐕 Pets welcome	
🧺 Laundry facilities		🧺 Shop on site	
🍷 Licensed bar on site		W Wifi access available	

SOUTH WEST ENGLAND
Somerset

Somerset

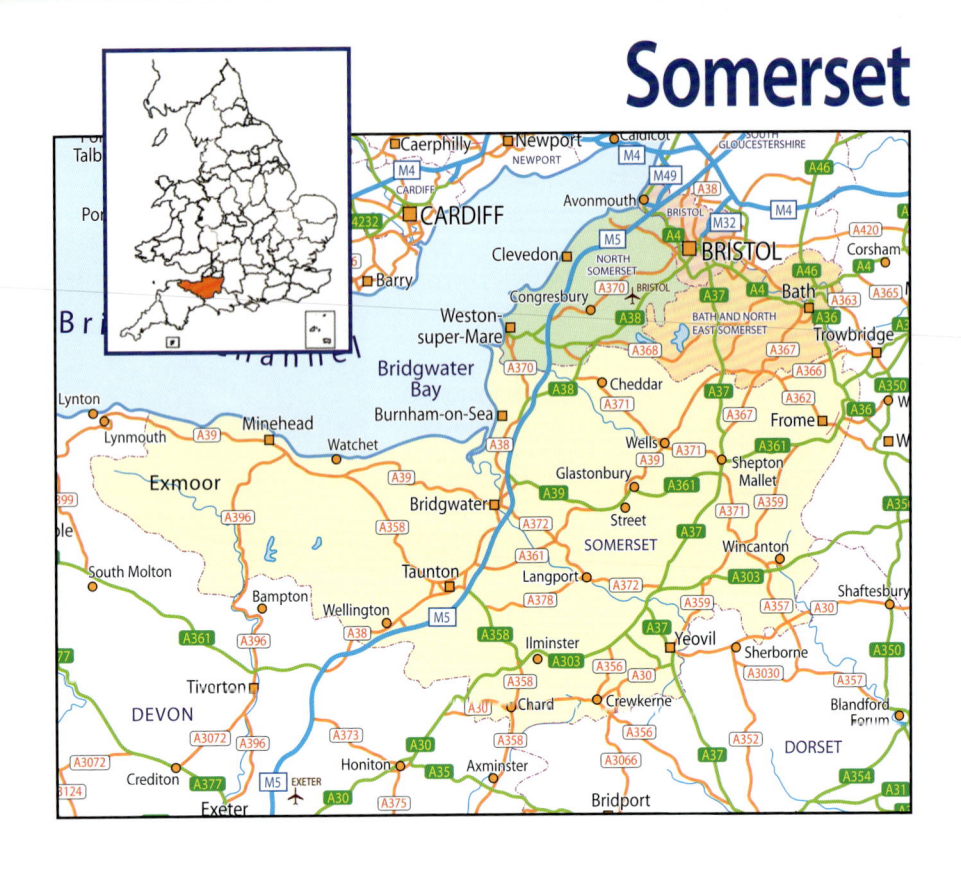

Other specialised holiday guides from FHG

PUBS & INNS OF BRITAIN • **COUNTRY HOTELS** OF BRITAIN
WEEKEND & SHORT BREAK HOLIDAYS IN BRITAIN
THE GOLF GUIDE WHERE TO PLAY, WHERE TO STAY
500 GREAT PLACES TO STAY • **SELF-CATERING HOLIDAYS** IN BRITAIN
BED & BREAKFAST STOPS • **PETS WELCOME!**
FAMILY BREAKS IN BRITAIN

Published annually: available in all good bookshops or direct from the publisher:
FHG Guides, Abbey Mill Business Centre, Seedhill, Paisley PA1 1TJ
Tel: 0141 887 0428 • Fax: 0141 889 7204
e-mail: admin@fhguides.co.uk • www.holidayguides.com

Somerset
Bath, Brean

SOUTH WEST ENGLAND 53

NEWTON MILL BATH

Idyllic setting in a hidden valley near the centre of Britain's most elegant city

Open All Year

LOO OF THE YEAR Awards 2008

- Family owned and cared for
- Frequent buses & level car-free cyclepath to city centre and to Bristol
- Superb award winning heated toilets with bathrooms, free showers & private cubicles
- All caravan/motorhome pitches are hardstandings with electric/TV hook-up.
- Well-drained Tent Meadows (Electric hook-up available)
- Attractive Old Mill Pub, Restaurant and Garden beside the millstream (free fishing)

Newton Rd, Bath, BA2 9JF   Tel 01225 333909

www.campinginbath.co.uk   newtonmill@hotmail.com

BEACHSIDE HOLIDAY PARK

- Chalets and Caravan holiday homes on quiet park
- Direct access to beach • Pets from £5 per night
- Full facilities • Colour television • Cafe/Bar
- Golf courses nearby • Free brochure

Coast Road, Brean Sands, Somerset TA8 2QZ
Tel: 01278 751346 • Fax: 01278 751683

**FREEPHONE
08000 190322**

www.beachsideholidaypark.co.uk

54 SOUTH WEST ENGLAND

Somerset
Bridgwater, Burnham-on-Sea

Mill Farm Caravan & Camping Park

FIDDINGTON, BRIDGWATER, SOMERSET TA5 1JQ

SWIMMING – TROPICAL INDOOR HEATED POOLS AND TWO OUTDOOR POOLS WITH GIANT WATER SLIDE ★ RIDING ★ BOATING ★ HOLIDAY APARTMENTS TO LET

Attractive, sheltered farm site. Between beautiful Quantock Hills and the sea. Boating, swings, table tennis, TV, tourist information, large sand pit.

FOR HIRE: Canoes, trampolines and ponies.

★ Club Entertainment ★ Caravan storage available.

CLEAN TOILETS ETC, LAUNDRY ROOM, ELECTRIC HOOK-UPS, CAMP SHOP, GOOD LOCAL PUBS. OPEN ALL YEAR.

WRITE OR PHONE FOR BROCHURE

Tel: M. J. Evans:
01278 732286
www.millfarm.biz

HOLIDAY PARKS & CENTRES

BURNHAM-ON-SEA. Burnham-on-Sea Holiday Village, Marine Drive, Burnham-on-Sea. Set around a lovely picturesque fishing lake, this beautifully landscaped Park is situated close to the wide sandy beach. Burnham-on-Sea offers something for everyone – it's ideal for a relaxing family holiday, whilst tempting you with many great outdoor activities such as its very own nature reserve and FunZone Play Area – to name but two, not forgetting fantastic nights in the bars and entertainment venues. Burnham-on-Sea also offers customers excellent Touring facilities and on-site amenities to make your stay as perfect as possible. **See also Colour Advertisement.**

Call our UK Central Team: 0871 230 1933 (open 7 days, 9am-9pm) or book on-line (quote: TO_FHG) www.touringholidays.co.uk

• Great for Groups! Just book 5 or more holiday homes for extra benefits and savings. Visit www.havengroups.co.uk Or call 0871 230 1911.

symbols

☀ Holiday Parks & Centres

🚐 Caravans for Hire

Ⓢ Caravan Sites and Touring Parks

▲ Camping Sites

Somerset
Dulverton, Minehead

SOUTH WEST ENGLAND 55

HIGHER TOWN
Dulverton, Somerset TA22 9RX
Tel: 01398 341272

Our farm is situated half-a-mile from open moorland, one mile from the Devon/Somerset border and four miles from Dulverton. 80 acres of the farm is in the Exmoor National Park. We let two caravans which are quarter-of-a-mile apart and do not overlook each other. Both have lovely views, situated in lawns with parking space. Both are 8-berth, with a double end bedroom, bunk bedroom, shower, flush toilet, hot/cold water and colour TV.

The caravans are modern and fully equipped except linen. Cot and high chair available. One caravan with three bedrooms. Visitors are welcome to watch the milking or walk over our beef and sheep farm. Riding and fishing nearby. Open May to October.

Price from £120, includes gas and electricity.

ST AUDRIES BAY Holiday Club

- Family-owned and run award-winning Park near Exmoor and The Quantocks
- 15 miles from the M5 • Fantastic views across the sea and beach access
- Sport & leisure facilities • Entertainment
- Licensed bars and restaurant
- Coffee Shop • On-site shop
- Children's play area
- Peaceful relaxing Park with family time in school holidays

Self-Catering & Half-Board Holidays
- Touring Caravans & Camping
- Luxury Holiday Homes for sale

e-mail: info@staudriesbay.co.uk
www.staudriesbay.co.uk

West Quantoxhead, Near Minehead, Somerset TA4 4DY
Tel: 01984 632515

In the heart of Exmoor Country
BURROWHAYES FARM
Caravan & Camping Site and Riding Stables
West Luccombe, Porlock, Near Minehead, Somerset TA24 8HT
Tel: 01643 862463

A select family site in the heart of the Exmoor National Park, just 2 miles from the coast.

The surrounding moors and woods of the glorious Horner Valley provide a walker's paradise and children enjoy playing and exploring for hours.

Riding Stables offer pony trekking for all ages and abilities.

Heated shower block with disabled and baby changing facilities, launderette and pot wash. Shop on site.

Sites for Touring Caravans, tents and motorhomes with or without hook-ups. Caravan holiday homes for hire.

Proprietors Julian & Marion Dascombe
e-mail: info@burrowhayes.co.uk
www.burrowhayes.co.uk

Somerset

Porlock, Taunton

SOUTH WEST ENGLAND 57

PORLOCK CARAVAN PARK
HIGH BANK, PORLOCK, NEAR MINEHEAD SOMERSET TA24 8ND

- Small family run park • A few minutes walk from Porlock village set in the heart of Exmoor
- Luxury, central heated holiday homes for hire • Full facilities for tourers, tents and motorhomes
- Village offers several pubs, restaurants and shops selling local produce
- Ideal base from which to explore Exmoor, whether walking, cycling or riding

Facilities on Site include: • Reception & Information Area • Free Showers and hot water • Hair dryer and shaver points • Disabled facilities • Dishwashing room • Laundry room and drying area • Microwave oven • Free freezer block facility • Electric hook-up • Grass or hardstanding pitches • Chemical waste disposal room • Dog exercise area • Calor gas exchange • Cars park beside units • WiFi

Phone for brochure 01643 862269 or e-mail: info@porlockcaravanpark.co.uk • www.porlockcaravanpark.co.uk

Ashe Farm Touring Park
Thornfalcon, Taunton, Somerset TA3 5NW
TEL: 01823 442567

Ashe Farm Touring Park is a quiet, informal family-run site, part of a working farm situated in the Vale of Taunton between the Quantock and Blackdown Hills. The six acre site has two sheltered meadows with lovely views of the hills and an atmosphere of peace and seclusion. Towing approach from the M5 motorway is easy and the site is easy to find at the end of your journey.

There are electric hook-ups in both fields. The first field has a new toilet block with showers, hot water, hair dryers and razor points. There are toilet facilities for the disabled and a laundry with tumble dryer and iron. Nearby is the information Room and a play area for small children. also wash up sinks and waste disposal points.

Visit the FHG website
www.holidayguides.com

for details of the wide choice of accommodation featured in the full range of FHG titles

Somerset

Taunton, Wookey Hole

Quantock Orchard Caravan Park

Welcome to Quantock Orchard Caravan Park.

A small, family-run touring caravan and camping park situated in the quiet rural heart of West Somerset.
Close to Exmoor and the coast at the foot of the beautiful Quantock Hills, this peaceful park is set in a designated Area of Outstanding Natural Beauty and an ideal touring base for Somerset, Exmoor and the North Devon coast.
Personally supervised by the proprietors, Michael and Sara Barrett.

The small, clean, friendly park for touring and camping

STATIC CARAVANS FOR HIRE.

For colour brochure and tariff call:
01984 618618
or write to: Michael & Sara Barrett,
Quantock Orchard Caravan Park, Flaxpool,
Crowcombe, Near Taunton, Somerset TA4 4AW
e-mail: qocp@flaxpool.freeserve.co.uk
www.quantockorchard.co.uk

DE LUXE PARK

Ebborlands Farm & Riding Centre

SIX-BERTH LUXURY CARAVAN. Two separate bedrooms, bathroom with toilet/shower/washbasin, bedroom/lounge, kitchen. Own private site situated on the southern slopes of the Mendip Hills, a few minutes' walk from Wookey Hole village, but away from the main traffic route to the caves. 2½ miles from the city of Wells.
Good touring area for Somerset, surrounding counties and Severn crossings into Wales.
Lots of country footpaths - near West Mendip Way, Ebbor Gorge and surrounding hills.
Horse riding available from our centre nearby.
Rates from £100 to £250 per week according to season.

Mrs E.A. Gibbs, Ebborlands Farm & Riding Centre, Wookey Hole, Wells BA5 1AY
(Tel & Fax: 01749 672550)
e-mail: eileen.gibbs1@btinternet.com • www.ebborlandsridingcentre.co.uk

Somerset
Watchet

SOUTH WEST ENGLAND 59

Hawkchurch Country Park

Hawkchurch Country Park boasts a superb rural setting offering stunning views across the Axe Valley, visible through the mature woodland surrounding the park. Situated on the Devon/Dorset border, we offer a variety of accommodation & facilities including:

- Static Holiday Homes
- Camping Meadows
- Touring Caravans
- Restaurant & Licensed Bar
- Convenience Shop
- Laundry Facilities

Pet Friendly

CALL NOW TO REQUEST YOUR BROCHURE

tel: 01297 678402
email: enquiries@hawkchurchpark.co.uk
web: www.hawkchurchpark.co.uk

hawkchurch
country park

Wiltshire

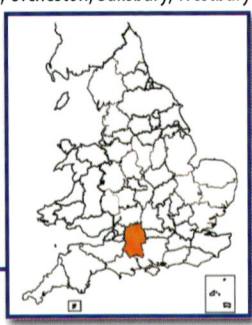

Calne, Devizes, Orcheston, Salisbury, Westbury

CALNE. Blackland Lakes, Stockley Lane Calne SN11 0NQ
Tel: 01249 813672 • www.blacklandlakes.co.uk
Ideal for a family holiday, this peaceful site set over 15 acres comprises 7 tree-lined paddocks and 3 small lakes (two for fishing and one a nature reserve. 180 caravan/tent pitches and 15 superpitches.

Colin and Cynthia Fletcher
FOXHANGERS CANALSIDE FARM
Lower Foxhangers, Rowde, Devizes SN10 1SS
Tel & Fax: 01380 828254
e-mail: sales@foxhangers.co.uk
www.foxhangers.com

Small farm/marina with its many diverse attractions situated alongside the famous "Caen Hill" flights of 29 locks. Hear the near musical clatter of the windlass heralding the lock gate opening and the arrival of yet another colourful narrowboat. Relax on the patios of our rural retreats - 4 holiday mobile homes, all new models, sleeping 4/6. Ideally situated for fishing, cycling or walking. Pubs within easy walking distance. Short breaks when available. Secluded campsite nestling under the hedgerows, with electricity and facilities.
Also narrowboat hire for weekly or short breaks. Avebury, Stonehenge, Bath and Longleat all close by.

ORCHESTON. Stonehenge Touring Park, Orcheston, Near Shrewton, Salisbury SP3 4SH
Tel: 01980 620304 • www.stonehengetouringpark.com
Located on the edge of Salisbury Plain and just 4 miles from historic Stonehenge, this small site is maintained to the highest standards. Some hardstandings are available and there are 20 electric hook-ups. Open all year.

SALISBURY. Alderbury Caravan & Camping Park, Southampton Road, Whaddon, Salisbury SP5 3HB
Tel: 01722 710125 • www.alderburycaravanpark.co.uk
A small, friendly, family-run site, convenient for visiting Salisbury and just a short drive from the New Forest. A pub serving meals is located just opposite and the village shops are close by. Tourers and tents welcome.

WESTBURY. Brokerswood Country Park, Westbury BA13 4EJ
Tel: 01373 822238 • www.brokerswood.co.uk
Spacious pitches are available for tents and caravans in 80 acres of woodland just a few minutes from Longleat. Attractions include woodland walks, a fishing lake, and a cafe serving meals until 5pm. A pub is just a short walk away.

London (Central & Greater)

Edmonton, London, Loughton

London
(Central & Greater)

LONDON & SOUTH EAST ENGLAND

EDMONTON. Lee Valley Camping And Caravan Park, Meridian Way, Edmonton, London N9 0AS
Tel: 0208 803 6900 • Fax: 020 8884 4975 • www.leevalleypark.org
Set within Lee Valley Regional Park which stretches over 26 miles, this is a ideal base for experiencing the attractions of London from a peaceful and good value base (40 minutes by Tube). Open all year.

LONDON. Abbey Wood Caravan Club Site, Federation Road, Abbey Wood, London SE2 0LS
Tel: 0208 311 7708 • Fax: 0208 311 1465
With good rail connections to the city centre just a short walk away, this popular rural site welcomes caravans, motorhomes and tents. The atmosphere is very rural, with local wildlife and mature trees providing a peaceful haven at the end of a busy day. Open all year.

LONDON. Crystal Palace Caravan Club Site, Crystal Palace Parade, Crystal Palace, London SE19 1UF
Tel: 0208 7787 155
On a direct bus route to the city centre, this site is popular with families from all over Europe. 150 pitches. Tourers and tents are welcome (but please note there are restrictions on motorhome length). Open all year.

LOUGHTON. The Elms Caravan & Camping Park, Lippitts Hill, High Beech, Loughton IG10 4AW
Tel: 0208 502 5652 • Fax: 0208 508 9414 • www.theelmscampsite.co.uk
Right on the edge of London and in the peaceful conservation area of Epping Forest, this 50-pitch site offers convenient access to the capital by Tube (station 3 miles away). Caravans, motorhomes and tents welcome. Open March to October.

Debden House Camp Site

15 miles north of London in Epping Forest, two miles north of Loughton. M25 to Junction 26 then A121 (Loughton). Left onto A1168 Rectory Lane, second left Pyrles Lane, over crossroads, right onto England's Lane, then second left. Epping Forest is 40 minutes from London (Underground nearby).

Site facilities include shop, café, launderette, showers, play area and much more. Electric hook-ups. Terms £7.00 adult, £3.50 child; family ticket £25.00. Day ticket £3.50. London Borough of Newham residents reduced rates. Open May to September. Brochure available.

Debden Green
Loughton,
Essex IG10 2NZ
Tel: 020 8508 3008
Fax: 020 8508 0284
www.debdenhouse.com

Berkshire

Berkshire — Wokingham

California Chalet & Touring Park

Small, family-run park alongside a lake. Secluded pitches in a wooded setting. Close to London, Windsor and Oxford. Also available, 10 self-catering holiday chalets. Terms on request.

California Chalet & Touring Park
Nine Mile Ride, Finchampstead,
Wokingham, Berkshire RG40 4HU
Tel: 0118 973 3928
Fax: 0118 932 8720

- Electric hook-ups available
- Children's play area
- Laundry facilities
- Licensed bar on site
- Facilities for disabled visitors
- Pets welcome
- Shop on site
- Wifi access available

Buckinghamshire

Beaconsfield, Milton Keynes, Newport Pagnell, Olney, Radnage

Buckinghamshire

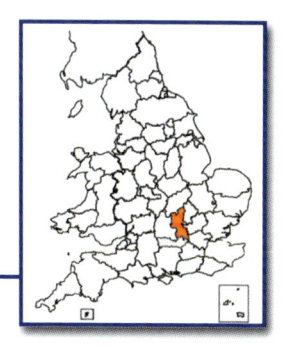

Quiet, level meadowland park. Ideal for touring London, train station one mile. 25 minutes to Marylebone, cheap day return fares available. Legoland 12 miles, with Windsor Castle and the Thames. Model village three miles, many local attractions, including rare breeds farm. Local inn for food quarter of a mile. Lots of walks, ideal for dogs. On suite accommodation available – room only. New shower block for 2008, new tenting area. 65 pitches available. Open March to January.

Tourers from £15 to £19, tents from £10, motor homes £13 to £18, electric point £2.50

~ HIGHCLERE FARM ~
New Barn Lane, Seer Green, Near Beaconsfield HP9 2QZ
Tel & Fax: 01494 874505 • e-mail: highclerepark@aol.com
website: www.highclerefarmpark.co.uk

MILTON KEYNES. Old Dairy Farm, Orchard Mill Lane, Stoke Hammond, Milton Keynes MK17 9BF
Tel & Fax: **01908 274206**
Picturesque farm site, with good walking nearby on Grand Union Canal towpath; Milton Keynes is just 5 miles away, with lots of shopping and leisure amenities. Ideal for anglers - River Ouzel adjacent. 10 caravan and 10 tent pitches.

NEWPORT PAGNELL. Lovat Meadow Caravan Park, London Road, Newport Pagnell MK16 0AE
Tel: **01908 610858** • Fax: **01908 617874**
This gently sloping site has 40 grass pitches and is bordered by woodland and by the River Ouzel where fishing is available in season. No shower or toilet facilities. The site is open March to October.

OLNEY. Emberton Country Park, Olney Road, Emberton, Near Olney MK46 5FJ
Tel: **01234 711575** • www.mkweb.co.uk/embertonpark
A former gravel works has been converted into an attractive 200-acre park which includes a camping and caravan park with five fishing lakes and two children's play areas. Just 12 miles from the MK Bowl; nearby Olney has shops.

RADNAGE. Home Farm Caravan & Camping Park, City Road, Radnage, High Wycombe HP14 4DW
Tel: **01494 484136** • www.homefarmradnage.co.uk
With superb views and lots of good walks along the Ridgeway Path and Icknield Way, this is a good base for visiting Oxford and the surrounding area. Local village has shop and two pubs. Tourers, motorhomes and tents welcome.

The FHG Directory of Website Addresses
on pages 235-250 is a useful quick reference guide for holiday accommodation with e-mail and/or website details

64 LONDON & SOUTH EAST ENGLAND Hampshire

Hayling Island, Milford-on-Sea

Hampshire

HAYLING ISLAND FAMILY CAMP SITES

Hayling Island is an ideal touring base for Portsmouth, the Isle of Wight and the New Forest, with excellent motorway access. We have safe, clean, award-winning beaches, and windsurfing, sailing, horse riding, golf, tennis and walking to be enjoyed locally. Our campsite has children's play areas, electric hook-ups, toilets and hot water, heated swimming pool. Many other extras included.

The Oven Campsite
Tel: 023 9246 4695 • Mobile: 077584 10020
e-mail: theovencampsite@talktalk.net
www.haylingcampsites.co.uk

Downton Holiday Park

Downton Holiday Park is a small, peaceful park are on the edge of the New Forest and close to the sea. Green fields are across the country lane from us.

We let only 22 static caravans on our small park; each caravan has shower and colour TV.

A laundry and children's play equipment are on premises. Swimming, riding and sailing are all nearby. Bournemouth is about 25 minutes away by car. The Isle of Wight can be reached by ferry from Lymington.

We believe our prices which start at £130 per week Low Season are excellent value. Please telephone or write for a free brochure. **CARAVANS FOR SALE**

Downton Holiday Park, Shorefield Road, Milford-on-Sea SO41 0LH
Tel: 01425 476131 or 01590 642515
info@downtonholidaypark.co.uk
www.downtonholidaypark.co.uk

For a Happy, marvellous seaside holiday

Hampshire
LONDON & SOUTH EAST ENGLAND

Ringwood, Romsey

Beautifully situated in the heart of the NEW FOREST, yet only half-an- hour's drive to Bournemouth and coast. Four acres of close mown meadow. Ideal centre for walking and touring and for nature lovers. Pets welcome. Open 1st March to 31st October *Approved site - tents, caravans and motor caravans *Amenities block recently upgraded to very high standard *Facilities for disabled visitors *Well stocked shop *Safe playground *Mountain bike hire *Laundry room *Electric hook-ups *Forest Inn adjacent - families and dogs welcomed *Owner-managed to high standard. Please send SAE for brochure. From east turn off M27 at Exit 1 and follow signs to Linwood. From west turn off A388 2 miles north of Ringwood and look for our sign.

Red Shoot Camping Park, Linwood, Near Ringwood BH24 3QT
Tel: 01425 473789 • Fax: 01425 471558
e-mail: enquiries@redshoot-campingpark.com
www.redshoot-campingpark.com

A friendly welcome awaits you from Tony and Jane at their family-run farm and campsite. All types of touring units are catered for. Cleanliness is top priority with our toilet facilities, and free hot showers are available. We have a toilet and shower for the disabled; washing machine and dryer; washing-up sinks; electric hook-ups; small shop; Calor and camping gas; payphone. Well-controlled dogs are welcome. Daytime kennels are available. Children love the space, where they can play in full view of the units (parents appreciate that too). 20 minutes' walk to local pub, serving good food. Fishing and golf nearby.

Tel: 023 8081 4444
e-mail: enquiries@greenpasturesfarm.com   www.greenpasturesfarm.com

Green Pastures Farm
Ower, Romsey, Hampshire
SO51 6AJ

---

symbols

- ☼ Holiday Parks & Centres
- 🚐 Caravans for Hire
- Ⓢ Caravan Sites and Touring Parks
- ▲ Camping Sites

Hampshire
Southsea

You couldn't get closer to the beach

Southsea HOLIDAY & LEISURE PARK

The warmest welcome awaits you at Southsea Leisure and Holiday Park. This privately owned Holiday Park is ideally situated by the Solent, adjacent to the beach and with breathtaking views over to the Isle of Wight.

Whether you are seeking a quiet holiday on our popular 12 acre site, intend using it as a centre to go out and about to discover the delights of the region or, simply having a well earned rest before taking the ferry to France or Spain, the management and team of Southsea Leisure and Holiday Park will make your stay one to remember.

Our fabulous Self Catering Holiday Homes are fully equipped for family use, they are modern and offer perfect accomodation for your family, ranging from basic accomodation up to the luxury of extra added space and heating throughout.

Alternatively you can join the 1000's of people who come each year and enjoy the freedom of bringing along their own Touring Caravan, Motorhome or Tent, these pitches range from standard pitch only to full electric hook-up with grass or gravel standing.

So much to see and do

Enjoy a round-the-city bus trip, stopping at various places of interest, or how about a day's excursion to the Isle of Wight. Travel by coach via the ferry and tour the Island's beauty spots and unique places of interest. Or discover the City of Portsmouth's 800 years of maritime history during a cruise around the harbour. There are mountain and BMX bikes for hire.

On site are table tennis and pool tables and amusement arcade. A heated outdoor pool. A great playpark for children under 12years, pitch and putt golf course, sailing, swimming off the beach.

Southsea also offers a wealth of restaurants, cafes, nightspots and summer shows to suit all tastes, or a short walk away you can soak up the atmosphere while having a quiet drink in the Top Deck at Southsea Marina.

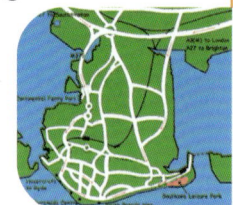

We are located at the very eastern end of Southsea seafront

SOUTHSEA HOLIDAY & LEISURE PARK
Melville Road, Southsea
Hampshire PO4 9TB
Tel: 023 9273 5070 • Fax: 023 9282 1302
e-mail: info@southsealeisurepark.com • www.southsealeisurepark.com

Kent

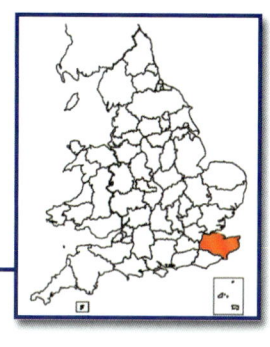

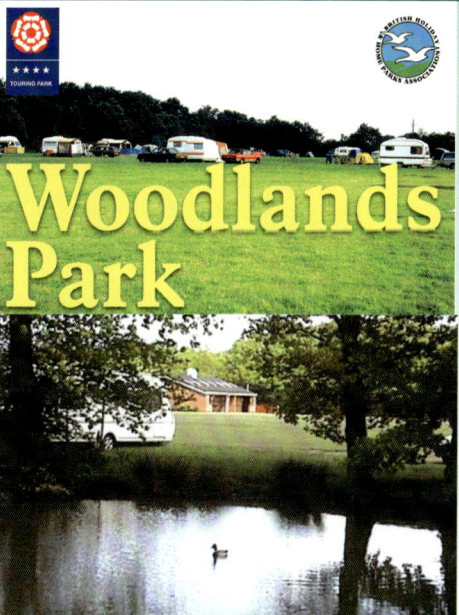

Biddenden

Woodlands Park

Situated in the heart of the beautiful Kent countryside, a quiet and tranquil environment to enjoy your holiday.
An ideal base for visiting the many historic Castles and other attractions throughout Kent and East Sussex.
Large open level grassland park with two ponds to enjoy a spot of fishing
Electric hook-ups available, modern toilet and shower block facility.
Plenty of space for children to run around and let off steam.
Small site shop where all essential items can be purchased from camping gaz to a bottle of milk. Friendly staff are on hand to answer any questions on the area and to provide tourist information.

Tenterden Road, Biddenden, Kent TN27 8BT
Tel: 01580 291216
e-mail: woodlandspark@overlinebroadband.com
www.campingsite.co.uk

Residential Park Homes, Leisure Homes and Tourist Park

Please note

All the information in this book is given in good faith in the belief that it is correct. However, the publishers cannot guarantee the facts given in these pages, neither are they responsible for changes in policy, ownership or terms that may take place after the date of going to press. Readers should always satisfy themselves that the facilities they require are available and that the terms, if quoted, still apply.

Kent
Birchington

Two Chimneys Caravan Park
www.twochimneys.co.uk

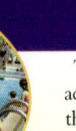

Two Chimneys is a family run, five star holiday park set in 40 acres of Kent countryside. We are just a few minutes drive from the coast, which boasts miles of golden sandy beaches and calm seas of the English Channel. In recent years Two Chimneys Caravan Park has undergone a large amount of expansion and improvement providing more modern facilities, Toilets, Showers, Launderette and a Telescopic Swimming Pool Enclosure, so the pool can still be enjoyed on those not so warm days.

Licensed Club House, on-site Shop, Take Away Food, Tennis Court, Children's Play Areas.

Two Chimneys has over 200 tent and touring pitches available on level grass fields. Open from March to October. Sorry no dogs.

Telephone: 01843 841068 / 843157
Fax: 01843 848099
Two Chimneys Caravan Park,
Shottendane Road, Birchington,
Kent CT7 0HD

St Nicholas at Wade Camp Site
Court Road
St Nicholas at Wade
CT7 0NH

Sheltered village site in easy reach of five major towns and seaside. Village (two pubs and post office) signposted off A299 and off A28 near Birchington.

Open from 1st March to 31st October

Three acres takes 75 units • Open meadow, hedged • Booking advised
Flush toilets, showers, lighting, shavers • Fishing • Gaz
Touring and motor caravans and tents welcome, electric hook-ups available.

**Prices: Tourers £14 to £16,
Motor Caravans £13.50 to £16.50, Tents £10 to £17**

Many places of interest including Ramsgate and Canterbury within easy reach. Birchington is a delightful resort with sand and cliffs.

Contact: E.B. Broadley - 01843 847245

Oxfordshire

Banbury, Charlbury, Chpping Norton, Standlake

Oxfordshire

BANBURY. Bo Peep Farm Caravan Park, Aynho Road, Adderbury, Banbury OX17 3NP
Tel: 01295 810605 • Fax: 01295 810605 • www.bo-peep.co.uk
Enjoy the clean air at this secluded farm with a 4-acre camping field and 84 acres of countryside. The site offers large and varied pitches and modern facilities. No facilities for children. Open March to October. 104 touring pitches available. Caravans, motorhomes and tents welcome.

BANBURY. Barnstones Caravan & Camping Park, Main Street, Great Broughton, Banbury OX17 1QU
Tel: 01295 750 289
Pets are welcome at this small caravan and camping park in Banbury, ideal for couples and families. There is easy access to the Cotswolds, Oxford and Stratford-upon-Avon. Caravans, motorhomes and tents welcome.

CHARLBURY. Cotswold View Caravan and Camping Park, Enstone Road, Charlbury OX7 3JH
Tel: 01608 810314 • Fax: 01608 811891• www.cotswoldview.co.uk/
This scenic park extends over 54 acres of rolling hills, with spacious pitches overlooking the Evenlode Valley and Wychwood Forest. Grass walks, farm trails, animals, playgrounds and sports facilities are among the many attractions for visitors. Open March to November. 125 pitches available. Caravans, motorhomes and tents welcome.

CHIPPING NORTON. Chipping Norton Camping and Caravanning Club Site, Chipping Norton OX7 3PE
Tel: 01608 641993
This site in the Cotswolds has easy access to local villages, including Stow-on-the-Wold and Bourton-on-the-Water. Oxford and Stratford-upon-Avon are only 20 miles away. 105 touring pitches available. Caravans, tents and motorhomes. Open from March to November.

STANDLAKE. Lincoln Farm Park Oxfordshire, High Street, Standlake OX29 7RH
Tel: 01865 300239 • Fax:01865 300127 • www.lincolnfarmpark.co.uk
This small family park has an impressive number of facilities, helping to make your stay as comfortable as possible. Special deals are available throughout the year. Tents, caravans and motorhomes are welcome; tent trailers permitted. Open from February to November. 90 touring pitches, 17 tent pitches available.

⚡	Electric hook-ups available	♿	Facilities for disabled visitors
🛝	Children's play area	🐕	Pets welcome
📺	Laundry facilities	🛒	Shop on site
🍷	Licensed bar on site	W	Wifi access available

Sussex

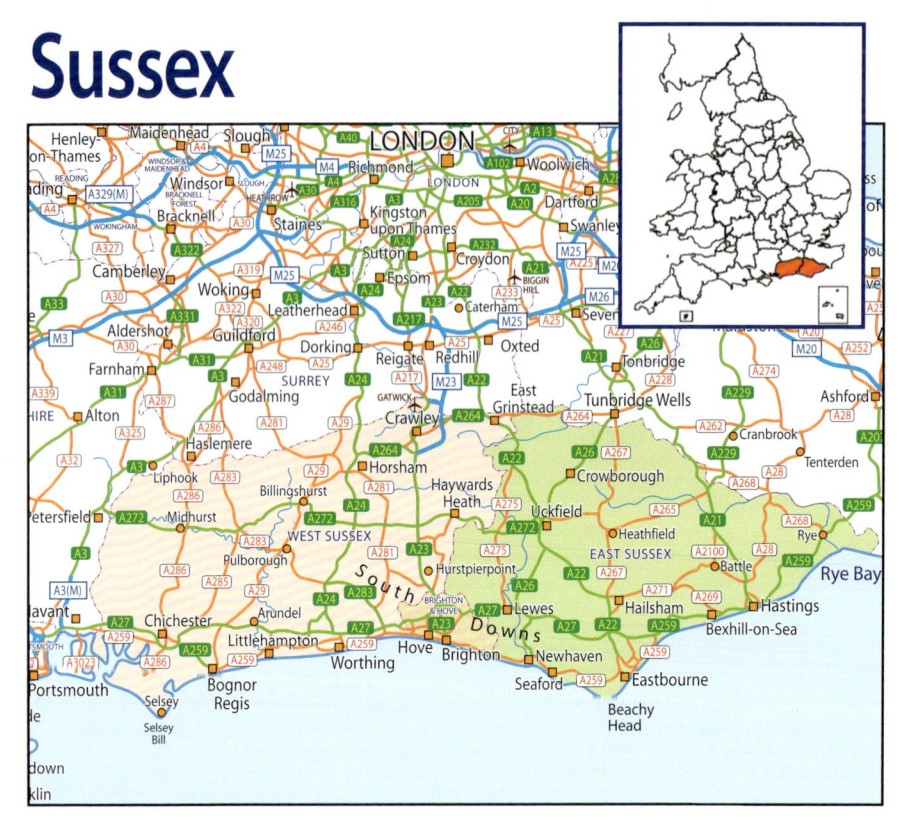

Beachy Head, near Eastbourne

East Sussex
Battle, Bodiam, Eastbourne

East Sussex

Crazy Lane Tourist Park
Camping & Caravanning in Sedlescombe,
Near Battle, East Sussex   ★★★

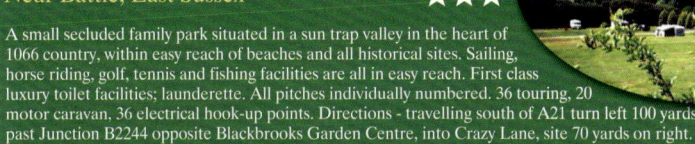

A small secluded family park situated in a sun trap valley in the heart of 1066 country, within easy reach of beaches and all historical sites. Sailing, horse riding, golf, tennis and fishing facilities are all in easy reach. First class luxury toilet facilities; launderette. All pitches individually numbered. 36 touring, 20 motor caravan, 36 electrical hook-up points. Directions - travelling south of A21 turn left 100 yards past Junction B2244 opposite Blackbrooks Garden Centre, into Crazy Lane, site 70 yards on right.
Rates: From £13.00 per night; book seven nights, only pay for six!
• Hardstanding for disabled with own fully equipped toilet facility. • Dogs are welcome on lead.
• Open 1st March to 31st October.   Whydown Farm, Sedlescombe, Battle TN33 0QT
Tel: 01424 870147 • e-mail: info@crazylane.co.uk • www.crazylane.co.uk

CAMPING SITES

BODIAM. Mr Richard Bailey, Park Farm Caravan and Camping Site, Park Farm, Bodiam TN32 5XA (01424 838433).
Quiet rural site in beautiful setting. Off B2244, signposted. Hot showers; children's play area. Small camp fires and barbecues permitted. Riverside walk to Bodiam Castle. Free fishing in River Rother.
Rates: : £8 per adult and £3 per child per night. Electric hookup £3
• Open Easter to October. • Dogs allowed.
e-mail: info@parkfarmcamping.co.uk
www.parkfarmcamping.co.uk

Fairfields Farm & Caravan and Camping Park, Eastbourne Road,
Westham, Pevensey BN24 5NG • Tel: 01323 763165; Fax: 01323 469175

Quiet country touring site on a working family-run farm. Close to the beautiful resort of Eastbourne, we offer an excellent base from which to explore the stunning scenery and diverse attractions of South East England.

• Drinking water taps • wash basins and showers • flush toilets • washing-up area • • laundry sinks • washing machine and tumble dryer • chemical sluice disposal •

Our farm spans an area of almost 200 acres, alongside the extensive views you will find a duck pond, numerous farm animals and pets, a recreational walk and a fishing lake.

Site open from 1st April to 31st October.

e-mail: enquiries@fairfieldsfarm.com • www.fairfieldsfarm.com

---

FREE or REDUCED RATE entry to Holiday Visits and Attractions – see our READERS' OFFER VOUCHERS on pages 205-234

East Sussex
Hastings

Hastings
Touring Park

Welcome to Hastings....

If it's the very best in camping, caravan or motor home holidays you're looking for then look no further. An ideal, easy to access location, thoughtfully placed pitches, and great facilities all add up to the perfect place to spend valuable holiday time, and that's before you begin to explore the stunning countryside!

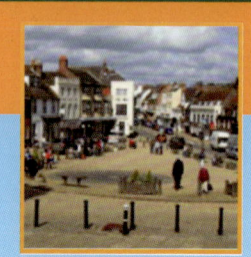

Shearbarn

Set in the rolling hills above the historic town of Hastings, Shearbarn's location offers the best of so many worlds.
Literally on the doorstep there's the rural beauty of the 660 acres of the Hastings Country Park to explore; then there's mile upon mile of unspoilt beaches stretching into the distance, and the charming town of Hastings itself, with its enviable selection of restaurants and bars as well as museums, galleries and interesting shops to browse in.

Facilities

With 131 pitches, over 100 of which have electrical hook-ups, we have plenty of room for you and your friends.
As a customer of Hastings Touring Park, you'll be able to use the neighbouring bar and restaurant at 'Shearbarn'. The restaurant offers a varied menu with regular specials. There's nothing better at the end of a long and enjoyable day.
A smart casual dress code operates in the Bar and Restaurant complex. And if you'd rather cook for yourselves and eat in, there is a small shop just perfect for daily essentials. For more choice, there is a wide range of shops a short drive away. And don't forget the kids, at Hastings Touring Park we have indoor soft play and outdoor play areas.

Hastings Touring Park
Barley Lane, Hastings, East Sussex TN35 5DX
Telephone: 01424 423583 • Fax: 01424 718740
e-mail: info@hastingstouring.co.uk
www.hastingstouring.co.uk

A superb sea view location for your perfect holiday...

West Sussex

Arundel, Bognor Regis, Chichester

ARUNDEL. Maynards Caravan & Camping Park, Crossbush, Arundel BN18 9PQ
Tel: 01903 882075 • Fax: 01903 885547
Just a mile from Arundel, this 3-acre level site caters for tents, caravans and motorhomes. The surrounding area has amenities to suit all the family, including golf, fishing and horseriding. The park has excellent facilities and is open all year.

BOGNOR REGIS. The Lillies Caravan Park, Yapton Road, Barnham, Bognor Regis PO22 0AY
Tel: 01243 552081 • www.lilliescaravanpark.co.uk
A quiet site set within 3 acres of secluded countryside within a short travelling distance of many local attractions. This is a grassy site with sheltered areas suitable for touring caravans, motor homes, trailer tents and tents.

CHICHESTER. Chichester Lakeside Holiday Park, Vinnetrow Road, Chichester PO20 1QH
Tel: 0845 815 9745 • www.parkholidaysuk.com
With superb facilities included a heated leisure pool, licensed clubhouse and entertainment complex, this is the perfect location for a relaxing family holiday. The large touring site is well lit and is open all year round.

CARAVAN SITES & TOURING PARKS

CHICHESTER. Bell Caravan Park, Bell Lane, Birdham PO20 7HY (01243 512264).
Holiday home (owner-occupied only) and small touring park with electric hook-ups, toilet blocks with showers. Local shop within walking distance. We are approximately within one/two miles from the beach and Chichester Harbour and Marina are a short drive away. The Roman city of Chichester is about five miles away and there are many places to visit in the area including Goodwood House and racecourse, Petworth House and Arundel Castle. Chichester is also ideal for visiting the historic town of Portsmouth. For prices please telephone or send a SAE.
• Children and dogs welcome.

🚐 Electric hook-ups available		♿ Facilities for disabled visitors	
🎢 Children's play area		🐕 Pets welcome	
🧺 Laundry facilities		🛒 Shop on site	
🍷 Licensed bar on site		W Wifi access available	

Honeybridge Park

Dial Post, Eastergate

A picturesque 15-acre touring, camping and caravan park set in an Area of Outstanding Natural Beauty, convenient for London, Gatwick & South Coast.

Large hardstanding and grass pitches, electric hook-ups, heated amenity blocks, licensed shop, laundry, games room and play area. Seasonal pitches and storage available. Luxury lodges and static caravans for sale on 11-month holiday licences. Dogs welcome. Open all year.

Tel: 01403 710923
web: www.honeybridgepark.co.uk
e-mail: enquiries@honeybridgepark.co.uk

Honeybridge Lane, Dial Post, West Sussex RH13 8NX

Wandleys Caravan Park

Eastergate, West Sussex PO20 3SE

Telephone:
01243 543235
or
01243 543384
(evenings/weekends)

You will find peace, tranquillity and relaxation in one of our comfortable holiday caravans. All have internal WC and shower. Dogs welcome.

The Sussex Downs, Chichester, Bognor Regis, Arundel, Littlehampton – all these historic and interesting places are only 15 minutes from our beautiful, small and quiet country park. Telephone for brochure. New and used holiday homes for sale when available.

Cambridgeshire

Comberton, Ely, Great Shelford, Huntingdon

Cambridgeshire

EAST OF ENGLAND 75

COMBERTON. Highfield Farm Touring Park, Long Road, Comberton CB3 7DG
Tel: 01223 262308 • Fax: 01223 262308 • www.highfieldfarmtouringpark.co.uk
Five miles from Cambridge, the park is set in 8 acres of secluded countryside, with outstanding views. The careful layout, with a central open area, gives a great feeling of space. 60 touring pitches available. Caravans, motorhomes and tents welcome. Open from April/Easter to October.

ELY. Riverside Camping & Caravan Park, 21 New River Bank, Ely CB7 4TA
Tel: 01353 860255 • www.riversideccp.co.uk/
The ideal fisherman's escape, this adults-only site is situated on 4 acres of well laid out parkland, with pleasant paths leading along the riverside to the local marina and pub and into town. Open all year round. 37 touring pitches, 37 tent pitches available. Caravans, motorhomes and tents welcome.

GREAT SHELFORD. Cambridge Caravanning Site, 19 Cabbage Moor, Great Shelford CB2 5NB
Tel: 01223 841185
Located just minutes from the University town of Cambridge, the site makes the perfect base from which to explore the old streets and colleges. Excellent facilities. Open from March to October. 120 touring pitches. Caravans, motorhomes, tents welcome.

HUNTINGDON. The Willows Caravan Park, Brampton, Huntingdon PE18 8NE
Tel: 01480 437566 • www.willowscaravanpark.com/
This park is ideal for an activity based holiday for all the family, including small children, with a choice of walking, cycling and fishing and other water-based activities nearby. 55 touring pitches available. Caravans, motorhomes and tents welcome.

HUNTINGDON. Old Manor Caravan Park, Church Road, Grafham, Huntingdon PE28 0BB
Tel: 01480 810264
This attractive, peaceful site a short walk form Grafham Water has received a David Bellamy Gold Award for conservation. Facilities include a heated outdoor pool and children's play area. 76 touring pitches available. Caravans, tents and motorhomes welcome. Open all year.

HUNTINGDON. Houghton Mill Caravan Site, Mill St, Houghton Mill, Huntingdon PE28 2AZ
Tel: 01480 466716
A National Trust-owned paradise for walkers, with bridleways for horse riders too. The ideal retreat for wildlife enthusiasts and bird watchers. 65 touring pitches. Caravans and tents welcome.

A useful index of towns/counties appears at the back of this book

76 EAST OF ENGLAND — Cambridgeshire

Huntingdon, Peterborough, Pidley, Wisbech

HUNTINGDON. Quiet Waters Caravan Park, Hemingford Abbots, Huntingdon PE28 9AJ
Tel: 01480 463405 • Fax: 01480 463405 • www.quietwaterscaravanpark.co.uk/
5 acres of well maintained parkland situated next to the banks of the Great Ouse River, with easy access into the nearest town, St Ives. Open from April to October. 20 touring pitches. 20 tent pitches. Caravans, motorhomes and tents welcome.

PETERBOROUGH. Ferry Meadows Caravan Club Site, Ham Lane, Peterborough PE2 5UU
Tel: 01733 233526 • Fax: 01733239880
The perfect family retreat, there is a wide range of activities available at this level parkland site, including local steam trains, a watersports centre, cycle and walking trails, as well as ice and roller skating, an indoor pool, bowling alley, cinema, and theatre in nearby Peterborough. Open all year round. 254 touring pitches available. Caravans, motorhomes and tents welcome.

PETERBOROUGH. Northey Lodge Touring Park, North Bank Whittlesey Road, Peterborough PE6 7YZ
Tel: 01733 223918 • Fax: 01733 221073 • www.northeylodge.co.uk
This quiet touring park is situated adjacent to the River Nene near Peterborough. Open all year round. Caravans, motorhomes and tents welcome.

PETERBOROUGH. Windmill Farm Caravan Park, Windmill Farm Baston Fen, Peterborough PE6 9PX
Tel: 01775 640215 • Fax:01775 640 133 • www.windmill-farm-caravan-park.co.uk
Adults-only park close to Bourne, Spalding, Peterborough and and their many attractions. The facilities are of a high standard. Open all year round. 26 touring pitches. Caravans, motorhomes and tents welcome.

PIDLEY. Stroud Hill Park, Fen Road, Pidley PE28 3DE
Tel: 01487 741333 • Fax: 01487 741365 • www.stroudhillpark.co.uk
Winner of AA Campsite of the Year & Overall Winner 2008; 5 stars for Loo of the Year! Stroud Hill is strictly adults-only and accessible by all major road links. Fishing lake on site. 54 touring pitches. Caravans and motorhomes welcome.

WISBECH. Little Ranch, Begdale, Elm, Near Wisbech PE14 0AZ
Tel: 01945 860066
Full serviced pitches are available at this family-run Cambridgeshire caravan park in the heart of the fenland countryside, near the villages of Elm and Friday Bridge, and the town of Wisbech. Open all year. Caravans welcome.

WISBECH. Virginia Lake & Caravan Park, Smeeth Road, St Johns Fen End, Wisbech PE14 8JF
Tel: 01945 430167 • www.virginialake.co.uk
This park is popular with dog-owners who appreciate the designated path that runs by the lake. Club with entertainment, welll stocked fishing lake. Open all year round. Caravans, motorhomes and tents welcome.

Key

- Electric hook-ups available
- Facilities for disabled visitors
- Children's play area
- Pets welcome
- Laundry facilities
- Shop on site
- Licensed bar on site
- Wifi access available

Essex

Clacton-on-Sea

Essex

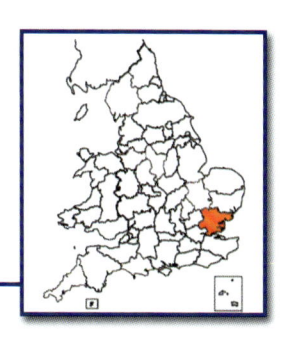

Essex - between London and England's East Coast lies the ancient county of Essex, a place of farms and forests, quiet villages and country towns, and also of seaside resorts offering traditional entertainments and exciting events. Thatched cottages and timber framed farmhouses are very characteristic as are the unmistakable outlines of windmills which still punctuate the horizon. Close to the European mainland, Essex has been influenced by many different cultures and historical events. The Normans left their mark in castles at Colchester, Castle Hedingham, Stansted and elsewhere, while Colchester's Roman walls remain to show the pedigree of Britain's oldest recorded town. Perhaps Essex is best known for its resorts. Southend, Clacton, Frinton, Walton and Dovercourt offer all the fun of the seaside but with much more besides. Down the centuries, Essex has been home to both the famous and the infamous. John Constable, England's greatest landscape painter, was inspired by the beauty of the Stour Valley; Hedingham Castle was once home to Edward de Vere, believed by many to be the true author of Shakespeare's works. Other famous names include the composers Gustav Holst and William Byrd, writers Dorothy L. Sayers, Sabine Baring-Gould and H.G. Wells, and the philosopher, John Locke.

CLACTON-ON-SEA. Highfield Grange Holiday Park, London Road, Clacton-on-Sea CO16 9QY
Tel: 0871 664 9746 • Fax: 01255 689805 • www.park-resorts.com
Highfield Grange is situated by Clacton's charming beaches and Victorian pier. This is the ideal getaway for the whole family, with plenty of amusements as well as activities to suit the mature traveller. The facilities include a bar and restaurant, and indoor swimming pool with a 200ft chute! 43 touring pitches available. Caravans and motorhomes welcome. Open from March to October.

CLACTON-ON-SEA. Martello Beach Holiday Park, Belsize Avenue, Jaywick, Clacton-on-Sea CO15 2LF
Tel: 01255 820372 • Fax: 01255 820060 • www.park-resorts.com
Sandy beaches and countryside to explore are among the attractions of this seaside site. There are facilities for all the family, including walking paths for those seeking peace and quiet. Open from March to October. 70 touring pitches, 100 tent pitches available. Caravans, motorhomes and tents welcome.

FREE or REDUCED RATE entry to Holiday Visits and Attractions – see our
READERS' OFFER VOUCHERS on pages 205-234

Essex

Colchester, Maldon

COLCHESTER. Colchester Camping & Caravan Park, Cymbeline Way, Colchester CO3 4AG
Tel: 01206 545551 • Fax: 01206 710405 • www.colchestercamping.co.uk
Surrounded by wildlife and idyllic landscapes and offering modern facilities, including free showers with hot water. There is easy access to the nearby town centre. Open all year round. 120 electric hook-ups available. 168 touring pitches, 40 tent pitches. Caravans, motorhomes and tents welcome.

COLCHESTER. Fen Farm Caravan Site, Moore Lane, East Mersea, Colchester CO5 8UA
Tel: 01206 383275
The perfect escape for those with an interest in wildlife, with Fingringhoe Wick nature reserve only 6 miles way. Open from March to September. 95 touring pitches. Caravans, motorhomes, tents welcome.

COLCHESTER. Waldegraves Holiday Park, Mersea Island, Colchester CO5 8SE
Tel: 01206 382898 • Fax: 01206 385359 • www.waldegraves.co.uk
Waldegraves provides entertainment for the whole family including a designated play area for children. Many attractions nearby including Colchester Zoo and museums. Open from March to November. 60 touring pitches. Caravans, motorhomes and tents welcome.

MALDON. Mundon Caravan Site, Hook Farm Nursery, Mundon Road, Maldon CM9 6PN
Tel: 0785 093 5240 • www.mundoncaravansite.com
Quiet site with views of the River Blackwater. Nearby attractions include golf, theatre and Colchester Zoo. Open all year round. Caravans, motorhomes and tents welcome.

Looking for Holiday Accommodation?

for details of hundreds of properties throughout the UK, visit our website

www.holidayguides.com

Essex

EAST OF ENGLAND 79

Southminster, Walton-on-the-Naze, Weeley

SOUTHMINSTER. Steeple Bay Holiday Park, Steeple, Southminster CM0 7RS
Tel: 0845 815 9766 • Fax: 01621 773967 • www.parkholidaysuk.com
This coastal family retreat in Southminster offers great facilities including a leisure pool, paddling pool, and nightly entertainment. Open March – November. 55 touring pitches available. Caravans, motorhomes and tents welcome.

SOUTHMINSTER. Waterside at St Lawrence Bay, Main Road St Lawrence Bay, Southminster CM0 7LY
Tel: 0871 664 9794 • Fax: 01621 778 106 • www.park-resorts.com
A coastal getaway perfect for the whole family, offering plenty of facilities including a small indoor pool, and activities including crabbing in the estuary. 70 touring pitches, 8 tent pitches available. Caravans, motorhomes and tents welcome. Open from March to October.

WALTON-ON-THE-NAZE. Naze Marine Holiday Park, Hall Lane, Walton-on-the-Naze CO14 8HL
Tel: 0871 664 9794 • Fax: 01255 682 427 • www.park-resorts.com
A park with a difference offering a great variety of facilities, including nature reserves, walking paths, beaches and a wonderful pier, as well as a pool and poolside café. Nightly entertainment. 44 touring pitches available. Caravans and motorhomes welcome. Open from March to October.

WEELEY. Homestead Lake Caravan Park, Thorpe Road, Weeley CO16 9JN
Tel: 0800 093 1966 • Fax: 01255 830031
This quiet site is situated in 25 acres of lovely countryside near Clacton. There is a well established fishing lake on site. Open from March to January. 50 pitches available. Caravans, motorhomes and tents welcome.

Windsurfing off the coast, Essex

Hertfordshire

Baldock, Hertford, Royston, Waltham Cross

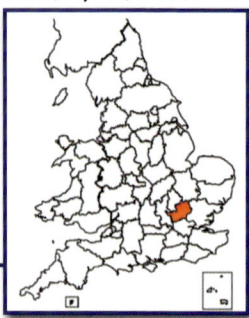

BALDOCK. Radwell Mill Lake Site, Radwell, Baldock SG7 5ET
Tel: 01462 730242
Small woodland site conveniently located for the A1(M), adjoining a lake and bird reserve. Modern toilets and wash house. Tourers, motorhomes and tents welcome.

HERTFORD. Hertford Camping and Caravanning Club Site, Mangrove Road, Hertford SG13 8AJ
Tel: 01992 586696
Surrounded by parkland, this well equipped site has two large camping fields, a tent field and a children's playing field. There are good public transport links to London. Open all year. Caravans, motorhomes and tents welcome.

ROYSTON. Highfields Farm, Old North Road, Bassingbourn, Royston SG8 5JI
Tel: 01763 248570
Small level site just outside the town of Royston, with generously spaced pitches and a large flat rally field. Tourers and motorhomes welcome. Open all year.

WALTHAM CROSS. Theobalds Park Camping & Caravanning Site, Waltham Cross EN7 5HS
Tel: 01992 620604 / 0870 243 3341
Set in Hertfordshire just outside London, this friendly country park provides exciting wildlife views and activities including boating, sailing and swimming. Non-members welcome. 90 pitches available.

---

symbols

- ☀ Holiday Parks & Centres
- 🚐 Caravans for Hire
- 🅢 Caravan Sites and Touring Parks
- ⛺ Camping Sites

Norfolk

Ashill, Attleborough

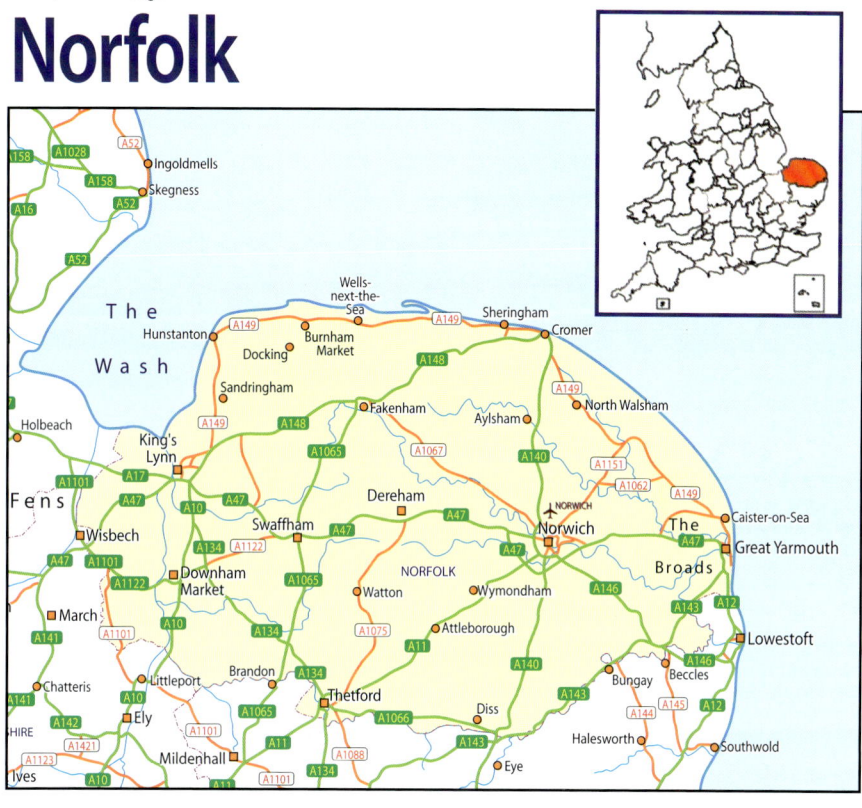

Norfolk

EAST OF ENGLAND 81

ASHILL. Brick Kiln Farm Caravan Park, Swaffham Road, Ashill, Thetford IP25 7BT
Tel: 01760 441300
This family-run park is set on 15 acres of meadow and woodland on the Norfolk/Suffolk border. 90 pitches available. Caravans, motorhome and tents welcome. Open all year round.

ATTLEBOROUGH. Moat Farm Caravan Park & Campsite, Low Road, Breckles, Attleborough NR17 1EP
Tel: 01953 498510 • Fax: 08714 336468 • www.moatfarm-cp.co.uk
Set within undisturbed fields, with a number of local attractions nearby, including Thetford Forest. Excellent facilities. Open all year round. Caravans, motorhomes and tents welcome.

Electric hook-ups available		Facilities for disabled visitors	
Children's play area		Pets welcome	
Laundry facilities		Shop on site	
Licensed bar on site		Wifi access available	

Norfolk
Caister-on-Sea, Cromer

NOW OPEN MARCH TO JANUARY

Elm Beach is a small, select, 4-star Caravan Park with unique, uninterrupted views of the Sea and Caister's golden, sandy beaches. We offer a range of 4-6 berth, fully equipped Heated Caravans, many of which overlook the sea or have sea views. We are a quiet, privately-run park with no entertainment facilities, but enjoy, free of charge, entertainment supplied by neighbouring parks, both within easy walking distance. Pets very welcome.

Elm Beach Caravan Park Manor Road, Caister-on-Sea NR30 5HG
Freephone: 08000 199 260 • www.elmbeachcaravanpark.com • e-mail: enquiries@elmbeachcaravanpark.com

---

CROMER. West Runton Camping & Caravan Club Site, Holgate Lane, West Runton, Cromer NR27 9NW
Tel: 01263 837544
This quiet, attractive site is convenient for the many attractions of West Runton and the surrounding area, including the beach, shops and excellent eateries. Open from March to November. 200 touring pitches available. Caravans, motorhomes and tents welcome.

CROMER. Deer's Glade Caravan & Camping Park, White Post Road, Hanworth, Cromer NR11 7HN
Tel: 01263 768633 • Fax: 01263 768328 • www.deersglade.co.uk
This family-run site is located within a delightful woodland clearing in north Norfolk. Children are welcome. Good facilities are available, and there is a new cycle hire and dog kennelling facility in place. Open all year round. Caravans, motorhomes and tents welcome.

CROMER. Wyndham Park, Runton Road, Cromer NR27 9NH
Tel: 01263 512 204 • www.parklandsleisure.co.uk/norfolk/wyndham
Situated ½ mile from Cromer town centre, this family-owned site is close to beaches and sporting and leisure attractions. 118 touring pitches available. Caravans, motorhomes and tents welcome.

CROMER. Woodhill Park, East Runton, Cromer NR27 9PX
Tel: 01263 512242 • Fax: 01263 515326 • www.woodhill-park.com
Woodhill Park is a welcoming, comfortable base from which to explore the natural beauty of Norfolk. The cliff top position guarantees wonderful sea and countryside views. Open from March to October. 300 touring pitches available. Caravans, motorhomes and tents welcome.

CROMER. Ivy Farm Holiday Park, High Street, Cromer NR27 0PS
Tel: 01263 579239 • www.ivy-farm.co.uk
An award-winning park set in a delightful area offering genuine peace and quiet. Minutes from sandy beaches; lots of country walks over farm meadows and lanes. 22 touring pitches; caravans, motorhomes and tents welcome.

CROMER. Laburnum Caravan Park, Water Lane, West Runton, Cromer NR27 9QP
Tel: 01263 837473
The park's cliff top position means visitors are guaranteed superb views of the beach. Children are welcome at Laburnum Park, with excellent facilities. Open from March to October. 6 touring pitches. Caravans and motorhomes welcome.

Norfolk
Diss, Fakenham, Great Yarmouth

EAST OF ENGLAND 83

WAVENEY VALLEY HOLIDAY PARK

★ Touring Caravan and Camping Site ★ Licensed Bar ★ Electric Hook-ups
★ Restaurant, Shop, Laundry ★ Self-Catering Mobile Homes
★ Outdoor Swimming Pool ★ Horse Riding on Site ★ Good Fishing in Locality

*Good access to large, level site, two miles east of Dickleburgh.
Midway between Norwich and Ipswich off A140.*

**Airstation Lane, Rushall, Diss,
Norfolk IP21 4QF
Telephone: 01379 741228/741690
Fax: 01379 741228
e-mail: waveneyvalleyhp@aol.com
www.caravanparksnorfolk.co.uk**

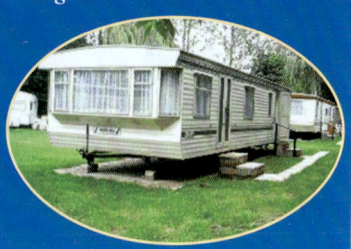

FAKENHAM. The Old Brick Kilns Caravan & Camping Park, Barney, Fakenham NR21 0NL
Tel: 01328 878305 • Fax: 01328 878948 • www.old-brick-kilns.co.uk
The spacious pitches at this family park are situated in 13 acres of quiet countryside, but convenient for all the attractions of north and west Norfolk. Open from March to January. 60 pitches available. Caravans, motorhomes and tents welcome.

GREAT YARMOUTH. Breydon Water Holiday Park, Burgh Castle, Great Yarmouth NR31 9QB
Tel: 01493 780481 • Fax: 01493 782383
The touring pitches are situated between two holiday park villages, Yare and Bure. Yare is ideal for a family day out, with an outdoor pool and waterside restaurant. Bure offers a more tranquil experience with scenic views. Guests of the park are entitled to use facilities at both villages. Open from March to October. 176 touring pitches, 54 tent pitches available. Caravans, motorhomes and tents welcome.

GREAT YARMOUTH. Grange Touring Park, Ormesby St Margaret, Great Yarmouth NR29 3QG
Tel: 01493 730306 • Fax: 01493 730188 • www.long-beach.co.uk/grange.htm
This peaceful touring park is only five minutes from Great Yarmouth and one mile from the sea. Open from March-October. 70 touring pitches available. Caravans, motorhomes and tents welcome.

GREAT YARMOUTH. Burgh Castle Marina, Butt Lane, Great Yarmouth NR31 9PZ
Tel: 01493 780331• Fax: 01493 780163 • www.burghcastlemarina.co.uk
The site covers 26 acres of informal parkland in a lovely area of natural beauty, with over 200 species of trees, shrubs and flowers. Pets not allowed. Open from March to December. 41 touring pitches available. Caravans, motorhomes and tents welcome.

Norfolk
Great Yarmouth

HOLIDAY PARKS & CENTRES

GREAT YARMOUTH. Wild Duck Holiday Park, Howard's Common, Belton, Great Yarmouth.
Set in a beautiful location not far from the Norfolk Broads and picturesque beaches, Wild Duck Holiday Park is a more relaxed holiday village-style Park surrounded by mature woodlands. This is the place to stay for wonderful surroundings and a relaxing family holiday. As well as first class Touring facilities and on-site amenities, Wild Duck boasts excellent sports and leisure facilities from heated indoor and outdoor pools to children's clubs for all ages. With so much to see and do you'll never be restless, enjoy a fabulous family holiday at Wild Duck Holiday Park.
See also Colour Advertisement.
Call our UK Central Team: 0871 230 1933 (open 7 days, 9am-9pm) or book on-line (quote: TO_FHG)
www.touringholidays.co.uk
- Great for Groups! Just book 5 or more holiday homes for extra benefits and savings.
Visit **www.havengroups.co.uk Or call 0871 230 1911.**

GREAT YARMOUTH'S Vauxhall 5 STAR HOLIDAY PARK

GREAT FUN, GREAT VALUE, GREAT TOURING
GREAT YARMOUTH

5 STAR TOURING FACILITIES
- Over 220 all electric sites • Awnings FREE
- Free car parking • Grass & hard standings
- Gas cylinder refills on site • Hair dryers
- Modern heated shower & toilet blocks
- Night security for late arrivals
- Baby changing facilities

SUPER PITCH: Full mains service pitch with hedged, landscaped and awning areas

FREE WITH YOUR HOLIDAY
★ Star Studded Entertainment ★ Electricity
★ Kid's Club ★ Indoor Tropical Waterworld
★ Satellite T.V. (super pitch only)
★ Louie's Adventure Playground
★ Sport & Fitness Fun

GREAT YARMOUTH'S Vauxhall 5 STAR HOLIDAY PARK

Call Now For a Free Colour Brochure
01493 857231
91 Acle New Road, Great Yarmouth, Norfolk NR30 1TB Ref: 91
visit the web site for great touring savers www.vauxhalltouring.co.uk

---

GREAT YARMOUTH. Wild Duck Holiday Park, Howards Common, Great Yarmouth NR31 9NE
Tel: 01493 780268 • Fax: 01492 782308
Charming country retreat with good modern facilities. Only three miles to sandy beach. Amenities include heated swimming pool, tennis court and adventure playground. Also pub, club and shows ideal for family entertainment. Open from March to November. 200 touring pitches. Caravans, motorhomes and tents welcome.

GREAT YARMOUTH. Broadlands Park, Johnson Street, Ludham, Great Yarmouth NR29 5NY
Tel: 01692 630357
Situated in the Norfolk Broads, with natural waterways, wildlife, marshland, windmills, and quaint towns. Ideal for visiting Norwich. Open from March to November. Caravans and motorhomes welcome.

Great Yarmouth. Long Beach Holiday Park, Long Beach, Hemsby, Great Yarmouth NR29 4JD
Tel: 01493 730023 • Fax: 01493 730188 • www.long-beach.co.uk
This family-run park is in a fantastic location, with access to a Nature Reserve and a beach. Shop and licensed bar. Open from March to November. 10 touring pitches. Caravans, tents and motorhomes welcome.

GREAT YARMOUTH. Rose Farm Touring Park, Stepshort, Belton, Great Yarmouth NR31 9JS
Tel: 01493 780 896 • www.rosefarmtouringpark.co.uk
Set amongst 8 acres of countryside. Personal service from the owners makes your stay at this park as cosy and relaxing as possible. 80 touring pitches. Open all year round. Caravans, motorhomes and tents welcome.

GREAT YARMOUTH. Willowcroft Caravan Park, Repps-with-Bastwick, Great Yarmouth NR29 5JU
Tel: 01692 670380
Small, family-run site just a short walk from the river and a delightful stroll into the nearby village. Only 15 miles from Norwich and Great Yarmouth. Open all year round. Caravans, motorhomes and tents welcome.

Norfolk

EAST OF ENGLAND

Harleston, Holt, Hunstanton, King's Lynn

HARLESTON. Little Lakeland Caravan Park, Wortwell, Harleston IP20 0EL
Tel: 01986 788646 • Fax: 01986 788646 • www.littlelakeland.co.uk
The 4 acres of lakeside accommodation at this site provide enough room for all touring visitors to feel secluded and relaxed. The wide range of facilities include an on-site shop, private fishing lake and library. Open from March to October. 38 touring pitches available. Caravans, motorhomes and tents welcome.

HOLT. Kelling Heath Holiday Park, Weybourne, Holt NR25 7HW
Tel: 01263 588181 • Fax: 01263 588599 • www.kellingheath.co.uk
Situated on 250 acres of idyllic open woodlands close to the north Norfolk coast at Weybourne, ideal for wildlife and walking. Open from February to December. 300 touring pitches available. Caravans, motorhomes and tents welcome.

Searles for superb holidays & fantastic facilities on the North Norfolk Coast.

Searles LEISURE RESORT • HUNSTANTON 2009

- Range of Quality Accommodation
- Underfloor Heated Toilets
- Range of Hook-Ups and Pitches
- Full Daytime and Evening Entertainment
- Swimming Pools and Health Club
- Bowls, Tennis and Fishing
- Captain Willies Activity Centre
- Golf Course and Driving Range
- Kids Club/Sports/Shows and Entertainment
- Three Bars & Restaurants and Country Club
- Reflections Hair & Beauty Salon
- Searles Seatours – Visit the Seals of the Wash

Call our friendly booking team today!
Tel: (01485) 534211
visit us at **www.searles.co.uk**

Quote Ref: **FHG**

Award Winning Tenting and Touring Park

KING'S LYNN. Pentney Park Caravan Site, Main Road, Pentney, King's Lynn PE32 1HU
Tel: 01760 337479 • Fax: 01760 338118 • www.pentney-park.co.uk
Pentney Park, set in woodland, is in an ideal situation for exploring north Norfolk. The facilities include indoor and outdoor pools, a gym and an area specially designated for dogs. Open all year round. 170 touring pitches available. Caravans, motorhomes and tents welcome.

KING'S LYNN. Gatton Water Caravan & Camping Site, Hillington, King's Lynn PE31 6BJ
Tel: 01485 600243 • www.gattonwaters.co.uk
Adults-only caravan park. 24 acres of countryside with beautiful wildlife, 8-acre lake for coarse fishing. Facilities of a high standard. Open from March to October. 30 touring pitches. Caravans, motorhomes and tents welcome.

EAST OF ENGLAND — Norfolk

King's Lynn, Mundesley, North Walsham, Norwich

KING'S LYNN. King's Lynn Caravan & Camping Park, North Runcton, King's Lynn PE33 0QR
Tel: 01553 840204 • www.kl-cc.co.uk
Set in 4 acres of carefully tended parkland, ideal for exploring the ancient market town and further afield. Modern facility block. Open from March to September. 35 touring pitches. Caravans, motorhomes, and tents welcome.

KING'S LYNN. Pentney Lakes Caravan and Leisure Park, Common Road, King's Lynn PE32 1NN
Tel: 01760 338668
285 acres of peaceful countryside with on-site water-sports activities such as water skiing, jet skiing, windsurfing and sailing. Open all year round. 100 touring pitches. 50 tent pitches. Caravans, motorhomes and tents welcome.

Sandy Gulls Caravan Park Ltd, Cromer Road, Mundesley NR11 8DF

Found on the Mundesley cliff tops, this quiet private park, managed by the owning family for over 30 years, offers a warm welcome to all visitors. The touring park has grass and non-turf pitches, all have uninterrupted sea views, electric/TV hook-ups and beautifully refurbished shower rooms. Holiday caravans for sale or hire, which are always the latest models.

Our charges include gas and electricity. Superbly situated for exploring the beauty of North Norfolk including The Broads National Park.

Sandy Gulls does not cater for children or teenagers.

Mr Shreeve • 01263 720513

KILN CLIFFS CARAVAN PARK

Peaceful family-run site with NO clubhouse situated around an historic brick kiln. Luxury six-berth caravans for hire, standing on ten acres of grassy cliff top. Magnificent view out over the sea; private path leads down to extensive stretches of unspoilt sandy beach. All caravans fully equipped (except linen) and price includes all gas and electricity. Caravans always available for sale or for hire. Within easy reach are the Broads, Norwich, the Shire Horse Centre, local markets, nature reserves, bird sanctuaries; nearby golf, riding and fishing. Facilities on site include general store and launderette. Responsible pet owners welcome.
Substantial discounts for off-peak bookings – phone for details. Call for brochure.

Mr R. Easton, Kiln Cliffs Caravan Park, Cromer Road, Mundesley, Norfolk NR11 8DF • Tel: 01263 720449

NORTH WALSHAM. Two Mills Touring Park, Yarmouth Road, North Walsham NR28 9NA
Tel: 01692 405829 • Fax: 01692 405829 • www.twomills.co.uk
Idyllically positioned in North Norfolk in unspoilt countryside, this adults-only 8 acre park has spacious pitches, all on level parkland. Open from March to December. Caravans, motorhomes and tents welcome.

NORWICH. Dower House Touring Park, Thetford Forest, East Harling, Norwich NR16 2SE
Tel: 01953 717214 • Fax: 01953 717843 • www.dowerhouse.co.uk
This picturesque site has a wide choice of facilities including an on-site pub and swimming pool. Ideal for walking and cycling, there is also an abundance of wildlife to watch. Open from March to September. 140 touring pitches available. Caravans, motorhomes and tents welcome.

Norfolk
Sandringham, Sea Palling, Sheringham

EAST OF ENGLAND 87

SANDRINGHAM. Sandringham Camping and Caravanning Club Site, Sandringham PE35 6EA
Tel: 01485 542555/ 01553 631614 • www.sandringham-estate.co.uk
This site is situated in the heart of the Sandringham Estate, but with King's Lynn close by. 275 touring pitches available. Caravans, motorhomes and tents welcome.

GOLDEN BEACH
HOLIDAY CARAVAN PARK

Golden Beach is a lovely quiet park situated in the small unspoiled village of Sea Palling on the Norfolk coast, just behind sand dunes which border miles of golden beaches with excellent sea fishing.

Golden Beach Holiday Centre
Beach Road, Sea Palling, Norfolk NR12 0AL
Tel: 01692 598269
e-mail: goldenbeach@keme.co.uk   www.goldenbeachpark.co.uk

SHERINGHAM. Beeston Regis Caravan Park, West Runton, Near Sheringham NR27 9NG
Tel: 01263 823614 • www.beestonregis.co.uk/
The 62-acre park stands on the cliff, 15 minutes' walk away from the attractive seaside town of Sheringham, ideal for walking by the sea or in the countryside. 45 seasonal touring pitches available. Caravans and motorhomes welcome. Open from March to October.

SHERINGHAM. Woodlands Caravan Park, Holt Road, Sheringham NR26 8TU
Tel: 01263 823802 • Fax: 01263 825700 • www.woodlandscaravanpark.co.uk
Situated close to Sheringham and Cromer, this attractive site is ideal for exploring north Norfolk. The adjacent leisure park provides a wide range of facilities. Open from March to October. 225 touring pitches available. Caravans and motorhomes welcome.

	Electric hook-ups available		Facilities for disabled visitors
	Children's play area		Pets welcome
	Laundry facilities		Shop on site
	Licensed bar on site	W	Wifi access available

Norfolk

Swaffham, Trimingham, Wells-next-the-Sea

SWAFFHAM. Breckland Meadows Touring Park, Lynn Road, Swaffham PE37 7PT
Tel: 01760 721246 • www.brecklandmeadows.co.uk
Adults-only park, with high standards of cleanliness. Situated just a short distance from Swaffham where visitors can go for a pub lunch or visit the Saturday street market. Open from January to December. 35 touring pitches. Caravans and motorhomes welcome; 13 tent pitches.

TRIMINGHAM. Woodland Leisure Park, Trimingham, Cromer NR11 8AL
Tel: 01263 579208 • Fax: 01263 576377 • www.woodland-park.co.uk
Relish the freedom of roaming the 55 acres of forestry. An idyllic location for a peaceful weekend or a midweek retreat. With live entertainment, bars, Sunday carvery and indoor heated pool and sauna. Open all year. 60 touring pitches. Caravans and motorhomes welcome.

WELLS-NEXT-THE-SEA. Pinewoods Holiday Park, Beach Road, Wells-next-the-Sea NR23 1DR
Tel: 01328 710439 • Fax: 01328 711060 • www.pinewoods.co.uk
A Norfolk treasure, rated 4 stars by the Tourist Board. Only ¾ mile from town. Situated adjacent to the beach with its distinctive beach huts. Open from March to October. 337 touring pitches. Caravans, motorhomes and tents welcome.

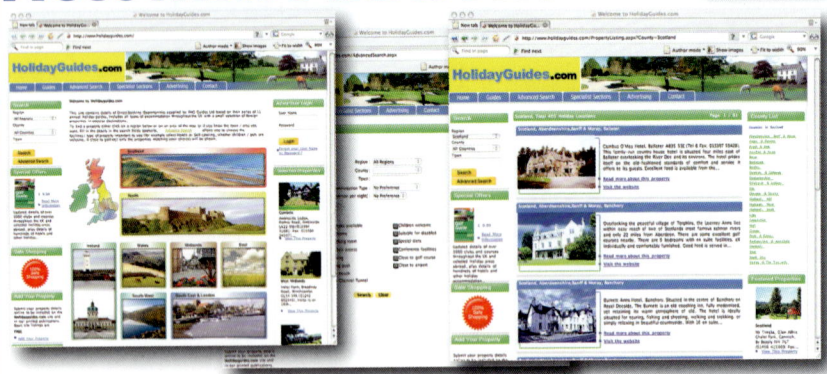

Looking for Holiday Accommodation?

FHG
K·U·P·E·R·A·R·D

for details of hundreds of properties throughout the UK, visit our website

www.holidayguides.com

Suffolk
Beccles, Bucklesham

Suffolk

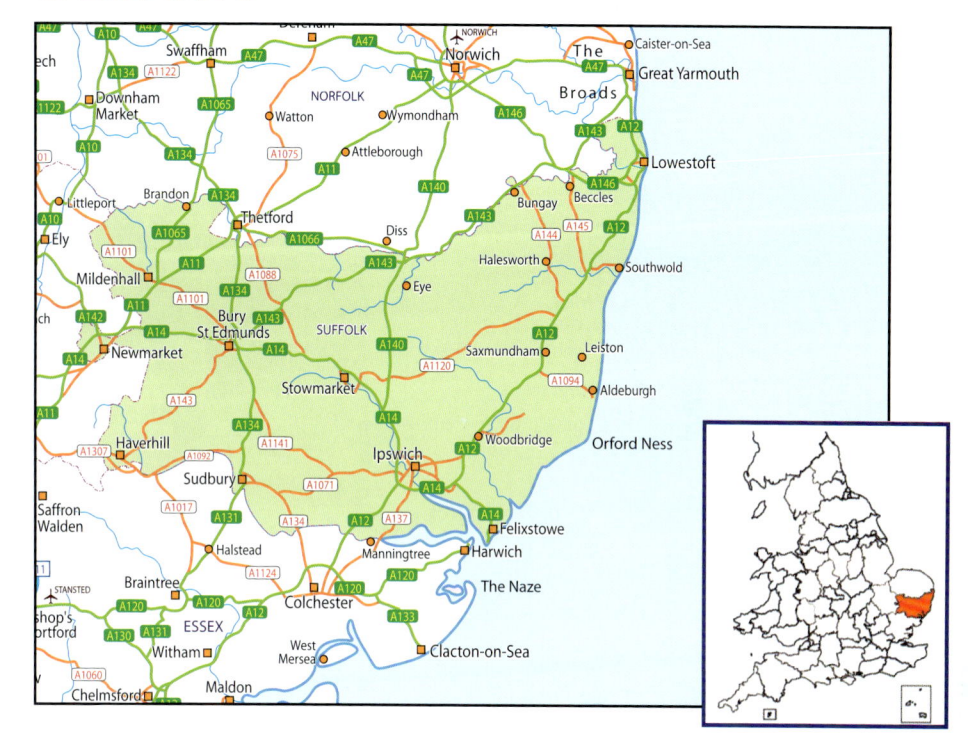

BECCLES. Waveney River Centre, Staithe Road, Burgh St Peter, Beccles NR34 0BT
Tel: 01502 677343 • Fax: 01502 677366 • www.waveneyrivercentre.co.uk
Efficiently run family park with conveniently positioned facilities including leisure centre, family pub, shop and off licence. Open from April to October. Caravans, motorhomes and tents welcome.

BUCKLESHAM. The Oaks Caravan Park, Chapel Road, Bucklesham, Near Ipswich PO10 0BT
Tel: 01394 448837 • www.oakscaravanpark.co.uk
This well maintained, adults-only park is surrounded by idyllic Suffolk countryside with easy access to the coast. Open from March to October. Caravans, motorhomes and tents welcome.

Please note

All the information in this book is given in good faith in the belief that it is correct. However, the publishers cannot guarantee the facts given in these pages, neither are they responsible for changes in policy, ownership or terms that may take place after the date of going to press. Readers should always satisfy themselves that the facilities they require are available and that the terms, if quoted, still apply.

Suffolk

Bungay, Felixstowe, Ipswich

Outney Meadow Caravan Park

This caravan and camping site in Suffolk is in a beautiful location, set in eight acres of ground on pleasant grassy areas beside the River Waveney, with screened pitches for tents, motor homes and caravans.

Toilets and shower block with hot showers and shaver points. Shop and launderette on site.

45 touring pitches and five hardstandings for motor caravans; some electric hook-ups.

Fishing, boat, canoe and bike hire. Barbecues are allowed; picnic tables. Pets welcome, special dog-walking area; dogs must be kept on leads.

The site is quiet day and night.

Please telephone or see our website for further details.

**Outney Meadow,
Bungay, Suffolk NR35 1HG
Tel: 01986 892338
www.outneymeadow.co.uk**

FELIXSTOWE. Peewit Caravan Park, Walton Avenue, Felixstowe IP11 2HB
Tel: 01394 284511 • www.peewitcaravanpark.co.uk/
Run by the same family for nearly 50 years! For 13 acres of peace and quiet, with Felixstowe's delightful seafront nearby, this four-star park is the ideal touring getaway. Open from April to October. 50 touring pitches. 15 tent pitches. Caravans, motorhomes and tents welcome.

IPSWICH. Orwell Meadows Leisure Park, Priory Lane, Ipswich IP10 0JS
Tel: 01473 726666 • www.parklandsleisure.co.uk/suffolk/orwell
This family-run leisure park adjacent to the country park and River Orwell estuary offers good facilities and live weekend entertainment in peak season, with a variety of activities also available in the surrounding area. Open March to January. 80 touring pitches available. Caravans, motorhomes and tents.

IPSWICH. Priory Park, Ipswich IP10 0JT
Tel: 01473 727239 • www.priory-park.com/touring.html
Surrounded by trees, this charming park nestles by the water's edge in 100 acres of parkland. Open from March to January. 75 touring pitches. Caravans and motorhomes welcome.

IPSWICH. Westwood Caravan Park, Old Felixstowe Road, Bucklesham, Near Ipswich IP10 0BN
Tel: 01473 659637 • www.westwoodcaravanpark.co.uk
Westwood is set in rural Suffolk, and the park is designed for families with caravans, motorhomes and/or tents. The site is set among country villages, yet is convenient for Ipswich and Felixstowe. Open from March to January.

Suffolk

EAST OF ENGLAND 91

Leiston, Lowestoft

LEISTON. Cliff House Park, Sizewell Common, Leiston IP16 4TU
Tel: 01728 830724 • www.cliffhousepark.co.uk/
With a frontage on the Suffolk coast, this site is ideal for active holidays, with cycle trails nearby, and the possibility of walking to Dunwich, Southwold or Thorpeness. There is also access to a private beach, and a games room. 60 touring and seasonal pitches available. Caravans and tents welcome. Open from March to November.

LOWESTOFT. Heathland Beach Caravan Park, London Road, Kessingland, Lowestoft NR33 7PJ
Tel: 01502 740337 • Fax: 01502 742355 • www.heathlandbeach.co.uk
This friendly resort overlooks Kessingland's fabulous sandy beach. The park has achieved a David Bellamy Gold Award. Open from March to October. 63 touring pitches available. Caravans, motorhomes and tents welcome.

LOWESTOFT. Kessingland Beach Holiday Park, Kessingland, Near Lowestoft NR33 7RN
Tel: 0871 664 9218 • Fax: 01502 740907 • www.park-resorts.com
Kessingland provides a tranquil base by the beach for the whole family, with a number of exciting attractions nearby. Lowestoft Blue Flag beach is only 5 miles from the park. Open from March to October. 93 touring pitches available. Caravans, motorhomes and tents welcome.

Beach Farm Residential & Holiday Park Ltd
1 Arbor Lane, Pakefield, Lowestoft, Suffolk NR33 7BD
Tel: 01502 572794 • Mobile: 07795 001449
e-mail: beachfarmpark@aol.com • www.beachfarmpark.co.uk

A friendly, peaceful family-run park set in six acres of attractive, sheltered surroundings only 500 yards from Pakefield beach and supermarket, two miles from the town centre.
* De luxe caravan holiday homes with central heating
* Deluxe Country Lodges (3-bed)
* Luxury residential Park homes for sale
* Limited spaces for touring / camping inc. hook-ups
* Licensed bar / beer garden with children's play area
* Seasonal entertainment • Outdoor heated swimming pool
* Launderette • Restaurant adjacent

The park is very close to many local attractions including Pleasurewood Hills Theme Park and Suffolk Wildlife Park.

Other specialised holiday guides from FHG

PUBS & INNS OF BRITAIN • **COUNTRY HOTELS** OF BRITAIN
WEEKEND & SHORT BREAK HOLIDAYS IN BRITAIN
THE GOLF GUIDE WHERE TO PLAY, WHERE TO STAY
500 GREAT PLACES TO STAY • **SELF-CATERING HOLIDAYS** IN BRITAIN
BED & BREAKFAST STOPS • **PETS WELCOME!**
FAMILY BREAKS IN BRITAIN

Published annually: available in all good bookshops or direct from the publisher:
FHG Guides, Abbey Mill Business Centre, Seedhill, Paisley PA1 1TJ
Tel: 0141 887 0428 • Fax: 0141 889 7204
e-mail: admin@fhguides.co.uk • www.holidayguides.com

Derbyshire

Ashbourne, Bakewell

Five modern six-berth caravans, fully equipped, each with gas cooker, fridge, TV; shower and flush toilet; mains electricity. Ashfield Farm overlooks the peaceful Dove Valley and is convenient for the Peak District. The old market town of Ashbourne is only two miles away, with golf courses, swimming pool, squash and bowling. Within easy reach of stately homes like Haddon Hall and Chatsworth, with the Potteries and Lichfield 25 miles distant, Uttoxeter 10 miles away while Alton Towers Theme Park is under five miles away.

Arthur Tatlow, Ashfield Farm, Calwich, Near Ashbourne DE6 2FR • 01335 324279 or 324443

- Prices and brochure on request.
- Write or telephone for further information.

ASHBOURNE. Callow Top Holiday Park, Buxton Road, Ashbourne DE6 2AQ
Tel: 01335 344020 • Fax: 01335 343726 • www.callowtop.co.uk
Visitors can take part in numerous activities in and around Callow Top. Enjoy the trails, fishing, swimming and hilltop climbing in this beautiful part of the Peak District. 150 touring pitches, 150 tent pitches.

ASHBOURNE. Rivendale, Buxton Road, Alsop-en-le-Dale, Ashbourne DE6 1QU
Tel: 01335 310311 • Fax: 01332 842311 • www.rivendalecaravanpark.co.uk
Holders of the David Bellamy Gold Award for conservation, this Leisure Park and camp site is set in the heart of the Peak district. Cycle trails and footpaths in the nearby national park. Open February to January. 95 touring pitches.

ASHBOURNE. Blackwall Plantation Caravan Club Site, Kirk Ireton, Ashbourne DE6 3JL
Tel: 01335 370903
This family-friendly club site is situated next to the beautiful Carsington Reservoir. The local villages contain numerous pubs full of character. 128 touring pitches. No tents. Caravans and motorhomes welcome.

BAKEWELL. Greenhills Caravan & Camping Park, Crow Hill Lane, Bakewell DE45 1PX
Tel: 01629 813052 • Fax: 01629 813467
Greenhills is situated in 12 acres of countryside, just a short walk from the old market town of Bakewell. The park welcomes families with children. 70 touring units and 100 tent pitches. Open February to end of October.

BAKEWELL. Bakewell Camping & Caravan Club Site, c/o Hopping Farm, Youlgreave, Bakewell DE45 1NA
Tel: 01629 636555
This peaceful camp site is located near the little town of Bakewell, with easy access to the Peak District National Park. Motorhomes, caravans and tents welcome. 100 touring pitches available. Open March to November.

Derbyshire
Buxton

MIDLANDS 93

BUXTON. Clover Fields Touring Caravan Park, 1 Heath View, Harpur Hill, Buxton SK17 9PU
Tel & Fax: 01298 78271 • www.cloverfieldstouringpark.co.uk
Clover Fields is open all year and has been awarded 3 Pennants by the AA. 25 touring pitches and a tent field. There is easy access to the Peak District National Park, Buxton and other surrounding market towns.

BUXTON. Lime Tree Park, Dukes Drive, Buxton SK17 9RP
Tel: 01298 22988
Situated in the historic town of Buxton in the Peak District, the park offers modern facilities including hot showers and heating (for those winter months!). Open March to November. 99 touring pitches and serviced pitches available. Motorhomes and tents welcome.

BUXTON. Longnor Wood Caravan & Camping, Longnor, Buxton SK17 0NG
Tel: 01298 83648 • Fax: 01298 83648 • www.longnorwood.co.uk
This secluded, adult-only park is designed to cater for the more mature visitor in pursuit of some peace and quiet. Surrounded by the rugged hills and moors of the Peak district, it is perfect for walks and gentle bike rides. Open March to December. 33 touring pitches available. Motorhomes, carvans and tents welcome.

BUXTON. Bank House Park, Hulme End, Buxton SK17 0EX
Tel: 01298 687 489 • Fax: 01298 687491 • www.bankhousepark.co.uk
This secluded park is situated in the village of Hulme End beside the Manifold River, ideal for enjoying all the outdoor activities of the Peak District, and visiting local market towns and nearby Alton Towers. Open March to October. Caravans, tents and motorhomes welcome.

NEWHAVEN
Caravan & Camping PARK

Delightful site in the heart of the Peak District providing an ideal centre for touring the Derbyshire Dales, walking, climbing, potholing, etc. Convenient for visiting Chatsworth, Haddon Hall, Hardwick Hall, Alton Towers, Matlock and the Dams. Two first class toilet blocks providing FREE hot water; electric hook-ups. Children's playground, playroom, fully-stocked shop supplying Calor and Camping gas, fresh groceries, etc. Laundry. Ice pack freezing facilities. Restaurant adjacent. Tents, motor vans, caravans. Pets and children welcome.

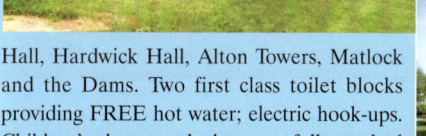

Terms from £11.25 per night – includes car and up to four people, discount for seven nights or more. SAE for brochure. Seasonal tourers welcome.

Newhaven Caravan and Camping Park, Newhaven, Near Buxton, Derbyshire SK17 0DT • 01298 84300 • www.newhavencaravanpark.co.uk

Derbyshire

Glossop, Hope Valley, Matlock, Ripley, Swadlincote

GLOSSOP. Crowden Camping & Caravanning Club Site, Woodhead Road, Crowden, Glossop SK13 1HZ
Tel: 01457 866057
Camp in classical style at this site located at Crowden. There are 45 touring pitches with breathtaking views of Peak District countryside and wildlife. Caravans and tents welcome. Open March to September.

HOPE VALLEY. Laneside Caravan Park, Laneside Farm, Station Road, Hope, Hope Valley S33 6RR
Tel: 01433 620215 • www.lanesidecaravanpark.co.uk
Situated at the foot of Derbyshire's Hope Valley in a quiet area of natural beauty. Campers and their families will find four friendly pubs in the village. Open mid March to early November. Motorhomes, motorvans and tents welcome.

HOPE VALLEY. Losehill Caravan Club Site, Castleton, Hope Valley S33 8WB
Tel: 01433 620 636.
This touring-only site located in the heart of the Peak National Park boasts a high standard of facilities and entertainment. Ideal for all kinds of outdoor activities, with shops and pubs in nearby Castleton. 78 touring pitches. Open all year round.

MATLOCK. Lickpenny Caravan Park, Lickpenny Lane Tansley, Matlock DE4 5GF
Tel: 01629 583040 • www.lickpennycaravanpark.co.uk
This new 4-star rated caravan park is located in Tansley, in 16 acres of Derbyshire countryside, near the market towns of Matlock and Bakewell. 100 touring pitches, 22 seasonal pitches and 25 serviced pitches available. Motorhomes and caravans welcome. Open March to December.

MATLOCK. Birchwood Farm Caravan Park, Wirksworth Road, Whatstandwell, Matlock DE4 5HS
Tel: 01629 822280 • Fax: 01629 822280 • www.birchwoodfcp.co.uk
On a working farm on the hills above the Derwent Valley, Birchwood is only ten minutes' walk from the High Peak Trail. Modern facilities and a small shop available on site. 40 touring pitches. Suitable for tourers, tents and motorhomes. Open March to October.

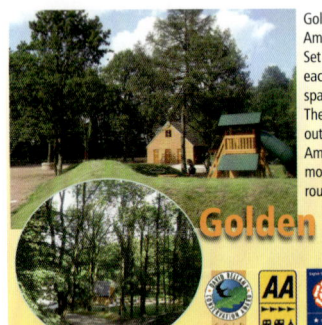

Golden Valley Caravan & Camping Park

Golden Valley Caravan and Camping Park is located in the beautiful hamlet of Golden Valley, in Amber Valley, the heart of Derbyshire.

Set within 26 Acres of secluded woodland and contains 24 super pitches for motor homes/caravans each having its own independent water supply, electric hook up point and mains drainage set in spacious bays within selected areas. There is also ample room for camping/tents.

The site has an independent toilet / shower block, laundry room, Jacuzzi, gym, children's play room, outside play area, cafe, bar and wildlife pond.

Amber Valley has many tranquil villages and bustling market towns nestled amongst some of the most beautiful scenery around. From historic houses and heritage sites, steam trains to walking routes there's something for you.

Coach Road, Golden Valley, Ripley, Derbyshire DE55 4ES
Tel: 01773 513881 • Fax: 01773 746786
e-mail: enquiries@goldenvalleycaravanpark.co.uk
www.goldenvalleycaravanpark.co.uk

SWADLINCOTE. Beehive Farm Woodland Lakes, Beehive Farm, Swadlincote DE12 8HZ
Tel: 01283763981 • www.beehivefarm-woodlandlakes.co.uk
The extensive grassy, open play areas make this a perfect site for a family break. Situated in the heart of the National Forest, there are shops and pubs serving food available in the village, just a short walk away. 25 touring pitches. Motorhomes and caravans welcome. Open all year round.

Herefordshire
Hereford, Leominster

Herefordshire

MIDLANDS 95

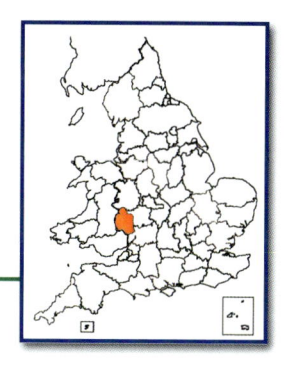

Herefordshire lies on the border with Wales, but is merely a stone's throw from Birmingham, Bristol, the Cotswolds and Cardiff. Green countryside, meandering rivers and acres of traditional cider orchards make up the landscape of this most rural of counties. It is home to the Hereford breed of cattle and has since become recognised for the standard of its local food and drink.

Hereford, a traditional Cathedral City but with the feel of a market town, offers visitors an interesting array of shops, cafes and bistros. The Norman Cathedral is home to the world famous Mappa Mundi, the oldest map of the world, and to the largest Chained Library in the world. The five market towns (Bromyard, Kington, Ledbury, Leominster and Ross-on-Wye) all offer something different to delight the visitor, and the 'Black and White Village' Trail explores a group of villages with beautiful half-timbered houses, cottages and country inns.

There is something for everyone – tranquil gardens, inviting tea-rooms, castles and historic houses, and of course, plenty of fresh country air in which to try canoeing, cycling, pony trekking, or maybe a good walk along one of the many long distance trails that intersect the county, including the recently opened Herefordshire Trail.

HEREFORD. Lucksall Caravan and Camping Park, Mordiford, Hereford HR1 4LP
Tel: 01432 870213 • Fax: 01432 870210 • www.lucksallpark.co.uk
This rural retreat is situated in the heart of the Wye valley, ideal for walking. There are also a number of tourist attractions nearby. Open from March to November. Caravans, motorhomes and tents welcome

Arrow Bank Holiday Park

Nun House Farm, Eardisland
Near Leominster, Herefordshire HR6 9BG

Arrow Bank Holiday Park is a family-run park enjoying peace and tranquillity in a spacious landscaped setting in the picturesque Tudor village of Eardisland. Touring caravans and motor homes are well catered for on a flat, level field with electric hook-up points.

Heated amenity block and Wi-Fi access. • Hardstanding seasonal pitches with hook-up available 1st March to 7th January.

Arrow Bank Holiday Park offers a superb opportunity to own your dream holiday Home from Home or to hire one of our new double glazed 2008 holiday homes with central heating. (Short breaks available).

An ideal touring base with many historic market towns and cathedral cities close by. The beautiful Elan Valley, Brecon Beacons and Shropshire Hills, perfect for walking, bird watching and fishing are easily accessible. From Leominster, follow the A44 west towards Rhayader for approx. 1 mile. As you pass Morrison's, bear right towards Eardisland (approx 4 miles).

Tel & Fax: 01544 388312 • e-mail: enquiries@arrowbankholidaypark.co.uk
www.arrowbankholidaypark.co.uk

MIDLANDS — Herefordshire

Leominster, Little Tarrington, Peterchurch, Ross-on-Wye, Stanford Bishop

---

LEOMINSTER. Townsend Touring Park, Townsend Farm, Pembridge, Leominster HR6 9HB
Tel: 01544 388527 • Fax:01544 388527 • www.townsend-farm.co.uk
Located on the edge of beautiful Pembridge, this five-star park covers 12 acres in rolling countryside. On site there is a luxurious facilities block, and award-winning farm shop. Open March to January. 60 fully serviced touring pitches available. Motorhomes, caravans and tents welcome.

LEOMINSTER. Pearl Lake Leisure Park, Shobdon, Leominster HR6 9NQ
Tel: 01568 708326
Winner of a Gold David Bellamy Award and with a five-star tourist board rating, Pearl Lake provides 80 acres of parkland for camping and caravanning. The park offers modern leisure facilities including golf, a 15- acre lake for fishing, a bowling green and beautiful stretches of land ideal for walks. Open all year round. 15 touring pitches available. Caravans, motorhomes and tents welcome.

LITTLE TARRINGTON. The Millpond Caravan & Camping Park, Little Tarrington HR1 4JA
Tel: 01432 890243 • Fax: 01432 890243 • www.millpond.co.uk
Situated in quiet open countryside, and with easy motorway access, the site is well situated for touring. There are modern facilities available; local pub. Open March to October. 40 touring pitches and 15 tent pitches available.

PETERCHURCH. Poston Mill Park, Peterchurch HR2 0SF
Tel: 01981 550225
A recipient of a David Bellamy Gold Award, the park is situated in 35 acres of open landscape. A high standard of service is provided for all visitors. The varied activities on offer include badminton, a tennis lawn, mini football pitch and croquet. Open all year round. 45 touring pitches available. Tents, motorhomes and caravans welcome.

ROSS-ON-WYE. Broadmeadow Caravan & Camping Park, Broadmeadows, Ross-on-Wye HR9 7BH
Tel: 01989 768076
This 5–star rated camping park is situated in the delightful country town of Ross-on-Wye. There are good facilities both on and off site, including numerous restaurants and pubs nearby. 150 touring pitches available. Caravans, motorhomes and tents welcome.

STANFORD BISHOP. Boyce Holiday Park, Stanford Bishop, Bromyard WR6 5UB
Tel: 01886 884 248 • Fax: 01886 884 187 • www.boyceholidaypark.co.uk
The location of this 100-acre family-run park on the Herefordshire-Worcestershire border is perfect for ramblers and for viewing woodland wildlife. Open March to October. 18 touring pitches available. Tents, caravans and motorhomes welcome.

Key

- Electric hook-ups available
- Facilities for disabled visitors
- Children's play area
- Pets welcome
- Laundry facilities
- Shop on site
- Licensed bar on site
- Wifi access available

Leicestershire & Rutland

Lutterworth, Market Harborough, Oakham, Wolvey

MIDLANDS 97

LUTTERWORTH. Stanford Park Caravan Site, Stanford Road, Swinford, Lutterworth LE17 6DH
Tel: 01788 860387 • Fax: 01788 860370 • www.stanfordhall.co.uk
A peaceful and tranquil site in the grounds of Stanford Hall Estate, with grass and hardstanding pitches for tourers and motorhomes (tents not accepted). Please note there are no toilet or shower facilities. Open all year.

MARKET HARBOROUGH. Brook Meadow Lakeside Holidays, Sibbertoft, Market Harborough LE16 9UJ
Tel: 01858 880886 • Fax: 01858 880485 • www.brookmeadow.co.uk
Brook Meadow's landscaped, lakeside camping and caravan area can accommodate 12 units on hardstanding plus 6 more on grass for tents, all with electric hook-up. Amenities include a laundry room, showers and disabled toilet facilities. Open all year.

OAKHAM. Greendale Farm Caravan & Camping Site, Pickwell Lane, Whissendine, Oakham LE15 7LB
Tel: 01664 474516 • www.rutlandgreendale.co.uk
Gold Award-winning site surrounded by rolling countryside, open exclusively to adults between April and September. This is an ideal retreat for friends or a couple. There are two pubs and a bistro in the village. 5 tent pitches, 15 caravan pitches.

CARAVAN SITES & TOURING PARKS

WOLVEY. Wolvey Caravan Park, Villa Farm, Wolvey, Near Hinckley LE10 3HF (01455 220493/220630).
A quiet site situated on the borders of Warwickshire and Leicestershire, ideally located to explore the many places of interest in the Midlands. Site facilities include shop (licensed), toilets, showers, washrooms, launderette, TV room, 9 hole putting green, fishing. Tariff and brochure available on request. Registered with the Caravan and Camping Club of Great Britain.
Rates: Tents £10.00 per night, two persons; car, caravan and two persons with hook-up £13.00 per night (extra person £1.50); dogs 50p per night; disabled unit, hook-ups £3.00.
• Dogs welcome
AA ★★★
www.wolveycaravansite.itgo.com

The FHG Directory of Website Addresses
on pages 235-250 is a useful quick reference guide for holiday accommodation with e-mail and/or website details

Lincolnshire

Boston

Orchard Holiday Park

perfect for fishing.. walking.. sightseeing.. shopping.. touring..cycling......or simply relaxing!

Nestling quietly in some 36 acres of delightfully landscaped parkland, Orchard Holiday Park is one of Lincolnshire's hidden jewels, where you can be as active or relaxed as you wish. Five-acre fishing lake. First-class amenities and services including licensed bar and new restaurant, shop, launderette, shower blocks etc. 120 luxury Holiday Homes, all with mains electricity, water and drainage. Separate area for touring caravans with mains electricity and water. Over 18s only.

Frampton Lane, Hubbert's Bridge, Boston, Lincs PE20 3QU
01205 290328/290368
Fax: 01205 290247

The White Cat Caravan & Camping Park

The park of 3½ acres is situated in quiet, rural surroundings and can be found 8 miles outside Boston on the A52 Skegness road; turn right opposite the B1184 Sibsey road, the park is 300 yards on the left. Flush toilets, handbasins, H&C, chemical disposal point, free showers, washroom, razor points, electric hook-ups, site shop and children's swings. Public houses and restaurants nearby. Ideal for touring and local fishing. Further details on request. Dogs allowed. Open April to October.

£11 per night for low season rising to £17 high season - these pitch prices include electric hook-up. Six-berth caravans for hire from £195 per week or nightly rate, min. two nights.

The White Cat Caravan & Camping Park,
Shaw Lane, Old Leake, Boston PE22 9LQ
Tel & Fax: 01205 870121 (*Mr & Mrs Lannen*)
e-mail: kevin@klannen.freeserve.co.uk
www.whitecatpark.com

BOSTON. Walnut Lake Lodges & Camping, Main Road, Algarkirk, Boston PE20 2LQ
Tel: 01205 460482 • www.campinglincolnshire.co.uk
Situated midway between Spalding and Boston, Walnut Lake is surrounded by tourist attractions. The site is for adults only. Lodges, touring and camping facilities available. Open March to October. 5 motorhome pitches.

FREE or REDUCED RATE entry to Holiday Visits and Attractions – see our READERS' OFFER VOUCHERS on pages 205-234

Lincolnshire
Alford

MIDLANDS 99

WOODTHORPE HALL
CARAVAN & LEISURE PARK

ETC ★★★★ COTTAGES

Ideally Situated to Make Your Holiday Special

- Tourers • Static Van Lettings • Static Van Sales
- Holiday Cottages • Leisure Activities • Bar & Restaurant
- Aquatics Centre • Garden Centre • Family Camping

Woodthorpe Hall Leisure Park is ideally situated, nestled between the rolling hills of the Lincolnshire Wolds and the wide open spaces of the marshes leading down to the sea, close to the seaside resorts of Skegness, Sutton on Sea and Mablethorpe.
The historic city of Lincoln with its 1200 year old cathedral and castle is only 40 minutes' drive.

We have about twenty static vans for letting along with plenty of room for tourers, motor homes and family tents.

The caravans are of the highest standard and equipped with all bedding, cookery utensils, crockery and cutlery. Letting charges are fully inclusive of gas, electricity TV and water.

Fully equipped with electricity hook-ups, shower, water, waste and chemical waste facilities.

Car parking is adjacent to your caravan or tent, there is a shop, and full disabled access and golf and fishing on site.

The park is in a quiet, secure location with groups and rallies also catered for. Don't forget to visit Woody's Bar and Restaurant where you can relax and a meal and drink can be enjoyed.

Also available, very well appointed one and three bedroom cottages overlooking the golf course. All have central heating, colour TV, microwave, washer, dryer, dishwasher and fridge freezer.

Leisure Park: 01507 450294 • Golf Course: 01507 450000
Woody's Bar: 01507 450079 • Garden Centre: 01507 450509
Aquatics Centre: 01507 451000

www.woodthorpehallleisure.co.uk
e-mail: enquiries@woodthorpehallleisure.co.uk

Woodthorpe Hall • Woodthorpe • Near Alford • Lincolnshire LN13 0DD

100 MIDLANDS
Lincolnshire
Cleethorpes, Grantham, Horncastle, Mablethorpe

HOLIDAY PARKS & CENTRES

CLEETHORPES. Thorpe Park Holiday Centre, Cleethorpes.
This carefully landscaped Park offers families the best of outdoor pleasure and indoor fun. Close to the busy resort of Cleethorpes and Pleasure Island Theme Park and with beach access nearby, you can opt for an easy going holiday experience, or full-on fun both day and night. Thorpe Park has a wonderful heated indoor pool with spa bath so you can kick back and relax, alternatively you could try your hand on the 9-hole golf course. Whatever your needs, with great Touring facilities and on-site amenities, you will have a perfect family holiday at Thorpe Park. **See also Colour Advertisement.**
Call our UK Central Team: 0871 230 1933 (open 7 days, 9am-9pm) or book on-line (quote: TO_FHG) www.touringholidays.co.uk
* Great for Groups! Just book 5 or more holiday homes for extra benefits and savings.
Visit www.havengroups.co.uk Or call 0871 230 1911.

WOODLAND WATERS Willoughby Road, Ancaster, Grantham NG32 3RT
Tel & Fax: 01400 230888
e-mail: info@woodlandwaters.co.uk
website: www.woodlandwaters.co.uk

Set in 72 acres of parkland. Five fishing lakes. Large touring and camping site with electric hook-ups. Luxury holiday lodges from £360 weekly. Excellent toilets, shower block with disabled facilities. Bar/restaurant on site. Children's play area. Dogs welcome. Four Golf Courses nearby. Rallies welcome. New function room " Malden Suite" available for weddings, events and conferences. Short Breaks available. Open all year.

HORNCASTLE. Ashby Park, West Ashby, Horncastle LN9 5PP
Tel: 01507 527966 • Fax: 01507 524539
Set within 70 acres of Lincolnshire countryside, this friendly site offers you peace and tranquillity, good walks and a diversity of wildlife. There are 7 fishing lakes, and good eateries and pubs nearby. Open March to January. 60 touring pitches available. Motorhomes, caravans and tents welcome.

MABLETHORPE. Lakeside Caravan Park, Alford Road, Sutton-on-Sea, Mablethorpe LN12 2RW
Tel: 01507 443355 • www.lakesideholidays.co.uk
The ideal holiday for all the family, with children's entertainment and great fishing facilities. Open from May to September. Caravans only. LPG stockist.

HOLIDAY PARKS & CENTRES

MABLETHORPE. Golden Sands Holiday Park, Quebec Road, Mablethorpe.
With a long, Blue Flag beach stretching to nearby Mablethorpe, Golden Sands is a big favourite with families. Buckets and spades at the ready! From superb Touring facilities and on-site amenities to fantastic activities and free children's clubs for all ages, Golden Sands goes all out to offer something for everyone so you can simply sit back and relax or join in the fun when the moment takes you. A fantastic family holiday Park with both daytime and evening entertainment, you'll be spoilt for choice at Golden Sands.**See also Colour Advertisement.**
Call our UK Central Team: 0871 230 1933 (open 7 days, 9am-9pm) or book on-line (quote: TO_FHG) www.touringholidays.co.uk
* Great for Groups! Just book 5 or more holiday homes for extra benefits and savings.
Visit www.havengroups.co.uk or call 0871 230 1911.

The FHG Directory of Website Addresses
on pages 235-250 is a useful quick reference guide for holiday accommodation with e-mail and/or website details

Lincolnshire
Market Rasen, Saltfleet, Skegness

MIDLANDS 101

Lincolnshire Lanes Log Cabins
Manor Farm, East Firsby, Market Rasen, Lincolnshire LN8 2DB
Ideal for Camping and Caravans • Come and try us!

Two pine log cabins in peaceful woodland setting offering a relaxing holiday, ideally situated for the Wolds and the beautiful city of Lincoln. Each has three bedrooms, one double, one twin, one child's bunkbed; large lounge, bathroom, kitchen, large veranda. Gas central heating, gas cooking. Car parking by unit. Near bus route. Linen provided. Pick up from Lincoln or Market Rasen Station available.

Terms £200 to £400 per week,
£100 to £200 per 3-day stay.
Complimentary local food hamper.
Visit our website or ask for a brochure.

Mr R. Cox
Tel: 01673 878258
e-mail:
info@lincolnshire-lanes.com
www.lincolnshire-lanes.com

SALTFLEET. Sunnydale Holiday Park, Sea Lane, Saltfleet LN11 7RP
Tel: 0871 664 9776 • Fax: 01507 339 100 • www.park-resorts.com
Come with all the family to this friendly 38-pitch holiday park located a stone's throw from the award-winning Mablethorpe beach. Attractions include regular entertainment, an indoor swimming pool and a well stocked fishing pond. Open March to October. Caravans and motorhomes welcome.

SKEGNESS. Coral Beach Leisure, Skegness Road, Ingoldmells, Skegness PE25 1JW
Tel: 01754 872402 • www.coral-beach.net
A fun-filled family caravan park for visitors, both young and old, situated off the A52 in a great location just by the golden Ingoldmells beach. The ideal place for those heading for Butlins and Fantasy Island.

SKEGNESS. North Shore Holiday Centre, Elmhirst Avenue, Roman Bank, Skegness PE25 1SL
Tel: 01754 763815 / 762291 • Fax: 01754 761423 • www.northshore-skegness.co.uk
A large holiday park for all the family, located near the beach. Licensed club on site. North Shore is open beween March to October. 164 pitches (all with electric hook-ups), 35 water hook-ups. Caravans and motorhomes only, no tents.

SKEGNESS. Skegness Water Leisure Park, Walls Lane, Skegness PE25 1JF
Tel: 01754 899400 • Fax: 01754 897867 • www.skegnesswaterleisurepark.co.uk
185 acres of Lincolnshire countryside located between Skegness and Ingoldmells, with easy access to the beach. Suitable for all ages. Caravans and tents welcome. Open March to October.

MIDLANDS — Lincolnshire

Skegness, Sutton-on-Sea, Tattershall

SKEGNESS. Skegness Sands Touring Site, Winthorpe Avenue, Skegness PE25 1QZ
Tel: 01754 761484 • www.skegness-sands.co.uk
This privately-owned Caravan Club site, situated in Skegness, has a wide range of modern facilities to make your family's stay an easy and enjoyable one. 82 touring pitches available.

SUTTON-ON-SEA. Cherry Tree Site, Huttoft Road, Sutton-on-Sea LN12 2RU
Tel: 01507 441626 • www.cherrytreesite.co.uk
Idyllic, dog-friendly site located in Sutton-on-Sea. Maintained to a high standard, there is easy access to beaches and the Wolds countryside. The site is adults only, and no travelling parties, single sex parties or commercial vehicles are permitted. Open all year round.

TATTERSHALL. Tattershall Lakes Country Park, Sleaford Road, Tattershall LN4 4LR
Tel: 01526 348800 • Fax: 01526 345796 • www.tattershallpark.co.uk
With a view of the castle wherever you look, Tattershall Park is set in over 350 acres of woods and lakes. Ideal for families in search of relaxation as well as adventure. Activities include golf, waterskiing, wakeboarding, jetskiing and fishing. Open March to January. 100 touring pitches including 14 motorhome pitches. 300 serviced pitches.

⚡	Electric hook-ups available
♿	Facilities for disabled visitors
⛺	Children's play area
🐕	Pets welcome
🧺	Laundry facilities
🛒	Shop on site
🍷	Licensed bar on site
W	Wifi access available

Kite flying on a Lincolnshire beach

Nottinghamshire

Mansfield, Newark, Radcliffe-on-Trent

MANSFIELD. Sherwood Forest Caravan Park, Edwinstowe, Mansfield NG21 9HW
Tel: 01623 823132 • Fax: 01623 824637 • www.sherwoodforestholidaypark.co.uk
The ideal getaway for cyclists and walkers, the park is set in 26 acres of secluded countryside in North Nottinghamshire, in the heart of Robin Hood country. Facilities include on-site shop and children's play areas. 170 touring pitches. Motorhomes, caravans and tents welcome. Open all year round.

MANSFIELD. Bridleways Holiday Homes and Guest House, Newlands Road, Mansfield NG19 0HU
Tel: 01623 635725; Fax 01623 635725 www.stayatbridleways.co.uk
Self-catering accommodation in static caravans or neighbouring cottage, quietly situated only a five minute drive from Mansfield. Sherwood Forest Visitor Centre 10 minutes; direct access to Vicar Water Country Park. Strictly no smoking. Open all year round.

NEWARK. Milestone Caravan Park, Great North Road, Cromwell, Newark NG23 6JE
Tel: 01636 821244
Situated within 15 acres of beautiful open landscape near the A1, with a good range of modern facilities. Activities available nearby include cycling, fishing and walking. Close to local pubs and restaurants. Open all year round.

NEWARK. Robin Hood View Caravan Park, Belle Eau Park, Bilsthorpe, Newark NG22 8TY
Tel: 07882 397217 • www.robinhoodviewcaravanpark.co.uk
In a tranquil setting, this modern camping park is ideal for nature lovers. Caravan storage available. Open all year round. 15 touring pitches available. Caravans, motorhomes and tents welcome.

RADCLIFFE-ON-TRENT. Thornton's Holt Camping Park, Stragglethorpe, Radcliffe-On-Trent NG12 2JZ
Tel: 0115 9332125 • Fax: 0115 9333318 • www.thorntons-holt.co.uk
Enjoy the charms of the Trent Valley, the Vale of Belvoir and Sherwood Forest, as well as visits to Nottingham, all a short distance from this attractive 14.5 acre site. 90 touring pitches available. Caravans welcome.

Visit the FHG website
www.holidayguides.com
for details of the wide choice of accommodation featured in the full range of FHG titles

Nottinghamshire

Sutton in Ashfield, Tuxford, Worksop

SUTTON IN ASHFIELD. Teversal Camping and Caravan Site, Teversal, Sutton in Ashfield NG17 3JJ
Tel: 01623 551838
Surrounded by breathtaking countryside on the Nottinghamshire/Derbyshire border, this is the ideal place from which to explore the beauty of the East Midlands. 100 tent pitches, 100 touring pitches available. Tents, caravans, motorhomes welcome. Open all year.

Orchard Park

Quiet, sheltered Park set in an old orchard. Ideal for Sherwood Forest and many attractions, all pitches with electric hook-up, children's play trail, dog walk, excellent heated facilities with free hot showers and facilities for disabled. Brochure available on request.

Orchard Park Touring Caravan and Camping Park
Marnham Road, Tuxford NG22 0PY
Tel: 01777 870228 • Fax: 01777 870320

www.orchardcaravanpark.co.uk

WORKSOP. Clumber Park Caravan Club Site, Lime Tree Avenue, Clumber Park, Worksop S80 3AE
Tel: 01909 484 758
At Clumber Park, guests have the freedom to roam, cycle and ride around the 20 acre parkland. Ideal for all the family, with lots of reminders of the Forest's most famous resident, Robin Hood. Open all year. 183 touring pitches.

Other specialised holiday guides from FHG

PUBS & INNS OF BRITAIN • **COUNTRY HOTELS** OF BRITAIN
WEEKEND & SHORT BREAK HOLIDAYS IN BRITAIN
THE GOLF GUIDE WHERE TO PLAY, WHERE TO STAY
500 GREAT PLACES TO STAY • **SELF-CATERING HOLIDAYS** IN BRITAIN
BED & BREAKFAST STOPS • **PETS WELCOME!**
FAMILY BREAKS IN BRITAIN

Published annually: available in all good bookshops or direct from the publisher:
FHG Guides, Abbey Mill Business Centre, Seedhill, Paisley PA1 1TJ
Tel: 0141 887 0428 • Fax: 0141 889 7204
e-mail: admin@fhguides.co.uk • www.holidayguides.com

Shropshire

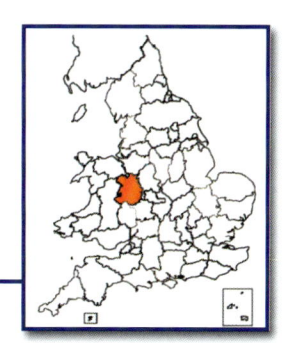

Shropshire is perhaps less well-known than other English counties. This is despite being the birthplace of Charles Darwin, home to the world's first iron bridge (now a World Heritage Site), having not one, but two of the finest medieval towns in England, inspiring the creation of the modern Olympics, and being the kingdom of the real King Arthur. After all, Shropshire is easy enough to find and get to from almost anywhere. (Hint: just north of Birmingham or south of Manchester depending on your direction of travel, and sitting snugly on the Welsh borders). It may also come as a surprise to find out just how much is on offer. There are plenty of indoor and outdoor attractions, so the weather isn't a problem either. In Ironbridge, you can step into the past at the Ironbridge Gorge Museums where you'll find 10 museums to visit, all following the history of the Industrial Revolution. For retail therapy at its best, small independent shops can be found in all its market towns, full of those special 'somethings' you were looking for and even some things you weren't.

Shrewsbury is the beautiful county town, and home (naturally enough) to the Shrewsbury Summer Season – packed with over 200 events including the Shrewsbury Flower Show and the Cartoon Festival. There is also the Darwin Festival to celebrate the town's most famous son, and the foot-tapping Folk Festival. Ludlow, a medieval town, once the seat of the Welsh parliament, and now famed equally for its events and food, is also full of surprises. The Ludlow Festival is an annual two week gathering of actors, musicians, singers, entertainers, and generally some blooming interesting people to keep you rather amused.

All in all, Shropshire has a surprising amount to offer. So take the Shropshire option – for a great day out, fresh clean air and no jams (except those the W.I. make!)

The Long Mynd, near Church Stretton

Shropshire

Ellesmere, Prees, Shrewsbury, Telford

ELLESMERE. Fernwood Caravan Park, Lyneal, Ellesmere SY12 0QF
Tel: 01948 710221 • Fax: 01948 710324 • www.fernwoodpark.co.uk
An attractive, family-run holiday park only 4 miles from Ellesmere in Shropshire, Fernwood is surrounded by unspoiled countryside, lakes and woods. 60 touring pitches available. Motorhomes welcome. Seasonal tariff.

ELLESMERE. Birch Hill, Birch Hill, The Cross, Ellesmere SY12 0LP
Tel: 01691 622951 • www.birchhill.co.uk
Set in two acres of regularly mown grass, Birch Hill is the perfect site for a quiet getaway. Only up to 5 touring caravans are accommodated at a time. Open all year round (subject to weather conditions). Motorhomes and caravans welcome.

PREES. Green Lane Farm, Green Lane Farm, Prees SY13 2AH
Tel: 01948 840 460
Set in North Shropshire's rolling hills, this spacious campsite is ideal for children. 20 pitches for motor caravans and tents. Open all year round.

SHREWSBURY. Beaconsfield Farm, Battlefield, Shrewsbury SY4 4AA
Tel: 01939 210370 • Fax: 01939 210349 • www.beaconsfield-farm.co.uk
Caravan in luxury at this adults-only farm situated north of Shrewsbury. Close by are museums, parks and a shopping centre. 20 tent pitches, 60 touring pitches available. Motorhomes, caravans and tents welcome. Open all year round.

TELFORD. Severn Gorge Park, Bridgnorth Road, Tweedale, Telford TF7 4JB
Tel: 01952 684789
This adults-only park is located in the pretty Shropshire town of Tweedale just ten minutes from Telford. Open all year round. 10 touring pitches available. Caravans and motorhomes welcome.

TELFORD. Church Farm, Rowton, Near Wellington, Telford TF6 6QY
Tel: 01952 770381 • Fax: 01952 77038 • www.churchfarmshropshire.co.uk
Good modern facilities are provided on this small farm site with uninterrupted views of Wrekin Hill. Breakfast is available at the farmhouse. 5 touring pitches, 20 tent pitches available. Caravans, campervans and tents welcome.

Looking for holiday accommodation?
for details of hundreds of properties
throughout the UK including
comprehensive coverage of all areas of Scotland try:

www.holidayguides.com

	Electric hook-ups available		Facilities for disabled visitors
	Children's play area		Pets welcome
	Laundry facilities		Shop on site
	Licensed bar on site		Wifi access available

Staffordshire

Stoke-on-Trent, Uttoxeter, Weston-under-Lizard

Staffordshire

MIDLANDS 107

Star Caravan and Camping Park, Cotton, Near Alton Towers, Stoke-on-Trent ST10 3DW
Tel: 01538 702219
www.starcaravanpark.co.uk

With Alton Towers so near - just over a mile away from our main gates - we are the number one choice for visitors who are looking for a great family-friendly camping and caravanning experience, that offers not only value for money, but also excellent facilities in one of the best locations near to Alton Towers.

Site amenities include large children's play area, toilet block with free showers, etc., laundry room with drying and ironing facilities, electric hook-ups, etc. Full disabled toilet and shower. Dogs welcome. Parent and baby toilet.

Park opens from the end of March to November.
From £14 per night for two persons.
Modern static caravans for hire.
Brochure and further details available.

UTTOXETER. Uttoxeter Racecourse Caravan Club Site, Wood Lane, Uttoxeter ST14 8BD
Tel:01889 564172
This friendly park at Uttoxeter racecourse is surrounded by 60 acres of dog-walking terrain. Beside the scenic Weaver Hills and with a golf course nearby; easy access to Alton Towers and Lichfield Cathedral. 76 touring pitches. Motorhomes, caravans and tents welcome. Open March to November.

WESTON-UNDER-LIZARD. White Pump Farm, Ivetsey Bank, Near Weston-under-Lizard ST19 9QU
Tel: 01785 841153/ 07990 607125 • www.whitepumpfarm.com
Situated in the depths of the Lincolnshire countryside, White Pump Farm is open all year round. There is easy access to events at Weston Park. Home produce for sale in the farm shop. 5 motorhome pitches, 100 tent pitches, 5 touring pitches available.

Warwickshire

Aston Cantlow, Market Bosworth, Rugby, Warwick

ASTON CANTLOW. Island Meadow Caravan Park, Aston Cantlow, Henley-in-Arden B95 6JP
Tel/Fax: 01789 488273 • www.islandmeadowcaravanpark.co.uk/
7 acres of flat Warwickshire countryside – with a weir for fishing and ideal terrain for cycling, walking or simply taking a break from it all. 24 touring pitches and 10 tent pitches available. Motorhomes, caravans and tents.

MARKET BOSWORTH. Bosworth Caravan Park, Cadeby Lane, Cadeby, Market Bosworth CV13 0BA
Tel: 01455 292259 • Fax: 01455 292922 • www.bosworthcaravanpark.co.uk
An ideal venue for rallies, the facilities at this 5-acre site include a large free car park, licensed restaurant, tearooms, bed and breakfast or self-catering accommodation. Caravans and motor homes welcome.

RUGBY. Lodge Farm, Bilton Lane, Rugby CV23 9DU
Tel: 01788 560193 • www.lodgefarm.com
Pets are welcome at this environmentally aware camp site. Lodge Farm offers level pitches in peaceful, countryside with a range of modern facilities. Open from February to October. Caravans, motorhomes and tents welcome.

WARWICK. Warwick Racecourse Caravan Club Site, Hampton Street, Warwick CV34 6HN
Tel: 01926 495448
The site is only six minutes from Warwick town, with a nearby golf course and numerous walking routes. Medieval Warwick Castle nearby provides an interesting day out for all the family. 55 touring pitches available. Caravans welcome. Open from March to January.

- Electric hook-ups available
- Facilities for disabled visitors
- Children's play area
- Pets welcome
- Laundry facilities
- Shop on site
- Licensed bar on site
- Wifi access available

Stratford-upon-Avon

RIVERSIDE LOCATION – ONLY ONE MILE FROM THE TOWN CENTRE

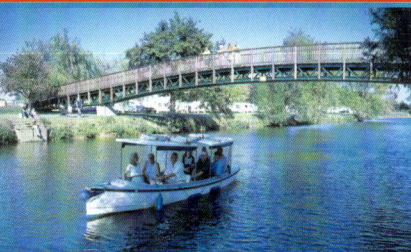

LUXURY HOLIDAY HOMES FOR HIRE • TOURING CARAVANS AND MOTORHOME PITCHES • RIVERFRONT COTTAGES TO RENT

Short Stay Bookings Welcome & 3-day Long Weekend Deals

Set in the heart of the lovely Warwickshire countryside and right on the banks of the beautiful River Avon, is Riverside Caravan Park, the perfect location for exploring Shakespeare Country and the Cotswolds. Holiday Home units accommodate 6 persons and Riverford Cottages 4 persons comfortably.

RIVER TAXIS TO AND FROM TOWN • ADJACENT LOCAL VILLAGE • FREE FISHING • RIVERSIDE WALKS ON SITE SHOP & CAFE • CLUB HOUSE • KIDS PLAYGROUND

Riverside Caravan Park

Tiddington Road
Stratford-upon-Avon
Warwickshire CV37 7AB

01789 292312

www.stratfordcaravans.co.uk

Warwickshire

Stratford-upon-Avon

dodwell park

A small touring park, very clean and quiet, set in the countryside two miles south west of Stratford-upon-Avon. An ideal location from which to visit Shakespeare's birthplace, Anne Hathaway's Cottage, Warwick Castle and the Cotswolds. There are country walks to the River Avon and the village of Luddington. From Stratford-upon-Avon take B439 (formerly A439) towards Bidford-on-Avon for two miles. The park lies on the left, signposted. Free brochure on request.

From £14.00 to £18.00 including electricity • Open all year.

A warm welcome awaits!

Dodwell Park is very well equipped to make your camping stay homely and comfortable. These are some of our facilities: -
Toilets • Free hot showers • Washhand basins with hot water
Hand and hair dryers • Shaving points
Calor and Camping Gaz • Dishwashing facilities
Shop and off-licence • Hard standings • Electric hook-ups
Public telephone and post box • Dogs are welcome

Evesham Road (B439)
Stratford-upon-Avon
Warwickshire
CV37 9SR

Tel: 01789 204957
enquiries@dodwellpark.co.uk
www.dodwellpark.co.uk

West Midlands

Halesowen, Meriden, Sutton Coldfield

West Midlands

HALESOWEN. Clent Hills Camping & Caravaning Club Site, Romsley, Halesowen B62 0NH
Tel: 01562 710015
Situated 15 miles from Birmingham, Clent Hills comprises 95 touring pitches set in an area of natural beauty. Open March to October. Caravans, motorhomes and tents welcome. Serviced pitches available.

MERIDEN. Somers Wood Caravan Park, Somers Road, Meriden CV7 7PL
Tel: 01676 522978 • Fax: 01676 522978 • www.somerswood.co.uk
This adults-only caravan park is set in beautiful North Warwickshire, overlooking a golf course and only 3 miles from Birmingham NEC. Open February to December. 48 pitches available. Caravans and motorhomes welcome. No tents.

SUTTON COLDFIELD. Kingsbury Water Park, Bodymoor Heath Lane, Sutton Coldfield B76 0DY
Tel: 01827 874101
There are at least 200 species of birds to see in this peaceful area of natural beauty. Discover the 600-acre Tame Valley Water Park or have a day out to Staffordshire's best loved theme park, Drayton Manor. 120 touring pitches available. Caravans, motorhomes, tents and trailer tents welcome. Open January to December.

MARSTON CAMPING AND CARAVAN PARK
KINGSBURY ROAD, MARSTON B76 0DP
NEAR SUTTON COLDFIELD AND BIRMINGHAM
Tel: 01675 470902 or 01299 400787

One mile off Junction nine of the M42, towards Kingsbury on the left hand side. Brand new park for 120 caravans, tents and motor homes. Site is open all year round.

All pitches have electricity and fully hard standings. Brand new toilet/shower block, laundry room. Play area. Pets welcome.

Kingsbury Water Park • Hams Hall • Drayton Manor Park • Belfry Golf Course National Exhibition Centre • Tamworth Ski Slope • Lee Manor Leisure Complex.

The FHG Directory of Website Addresses
on pages 235-250 is a useful quick reference guide for holiday accommodation with e-mail and/or website details

MIDLANDS
Worcestershire

Bewdley, Broadway, Bromyard, Evesham, Hanley Swan, Kidderminster

BEWDLEY. Bank Farm Holiday Park, Bank Farm, Bewdley DY12 3ND
Tel: 01299 401277 • Fax: 01299 404960 • www.bankfarmholidaypark.co.uk
Ideal for a family holiday or a quiet break, this family-run site has fishing access to the River Severn and an abundance of wildlife. Open all year. 10 touring pitches available. Caravans welcome.

BROADWAY. Leedons Park Broadway, Childswickham Road, Broadway WR12 7HB
Tel: 01386 852423 • Fax: 01386 853655
Leedon's Park in Worcestershire is perfectly placed for exploring the Cotswolds and visiting Shakespeare's Stratford-upon-Avon as well as Warwick and the Malvern Hills. Open March to January. Caravans welcome.

BROMYARD. Boyce Holiday Park, Stanford Bishop, Bromyard WR6 5UB
Tel: 01886 884 248 • Fax: 01886 884 187 • www.boyceholidaypark.co.uk
The location of this 100-acre family-run park on the Herefordshire-Worcestershire border is perfect for ramblers and for viewing woodland wildlife. Open March to October. 18 touring pitches. Tents, caravans and motorhomes welcome.

EVESHAM. Ranch Caravan Park, Honeybourne, Evesham WR11 7PR
Tel: 01386 830744 • Fax: 01386 833503 • www.ranch.co.uk
Visitors will discover a number of interesting restaurants and pubs, churches and historic gardens around the Vale of Evesham area. This family-run park is situated between Bidford-on-Avon and Broadway in Honeybourne. All pitches have modern facilities. 120 touring pitches available. Caravans welcome. Open March to November.

HANLEY SWAN. Blackmore No.2 Camping and Caravanning Club Site, Hanley Swan WR8 0EE
Tel: 01684 310280
Non-members are welcome to this site in a beautiful area of the Malvern Hills, with 40 square miles of countryside in which to walk and explore. 200 touring pitches. Caravans, tents and motorhomes welcome. Open all year round.

KIDDERMINSTER. Wolverley Caravan Site, Brown Westhead Park, Near Kidderminster DY10 3PX
Tel: 01562 850909
Non-members are welcome at this peaceful club site located just a short drive from Birmingham. Local facilities include a pub, horseriding, golf and a canal to walk along. Open March to November. 120 touring pitches available.

🔌	Electric hook-ups available	♿	Facilities for disabled visitors
🛝	Children's play area	🐕	Pets welcome
🧺	Laundry facilities	🛒	Shop on site
🍷	Licensed bar on site	W	Wifi access available

Worcestershire

Malvern, Stourport on Severn

MALVERN. Three Counties Park, Sledge Green, Malvern WR13 6JW
Tel: 01684 833439
Charming caravan park located in attractive countryside with lovely views of the Malvern Hills. 50 touring pitches, 25 tent pitches available.

MALVERN. Kingsgreen Caravan Park, Berrow, Malvern WR13 6AQ
Tel: 01531 650272
This small park is located in Malvern at the foot of the Malvern Hills. The park land is level, with various convenient facilities including a shower block. Fishing available. Open from March to October. 45 touring pitches available. Caravans, motorhomes and tents welcome.

STOURPORT ON SEVERN. Lickhill Manor Caravan Park, Stourport on Severn DY13 8RL
Tel: 01299 871041 • Fax: 01299 877820 • www.lickhillmanor.co.uk
Tree-lined Lickhill Manor provides 65 acres of natural beauty and is located by the banks of the River Severn. There are plenty of local attractions for all ages. 120 touring pitches available. Caravans, motorhomes and tents welcome. Open April to September.

STOURPORT ON SEVERN. Lincomb Lock Caravan Park, Titton, Stourport on Severn DY13 9QR
Tel: 01299 823836 • Fax: 01299 827527 • www.hillandale.co.uk/lincomblock.htm
This popular, south-west facing camping area, restricted to adults only, is a great sun-trap. Fishing access to the Severn is available. Open March to January. 14 pitches available. Caravans and motorhomes welcome.

Looking for Holiday Accommodation?

for details of hundreds of properties throughout the UK, visit our website

www.holidayguides.com

ls
Yorkshire

North Yorkshire

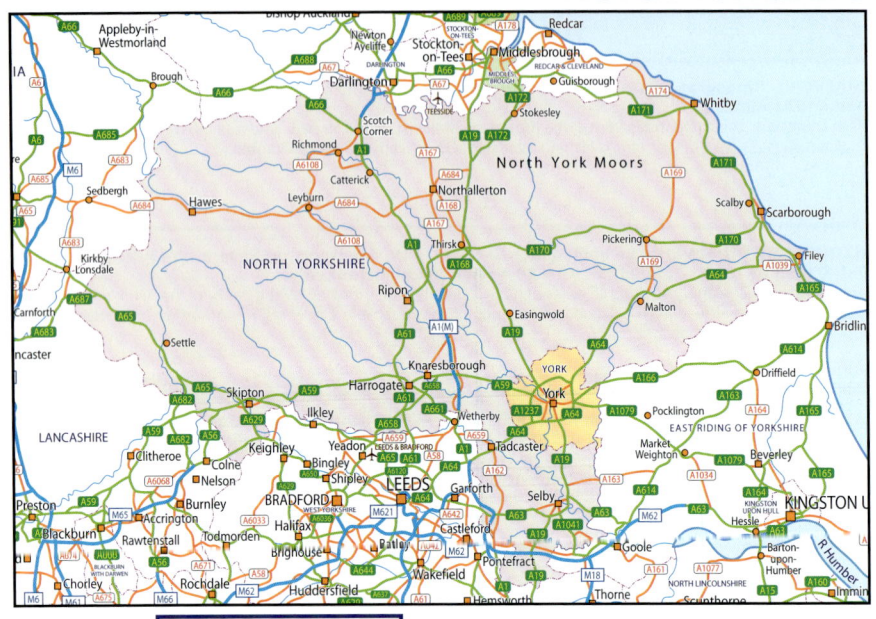

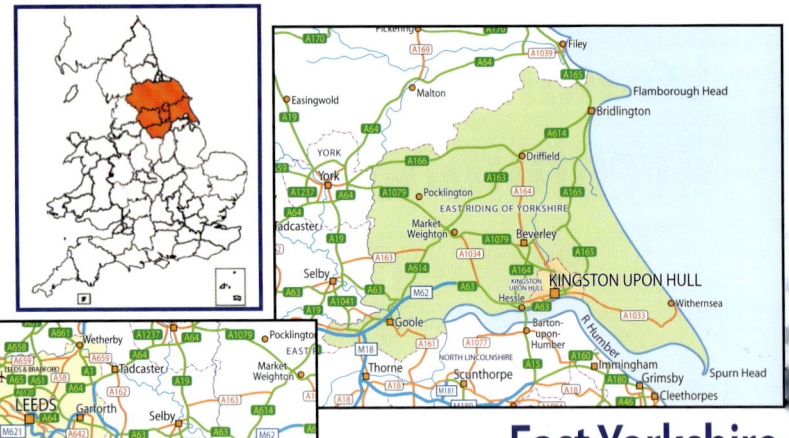

East Yorkshire

South & West Yorkshire

East Yorkshire
Bridlington, Flamborough, Sproatley, Withernsea

East Yorkshire

BRIDLINGTON. Fir Tree Caravan Park, Jewison Lane, Bridlington YO16 6YG
Tel: 01262 676442 • Fax:01262 676442 • www.flowerofmay.com/firTreePark
Enjoy the spacious pitches at this attractive holiday park standing on the stunning coastline at Flamborough Head and Bridlington. Open from March to November. 50 seasonal pitches. Caravans and motorhomes welcome.

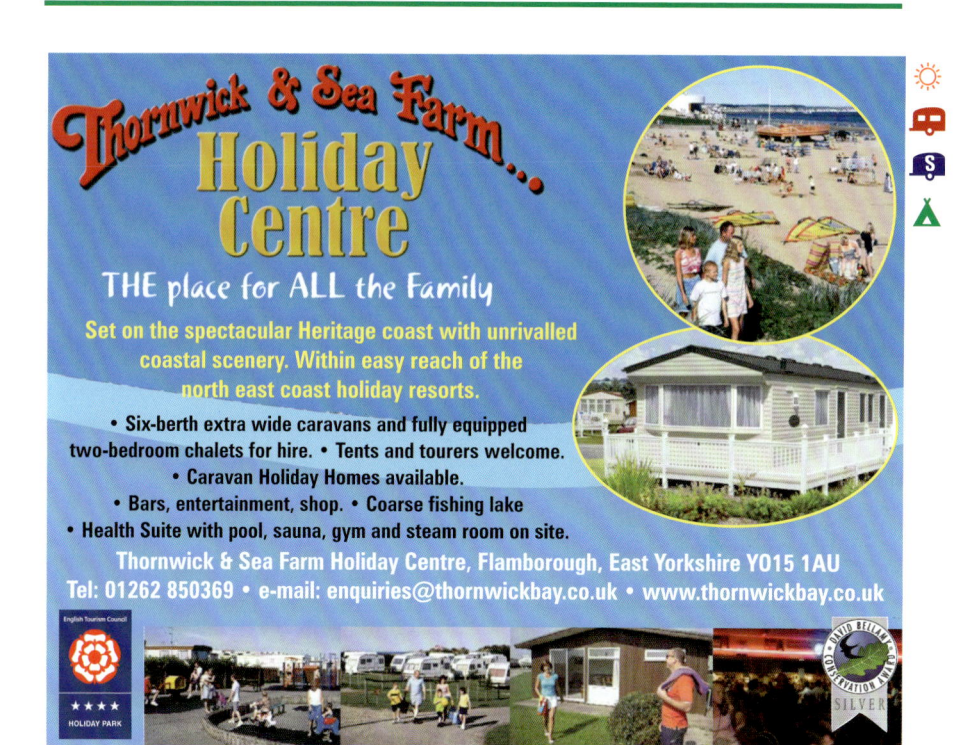

Thornwick & Sea Farm Holiday Centre

THE place for ALL the Family

Set on the spectacular Heritage coast with unrivalled coastal scenery. Within easy reach of the north east coast holiday resorts.

- Six-berth extra wide caravans and fully equipped two-bedroom chalets for hire. • Tents and tourers welcome.
- Caravan Holiday Homes available.
- Bars, entertainment, shop. • Coarse fishing lake
- Health Suite with pool, sauna, gym and steam room on site.

Thornwick & Sea Farm Holiday Centre, Flamborough, East Yorkshire YO15 1AU
Tel: 01262 850369 • e-mail: enquiries@thornwickbay.co.uk • www.thornwickbay.co.uk

SPROATLEY. Burton Constable Holiday Park, The Old Lodges, Sproatley HU11 4LN
Tel:01964 562 508 • Fax: 01964 563 420 • www.burtonconstable.co.uk
Winner of a White Rose Award for Tourism. In a peaceful setting with stunning views and an adventure play area for children. Open from March to October. 170 touring pitches. 50 tent pitches. Motorhomes welcome.

WITHERNSEA. Withernsea Sands Holiday Park, North Road, Withernsea HU19 2BS
Tel: 01964 611161 • Fax: 01964 612411 • www.withernseaholidays.com
Lively park with an indoor swimming pool and children's splash bath, the Boathouse Tavern for excellent meals, entertainment and to top it all off – a beach just minutes away! Open from March to October. 100 touring pitches. 8 tent pitches. Caravans, motorhomes and tents welcome.

North Yorkshire

North Yorkshire — Brompton-on-Swale, Easingwold, Filey

BROMPTON-ON-SWALE. Brompton-on-Swale Caravan & Camping Park, Brompton-on-Swale DL10 7EZ
Tel: 01748 824629 • www.bromptoncaravanpark.co.uk
Standing on the banks of the River Swale only two miles from Richmond, the Gateway to the Yorkshire Dales. Excellent on-site fishing. Open all year round. 170 touring pitches. Caravans, motorhomes and tents welcome.

EASINGWOLD. Holly Brook Adults Only Caravan Park, Penny Carr Lane, Easingwold YO61 3EU
Tel: 01347 821906
Adults-only caravan park situated next to Easingwold Golf Club. Quiet, secluded and the ideal getaway for a relaxing break. 30 touring pitches. Caravans and tents welcome.

HOLIDAY PARKS & CENTRES

FILEY. Blue Dolphin Holiday Park, Gristhorpe Bay, Filey.
Take the great escape to where it's all happening! Blue Dolphin is a fabulous cliff top Park that spoils you for choice of family fun. This lively and extensive Park, high over the sea near Scarborough and Filey, is equally high on the list for non-stop fun and entertainment. It's all go in the heated indoor and outdoor pools. It's all to play for on the All-Weather Multi Sports Courts, and it's right on the scenic coastal Cleveland Way, perfect for strolls. With all this and fantastic Touring facilities and on-site amenities, you can't go wrong. **See also Colour Advertisement.**
Call our UK Central Team: 0871 230 1933 (open 7 days, 9am-9pm) or book on-line (quote TO_FHG) www.touringholidays.co.uk
• Great for Groups! Just book 5 or more holiday homes for extra benefits and savings.
Visit www.havengroups.co.uk or call 0871 230 1911.

CARAVANS FOR HIRE

FILEY near. Crow's Nest Caravan Park, Gristhorpe, Near Filey YO14 9PS (01723 582206).
Crow's Nest Caravan Park is situated on the glorious Yorkshire coast between Scarborough and Filey. Privately owned and operated, this Rose Award winning park is a perfect base for families and couples wishing to make the most of these two great seaside towns and their glorious sandy beaches. The facilities at Crow's Nest are of a very high standard. The heated indoor swimming pool with waterslide provides fun for all ages, and together with the safe children's play area and games room, ensures that there is always something to do. Our well stocked supermarket will supply your every need. The family bar welcomes children, and our relaxing lounge bar features evening entertainment. Our non-smoking conservatory is ideal for a peaceful evening of relaxation after your day's excitement. Touring caravans, motor homes and tents welcome. Hard-standing pitches with electric hook-up are standard. Calor Gas and Camping Gaz stocked.
ETC ★★★★ *HOLIDAY PARK, ROSE AWARD.*
e-mail: enquiries@crowsnestcaravanpark.com   www.crowsnestcaravanpark.com

---

HOLIDAY PARKS & CENTRES

FILEY near. Reighton Sands Holiday Park, Reighton Gap, Near Filey.
Located on top of one of Yorkshire's finest sandy beaches, Reighton Sands boasts beautiful surroundings. A green and spacious cliff top Park, Reighton Sands offers every excuse for you to simply kick-back and relax. When you're done relaxing, why not try your hand at one of the various activities - from a heated indoor fun pool with flume and children's clubs for all ages to fencing and Family Park jumpers, you'll be spoilt for choice. Add to this the fantastic daytime and evening entertainment as well as superb Touring facilities and on-site amenities and you're guaranteed a perfect family holiday. **See also Colour Advertisement.**
Call our UK Central Team: 0871 230 1933 (open 7 days, 9am-9pm) or book on-line (quote: TO_FHG) www.touringholidays.co.uk
• Great for Groups! Just book 5 or more holiday homes for extra benefits and savings.
Visit www.havengroups.co.uk Or call 0871 230 1911.

North Yorkshire
Filey, Harrogate

YORKSHIRE 117

HOLIDAY PARKS & CENTRES

FILEY near. Primrose Valley Holiday Park, Primrose Valley, Near Filey.
Last year we splashed out over £6m on a superb new multi-level pool complex that sets new standards for exhilarating family fun. After enjoying the pulsating turbulence, torrential waterfalls and fun water flows, you can continue into the evening with top-line entertainment. If that's not enough to satisfy your need for family fun, why not try your hand at one of the many activities - from fencing to wall climbing, Primrose Valley offers everything you need for a thrilling, fun-packed family holiday and with top-notch Touring facilities and on-site amenities, you can't go wrong! **See also Colour Advertisement.**
Call our UK Central Team: **0871 230 1933** (open 7 days, 9am-9pm) or book on-line (quote: TO_FHG) www.touringholidays.co.uk
• Great for Groups! Just book 5 or more holiday homes for extra benefits and savings.
Visit www.havengroups.co.uk Or call 0871 230 1911.

HARROGATE. Reynard Crag Holiday Park, Reynard Crag Lane, High Birstwith, Harrogate HG3 2JQ
Tel: 01423 772828 • www.reynardcragpark.co.uk
Well maintained holiday park surrounded by woodland in the the little village of Birstwith, just five miles from Harrogate. Plenty of activities whatever your interest. Open all year round. Caravans and motorhomes welcome.

RIPLEY CARAVAN PARK

Situated adjacent to the delightfully quiet village of Ripley, dominated by its castle which has been occupied by the same family for over 600 years. Conveniently placed for the superb holiday and conference town of Harrogate and for historic Knaresborough; an ideal touring base with the Yorkshire Dales close by.

The site facilities include a leisure block with games room with colour TV, nursery playroom, telephone, shop and heated indoor swimming pool and sauna; toilet block with showers, ample washbasins, razor points and baby bath.
There is a room for our disabled guests with its own specialised facilities.
Laundry room, chemical toilet disposal. Electric hook-up points and hard standing for some pitches. Pets welcome by arrangement. Brochure and tariff available on request.

Ripley, Harrogate HG3 3AU
Tel: 01423 770050

Looking for holiday accommodation?
for details of hundreds of properties
throughout the UK including
comprehensive coverage of all areas of Scotland try:
www.holidayguides.com

YORKSHIRE
North Yorkshire
Harrogate, Hawes,

The Yorkshire Hussar Inn Holiday Park

Secluded family site nestling deep in the heart of picturesque Yorkshire, midway between Ripon and Harrogate, which is noted for its splendid flower gardens and shops. The park is situated behind the 'olde worlde' inn, in a peaceful garden setting, and is licensed for 75 caravans, plus space for some tourers and tents. **Five luxury six-berth caravans for hire** on a weekly basis; nightly lets allowed if available. Each caravan has a double and a twin bedroom, plus sofa bed in the lounge; bathroom/shower room. The caravans are connected to all services, and TV, cooking utensils, crockery, cutlery, duvets and pillows are supplied. Guests must supply own bed linen and towels. Children's play area. Village shop and Post Office.

Further details on request from Mrs Denton

Markington, Near Harrogate HG3 3NR • 01765 677327
e-mail: yorkshirehussar@yahoo.co.uk • www.yorkshire-hussar-inn.co.uk

---

CAMPING SITES

HAWES. Mr and Mrs Facer, Bainbridge Ings Caravan and Camping Site, Hawes DL8 3NU (01969 667354).
A quiet, clean, family-run site with beautiful views and only half-a-mile from Hawes. Good centre for walking and touring the Dales. You can be assured of a warm welcome.
Rates: from £13.00 per day.
• Pets welcome. • Children welcome.
ETC ★★
e-mail: janet@bainbridge-ings.co.uk   www.bainbridge-ings.co.uk

---

HELMSLEY. Golden Square Caravan & Camping Park, Oswaldkirk, Helmsley YO62 5YQ
Tel: 01439 788269 • Fax: 01439 788236 • www.goldensquarecaravanpark.com
Ideal for a family holiday, this spacious park offers panoramic views towards the North York Moors. Facilities include play areas, crazy golf and bike hire. Open from March to October. 129 touring pitches. Caravans, motorhomes, and tents welcome.

Hutton Le Hole Caravan Park

A family-run site at Westfield Lodge Farm, on the southern edge of the North Yorkshire Moors. A level, free-draining and secluded site with modern facilities in a picturesque and peaceful location just outside the village of Hutton Le Hole. This site has on-farm walks and is ideal for walking the North York Moors and touring the area. York is one hour's drive and Scarborough and the coast 45 minutes. Castle Howard is 20 minutes' drive away. Open Easter to 31st October. Prices from £10.00 per night.

**Enquiries/brochure: Mrs Annabel Strickland,
Westfield Lodge, Hutton Le Hole YO62 6UG
Tel: 01751 417261 • Fax: 01751 417876
e-mail: rwstrickland@farmersweekly.net
www.westfieldlodge.co.uk**

The FHG Directory of Website Addresses
on pages 235-250 is a useful quick reference guide for
holiday accommodation with e-mail and/or website details

North Yorkshire

Kirkbymoorside, Leyburn, Northallerton

YORKSHIRE 119

Welcome To Wombleton Caravan & Camping Park

The Willoughby family welcome you to a quiet retreat set in the middle of rural Ryedale. Wombleton is a five star touring park located halfway between Helmsley and Kirkbymoorside south of the A170. A good base to explore the North Yorkshire Moors and York and twenty miles from the east coast.

Wombleton Caravan & Camping Park
Moorfield Lane, Wombleton,
Kirkbymoorside, North Yorkshire YO62 7RY
Tel/Fax: 01751 431684

e-mail: info@wombletoncaravanpark.co.uk • www.wombletoncaravanpark.co.uk

---

LEYBURN. Akebar Caravan Park, Wensleydale, Near Leyburn DL8 5LY
Tel: 01677 450201 • Fax:01677 450046 • www.akebarpark.com
Akebar in the Yorkshire Dales is ideally placed between two National Parks, offering ample opportunites to enjoy outdoor pursuits. Amenities include a 27 hole floodlit golf course, pub and restaurant, and croquet/bowling green. Open from March-January. 200 touring pitches. 25 seasonal pitches. 50 tent pitches. 5 motorhome pitches.

Otterington Park

Situated in the Vale of York on a family-run farm, Otterington Park is a quality, purpose built 5-acre site designed to cater for up to 40 touring units. Electricity and luxury heated amenity block complete with individual bath/shower rooms, disabled facilities and laundry facilities available. Coarse fishing on site. Children and dogs welcome! There is also a brand new development, adjoining the Touring Caravan site, ready for 40 Luxury Holiday Lodges and Static Caravans. Full details on request.

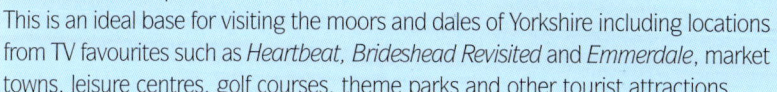

This is an ideal base for visiting the moors and dales of Yorkshire including locations from TV favourites such as *Heartbeat*, *Brideshead Revisited* and *Emmerdale*, market towns, leisure centres, golf courses, theme parks and other tourist attractions.

**Otterington Park, Station Farm,
South Otterington, Northallerton DL7 9JB
Tel: 01609 780656
www.otteringtonpark.com • info@otteringtonpark.com**

YORKSHIRE

North Yorkshire
Pickering, Scarborough

BLACK BULL CARAVAN PARK

Family Caravan and Camping Park one mile south of Pickering on the A169, behind a public house. The gateway to the North York Moors! Good base for walking, cycling, visiting the coast and numerous other local attractions.

On-site facilities: playground • games room • sports field refurbished amenities with free hot showers • dishwashing and laundry

Touring pitches in open level field with some shelter. Fully serviced and fully equipped holiday caravans also for hire. Double-glazed and heated.

Terms from £230 to £340.
Four caravans for hire, sleeping six.
36 pitches available, terms from £12 per night

Why not view our website for more photographs?
**Malton Road,
Pickering,
North Yorkshire
YO18 8EA**

www.blackbullpark.co.uk
Tel: 01751 472528

PICKERING. Vale of Pickering Caravan Park, Carr House Farm, Allerston, Pickering YO18 7PQ
Tel: 01723 859200 • Fax: 01723 850060 • www.valeofpickering.co.uk
First class facilities for the whole family, especially young children, at this friendly park where pets are also welcome. 120 touring pitches. Open from February to January. Caravans, motorhomes and tents welcome.

CARAVANS FOR HIRE

SCARBOROUGH. Sue and Tony Hewitt, Harmony Country Lodge, Limestone Road, Burniston, Scarborough YO13 0DG (0800 2985840).
Set in two acres of private land overlooking the National Park and sea. An ideal base for walking or touring in the beautiful North Yorkshire countryside. TWO miles to the north of Scarborough and within easy reach of many nearby attractions and amenities. Spacious five-berth, fully fitted static caravan with two bedrooms. Shower room with hand basin, hot and cold water, and flush toilet. Fully equipped kitchen, gas cooker and microwave, controlled electric heating and colour TV. Pillows, quilts and linen provided. Picnic table and lawned area. Parking.
Rates: from £150 to £340 per week, gas/electricity included.
• B&B available from £29.00 to £37.00
www.harmonycountrylodge.co.uk

e-mail: tony@harmonylodge.net

FREE or REDUCED RATE entry to Holiday Visits and Attractions – see our
READERS' OFFER VOUCHERS on pages 205-234

North Yorkshire
Scarborough, Wetherby

YORKSHIRE 121

The very best of coast and country. Luxurious facilities, adventure playground, site shop, dog walk, bus service at park entrance. Seasonal pitches, supersites, hardstanding and storage. Supersaver and OAP discounts. Open 1st March - 31st October. Location: half-a-mile to beach, three miles to Scarborough, four miles to Filey, adjoining village with pubs, chip shop, PO and bus service.

Prices: *Caravans and Motorhomes from £11.50 - £25, Tents from £9 - £20.*

Special Offers: *Low Season Savers: 7 nights £7 discount, Any 4 nights Sunday to Thursday inclusive £4 discount. Low Season OAP 7 night Special: £10 discount.*

Cayton Village Caravan Park Ltd, Mill Lane, Cayton Bay, Scarborough YO11 3NN
Tel: 01723 583171 • e-mail: info@caytontouring.co.uk • www.caytontouring.co.uk

ADULTS ONLY

MAUSTIN CARAVAN PARK

This award-winning Holiday Park is set in the beautiful surroundings of the Lower Wharfe Valley. It is a tranquil and peaceful setting for people without family responsibilities. Whether you hire our latest luxury holiday home or one of our country cottages, bring your own touring caravan or tent, or buy a luxury holiday home, you will be sure of a warm welcome. Visit the Stables Bar and Restaurant serving delicious home-cooked food and fine wines.

**Kearby, Near Wetherby,
North Yorkshire LS22 4BZ
Tel: 0113 288 6234
E-Mail: info@maustin.co.uk
www.maustin.co.uk**

symbols

- ☀ Holiday Parks & Centres
- 🚐 Caravans for Hire
- Ⓢ Caravan Sites and Touring Parks
- ▲ Camping Sites

YORKSHIRE
North Yorkshire
Whitby, York

Ladycross Plantation
Touring Caravan Park,
Ladycross Plantation, Egton,
Whitby YO21 1UA
01947 895502

A peaceful and well-screened 30-acre woodland site within the North York Moors National Park. Ideally situated for exploring Whitby, the North East Coast and Heartbeat Country. There are lots of activities and visits to suit all tastes within easy reach. Seasonal pitches. No charge for awnings or dogs; two heated amenity blocks, excellent dog walk, launderette, electric hook-ups. Open March – mid October.

enquiries@ladycrossplantation.co.uk
www.ladycrossplantation.co.uk

Middlewood Farm Holiday Park

Small, peaceful, family park. A walkers', artists' and wildlife paradise, set amidst the beautiful North Yorkshire Moors National Park, Heritage Coast and 'Heartbeat Country'. Relax and enjoy the magnificent panoramic views of our spectacular countryside. Five minutes' walk to the village PUB and shops. Ten minutes' walk to the BEACH and picturesque Robin Hood's Bay. SUPERIOR LUXURY HOLIDAY HOMES FOR HIRE, equipped to the highest standards (Open all year). TOURERS and TENTS: level, sheltered park with electric hook-ups. Superb heated facilities, free showers and dishwashing. Laundry. Gas. Children's adventure playground. Adjacent dog walk and cycle route. Credit cards accepted. Signposted. A warm welcome awaits you.

Robin Hood's Bay, Near Whitby, Yorkshire YO22 4UF
Tel: 01947 880414
e-mail: info@middlewoodfarm.fsnet.com • www.middlewoodfarm.com

---

YORK. Goosewood Holiday Park, Sutton-on-the-Forest, York YO61 1ET
Tel: 01347 810829 • Fax: 01347 811498 • www.goosewood.co.uk
A short distance from the centre of York, set in 45 beautiful acres of open countryside. A mixture of woodland and tranquil grassy areas make for the idyllic escape for adults, while there is an adventure playground and play barn for children. Open all year. 52 touring pitches. Caravans and motorhomes welcome.

YORK. Ashfield Holiday Cottages and Caravan Park, Hagg Lane, Dunnington, York YO19 5PE
Tel: 01904 488 631 • www.ashfieldtouringcaravanpark.co.uk
Friendly, family-run site only 10 minutes from the centre of York. Ideal for dog owners and fully equipped with modern, fully functional facilities and separate rally field. Caravans, motorhomes and tents welcome.

YORK. Naburn Lock Caravan Site, Naburn, York YO19 4RU
Tel: 01904 728697 • Fax:01904 728697 • www.naburnlock.co.uk
Well planned site with separate area for adults only. Regular bus service into the centre of historic York. Open from March to November. 96 touring pitches. Caravans, motorhomes and tents welcome.

⚡	Electric hook-ups available	♿	Facilities for disabled visitors
🎠	Children's play area	🐕	Pets welcome
🧺	Laundry facilities	🛒	Shop on site
🍷	Licensed bar on site	W	Wifi access available

York

MOOR END FARM (Established 1965)
Acaster Malbis, York YO23 2UQ • Tel/Fax: 01904 706727

Moor End Farm is a small, family-run caravan and camping site 4 miles south-west of York. The Tourist Board graded site has 10 touring pitches and 6 static caravans. Two of the static caravans are available for holiday lets starting from £44 a night or £210 a week. The hire caravans have colour TV, shower, toilet, fridge, microwave, 2 bedrooms, kitchen, dining/living area and accommodate up to 6 persons. Touring facilities available are electric hook-ups, hot showers, toilets, dish-washing sink, fridge/freezer and microwave oven. There are picnic tables around the site for our guests to use.

Moor End Farm is on a bus route to York and is 5 minutes' walk from the popular river bus service and the local inn. We are also very close to the York/Selby cycle track and the York park & ride scheme.

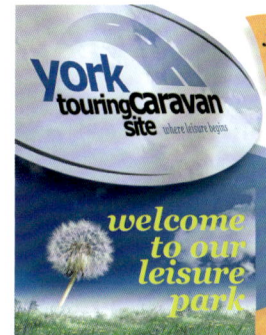

---

york touring caravan site — where leisure begins

just 5 miles ...from the centre of York!

OPEN ALL YEAR

This all-new park, which is open all year, has superb facilities including a full length Golf Driving Range and a 9 hole Putting Course.

Tel: 01904 499275
www.yorkcaravansite.co.uk

welcome to our leisure park
Come and see us soon...
...Perfect relaxation

The Alders has been sensitively developed in historic parkland on a working farm where visitors may escape from the hustle and bustle of life to peace and tranquillity. The water meadow, wild flowers and woodland walk combine to offer the nature lover an idyllic environment in which to stay. It is a level, dry site with electric hook-ups, fully equipped shower rooms, telephone and gas; nearby village cricket, golf and fishing. Near to A1 and A19 but convenient for York, Harrogate, Dales, Moors, Heritage Coast and National Trust properties. Brochure available.

The Alders CARAVAN PARK

Home Farm, Alne, York YO61 1RY
Tel & Fax: 01347 838722
e-mail: enquiries@homefarmalne.co.uk
www.alderscaravanpark.co.uk

Durham

BARNARD CASTLE. East Lendings Caravan Park, Abbey Lane, Barnard Castle DL12 9TJ
Tel: 01833 637271 • Fax: 01833 630578 • www.lakelandleisureestates.co.uk/eastlendings
Popular and sociable park located on the banks of the River Tees, with easy access to the market town of Barnard Castle. On-site pub and club. Open from March to October.

HOLIDAY HOMES IN THE HEART OF County Durham

Witton Castle
COUNTRY PARK County Durham

Situated in the heart of County Durham amidst 330 acres of beautiful landscape at the foot of the Pennines, the 14th century castle forms the centrepiece of the park and the surrounding countryside provides a peaceful haven in which to enjoy your holiday home.

Caravans start from only £9,995, fully sited, and our comprehensive facilities cater for your daily needs for all your family.

Only 25 minutes from Slaley Hall and even less for at least 3 or more local golf courses.

Call Mick or Steve on:
01388 488 230
Email: sales@wittoncastlecountrypark.co.uk
www.wittoncastlecountrypark.co.uk
Witton Castle Country Park, Witton-Le-Wear,
Bishop Auckland, County Durham, DL14 0DE

NEW CARAVAN PITCH DEVELOPMENT UNDER CONSTRUCTION

The FHG Directory of Website Addresses

on pages 235-250 is a useful quick reference guide for holiday accommodation with e-mail and/or website details

Northumberland
Bamburgh, Berwick-upon-Tweed

NORTH EAST ENGLAND 125

Northumberland

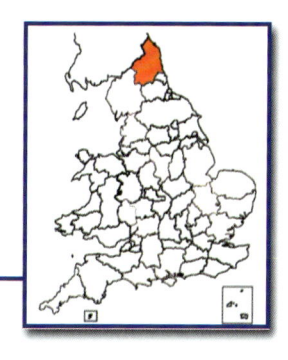

Glororum Caravan Park

Glororum, Bamburgh NE69 7AW
Tel: 01668 214457

Beautifully situated one mile from Bamburgh on the glorious Northumberland coast.
Set in peaceful surroundings within easy reach of Holy Island, the Farne Islands, the Cheviots and many historic castles.

There are ample opportunities locally for swimming, golf, tennis, sailing, water sports, etc.

The park facilities include a shop, toilet blocks with showers, laundry with washing machines and drying facilities and children's play area.

Please send for our colour brochure and tariff leaflet.

e-mail: enquiries@northumbrianleisure.co.uk
www.northumbrianleisure.co.uk

HOLIDAY PARKS & CENTRES

BERWICK-UPON-TWEED. Haggerston Castle Holiday Park, Beal, Near Berwick-upon-Tweed.
A 5-star Parkland and winner of Northumbria Park of the Year, Haggerston Castle is set within Northumberland's National Park and combines a wide range of outdoor pursuits with exceptional leisure and entertainment facilities. With wonderful sweeping beaches and historic castles on the door step, Haggerston Castle is the place to go for exploring and a wonderful Touring holiday. Haggerston Castle boasts fantastic Touring facilities and great on-site amenities to cater for all your Touring needs. With the setting for Hogwarts School of Witchcraft and Wizardry right on the doorstep, it's destined to make your holiday totally magical. **See also Colour Advertisement.**
Call our UK Central Team: 0871 230 1933 (open 7 days, 9am-9pm) or book on-line (quote: TO_FHG) www.touringholidays.co.uk
• Great for Groups! Just book 5 or more holiday homes for extra benefits and savings.
Visit www.havengroups.co.uk Or call 0871 230 1911.

Northumberland

Berwick-upon-Tweed, Corbridge, Hexham, Otterburn

BERWICK-UPON-TWEED. Barmoor Castle Country Park, Lowick, Berwick-upon-Tweed TD15 2DR
Tel: 01289 388376 • www.barmoorcastle.co.uk
Take a relaxing break at Barmoor Castle, located at the Gateway to the Cheviots, and just a short distance from Northumberland beaches. Lots of space, with 20 yards between each caravan, and set in 200 acres of tranquil woodland. Open from February to January.

Wellhouse Farm
Camping & Caravan Park
Newton, Stocksfield
Northumberland NE43 7UY
Tel: 01661 842193

A peaceful family-run site four miles east of Corbridge and ten miles from Hexham. 45 pitches for tourers, tents and motor homes, with hardstandings, electric hook-ups and internal road. Facilities include amenity block with modern toilets, showers, disabled access, laundry, dishwashing area and main reception. Well located for exploring Northumberland and surrounding areas; one mile from the Roman Wall and Hadrian's Wall Path; Newcastle and Metro Centre twelve miles.

e-mail: info@wellhousefarm.co.uk • www.wellhousefarm.co.uk

Greencarts is a working farm situated in Roman Wall country, ideally placed for exploring by car, bike or walking. It has magnificent views of the Tyne Valley. Campsite for 30 tents with facilities, and bunk barn with 12 beds, showers and toilet are now open from Easter until the end of October. Prices for campsite are £5 to £10 per tent, plus £1pp. Bunk barn beds from £10. Linen available.
Bed and Breakfast also available from £25 to £40.
Mr & Mrs D Maughan, Greencarts Farm,
Humshaugh, Hexham NE46 4BW
Tel/Fax: 01434 681320
e-mail: sandra@greencarts.co.uk

GREENCARTS FARM
www.greencarts.co.uk

THE BORDER FOREST CARAVAN PARK
Come and stay in Peaceful Northumberland on the edge of Kielder Forest • A paradise for dogs and nature lovers.
Small secluded family run park, ideal for touring, and with many outdoor pursuits and historic sites within easy reach.
- Touring Site • Timber Lodge • Self-catering Cottage • Heated Toilet Blocks
- Free Hot Showers • Electric Hook Ups • Washing-up Sink
- Chemical Disposal Point • Spring Water On Tap • Calor & Camping Gaz
- Public Telephone • Tourist Information Area • Plenty of Dog Walks

01830 520259

Cottonshopeburnfoot, Near Otterburn NE19 1TF
borderforest@btinternet.com
www.borderforest.com

FREE or REDUCED RATE entry to Holiday Visits and Attractions – see our READERS' OFFER VOUCHERS on pages 205-234

Tyne & Wear

Gateshead, Newcastle-upon-Tyne, South Shields

Tyne & Wear

NORTH EAST ENGLAND 127

GATESHEAD. Derwent Park Caravan and Camping Site, Rowlands Gill, Gateshead NE39 1LG
Tel: 01207 543383
Just a short walk from local shops and other amenities, this friendly site has all the facilities required for a peaceful and relaxing break. The city of Newcastle is just a short bus ride away. Open March to October.

Byreside Caravan Site

Hamsterley, Newcastle-upon-Tyne NE17 7RT
The caravan site is on the family-run farm in the beautiful countryside of the Derwent Valley. The site is open all year round and is quiet and secluded. It is very popular with walkers and cyclists as it is adjacent to the Derwent Walk Country Park which is also part of the Coast to Coast route. History looms large in the district with many places to visit in the surrounding area and only a short distance from both Durham and Northumberland. On site is a small shop and toilet block. All pitches have electric hook-up points. Camping area. Booking advisable.
Open all year • Contact: Mrs J. Clemitson • 01207 560280

SOUTH SHIELDS. Lizard Lane Caravan And Camping Site, Marsden, South Shields NE34 7AB
Tel: 0191 4544982
Small site catering for tents, tourers and motorhomes. Situated on the edge of town, it has easy access to the beach, and there are delightful walks along the cliff tops. The lively city of Newcastle is just 15 minutes' drive.

SOUTH SHIELDS. Sandhaven Caravan Park, Sea Road, South Shields NE33 2LD
Tel: 0191 454 5594
Miles of sandy beach and traditional seaside fun is on your doorstep at this well equipped park with easy transport links to Newcastle, Gateshead and Sunderland. 25 landscaped pitches include hardstanding. Open March to October.

	Electric hook-ups available		Facilities for disabled visitors
	Children's play area		Pets welcome
	Laundry facilities		Shop on site
	Licensed bar on site	W	Wifi access available

Cheshire

Holmes Chapel

Cheshire - soak in the atmosphere of the historic city of Chester, created by an abundance of black-and-white buildings set in a circuit of glorious city walls, the most complete in the country. Chester's crowning glory is the 13th century Rows – two tiers of shops running along the main streets, offering a unique and sophisticated shopping experience. A leisurely walk along the finest city walls in Britain will take you past most of the city's delights like the stunning Eastgate Clock and the 1000-year-old Cathedral, a haven of reflective tranquillity in a lively, bustling, cosmopolitan centre. The biggest archaeological dig in Britain is currently underway at the 2000-year-old Roman Amphitheatre; there is architectural splendour to enjoy at every turn. The lush countryside surrounding Chester is peppered with stately homes, award-winning gardens and chic market towns featuring characteristic black-and-white half-timbered buildings. Tatton Park near Knutsford is one of Britain's finest Georgian manors, with acres of parklands and formal gardens, a perfect attraction to enjoy in every season, and the host of the RHS Flower Show in July. Or visit Arley Hall and Gardens near Northwich, with its stunning herbaceous borders and Country Fair and Horse Trials in May. For super chic in super villages and towns, breeze into Tarporley, Nantwich, Knutsford and Wilmslow where sophisticated shopping, fine cuisine and contemporary pleasures ensure an afternoon of indulgence and fine delights, with food and drink festivals being held throughout the year.

CARAVAN SITES & TOURING PARKS

HOLMES CHAPEL (near). Woodlands Park, Wash Lane, Allostock WA16 9LG (01565 723429 or 01332 810818).
Woodlands Park is a 16-acre residential and holiday home park set in delightful shrubbery and mature woodland. The park offers homes for sale and has a flat, spacious area for tourers and tents. Facilities include toilet block with showers, laundry room, chemical toilet disposal, electric hook-up points and some hard standings. Brochure and tariff available upon request.
- Pets welcome by arrangement • Open 1st March to 7th January..

symbols

- ☼ Holiday Parks & Centres
- 🚐 Caravans for Hire
- $ Caravan Sites and Touring Parks
- ▲ Camping Sites

Cheshire

NORTH WEST ENGLAND

Chester, Macclesfield, Northwich, Wirral

CHESTER. Chester Fairoaks Caravan Club Site, Rake Lane, Little Stanney, Chester CH2 4HS
Tel: 01513 551600 • Fax: 01342 410258
Chester Fairoaks boasts 105 pitches on 8 acres of land. There are many attractions nearby, including the Roman amphitheatre, shops, restaurants and a town crier! Non-members welcome. 100 touring pitches available. Tents, caravans and motorhomes welcome. Open all year.

MACCLESFIELD. Stonyfold Caravan Park, Stonyfold Lane, Leek Road, Bosley, Macclesfield SK11 0PR
Tel: 07973 728547 • Fax: 01625 422832.
Adults-only caravan park located south of the market town of Macclesfield. Five touring van pitches available. Lodges, chalets and caravans available for hire. Designated parking.

NORTHWICH. Lamb Cottage Caravan Park, Dalefords Lane, Whitegate, Northwich CW8 2BN
Tel: 01606 882302 • Fax: 01606 888491 • www.lambcottage.co.uk
This caravan park is for adults only. Nearby recreational activities include golf, fishing and horseriding. Open March –end of October (approx.) Caravans and motorhomes are welcome.

WIRRAL. Wirral Country Park Caravan Club Site, Station Rd, Thurstaston, Wirral CH61 0HN
Tel: 0151 648 5228
Set in The Wirral, in an area of great natural beauty, the site offers visitors 2000 acres on which to cycle, explore with the family or simply meander. Open March to November. 93 touring pitches.

Looking for Holiday Accommodation?

FHG KUPERARD

for details of hundreds of properties throughout the UK, visit our website

www.holidayguides.com

Cumbria

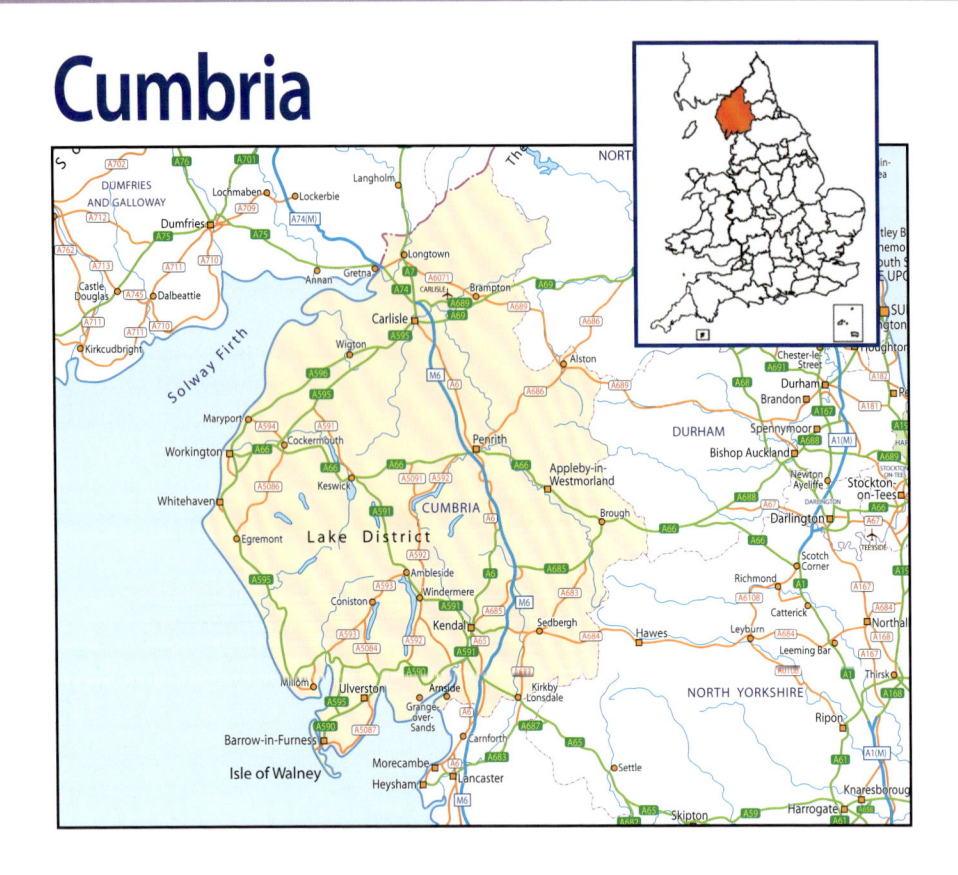

Cumbria - The Lake District is often described as the most beautiful corner of England, and it's easy to see why 15 million visitors head here every year. It is a place of unrivalled beauty, with crystal clear lakes, bracken-covered mountains, peaceful forests, quiet country roads and miles of stunning coastline.

At the heart of Cumbria is the Lake District National Park. Each of the lakes that make up the area has its own charm and personality: Windermere, England's longest lake, is surrounded by rolling hills; Derwentwater and Ullswater are circled by craggy fells; England's deepest lake, Wastwater, is dominated by high mountains including the country's highest, Scafell Pike. For those who want to tackle the great outdoors, Cumbria offers everything from rock climbing to fell walking and from canoeing to horse riding – all among stunning scenery.

Cumbria has many delightful market towns, historic houses and beautiful gardens such as Holker Hall with its 25 acres of award-winning grounds. There are many opportunities to sample local produce, such as Cumbrian fell-bred lamb, Cumberland Sausage, and trout and salmon plucked fresh from nearby lakes and rivers.

Cumbria is a county of contrasts with a rich depth of cultural and historical interest in addition to stunning scenery. Compact and accessible, it can offer something for every taste.

3 Great Sites in Beautiful Lakeland

Tarnside Caravan Park
Braystones, Beckermet, Cumbria CA21 2YL
Tel: 01946 822777 • Fax: 01946 824442
e-mail: reception@seacote.com • www.seacote.com

Situated on seafront on western fringe of Lake District, convenient for Ennerdale, Eskdale, Wasdale and some of England's highest mountains. Good range of tourist attractions in the vicinity.

Licensed club and restaurant on the park; pubs and shop in Beckermet village (½ mile); Egremont 10 min drive. Modern luxury static holiday caravans; pitches for tourers and motor homes. Dogs welcome.

Seven Acres Caravan Park

www.sevenacres.info
e-mail: reception@seacote.com

Holmrook, Cumbria CA19 1YD

Located alongside the A595 between the villages of Holmrook and Gosforth, Seven Acres is a quiet and peaceful park, with a variety of wildlife.

Modern luxury holiday caravans for hire, fully equipped to sleep up to 8. No additional charge for gas and electricity. Launderette on site. Holiday caravans also for sale. Fully serviced touring pitches and tents also available.

Tel: 01946 822777
Fax: 01946 824442

SEACOTE PARK

The Beach, St Bees, Cumbria CA27 0ET
Tel: 01946 822777
Fax: 01946 824442
reception@seacote.com
www.seacote.com

Adjoining lovely sandy beach on fringe of Lake District, modern luxury holiday caravans for hire, fully equipped to sleep up to 8. Full serviced touring pitches and tent area.
St Bees is convenient for touring, with Ennerdale, Eskdale and Wasdale, plus some of England's finest mountain scenery within easy reach.
Holiday caravans also for sale.

Greenhowe Caravan Park
Great Langdale, English Lakeland.

Greenhowe is a permanent Caravan Park with Self Contained Holiday Accommodation. Subject to availability Holiday Homes may be rented for short or long periods from 1st March until mid-November. The Park is situated in the heart of the Lake District some half a mile from Dungeon Ghyll at the foot of the Langdale Pikes. It is an ideal centre for Climbing, Fell Walking, Riding, Swimming or just a lazy holiday.

Please ask about Short Breaks.

**Greenhowe Caravan Park
Great Langdale,
Ambleside
Cumbria LA22 9JU**

For free colour brochure
**Telephone: (015394) 37231
Fax: (015394) 37464
www.greenhowe.com**

Cumbria
NORTH WEST ENGLAND 133
Ambleside, Appleby-in-Westmorland, Coniston

AMBLESIDE. Skelwith Fold Caravan Park, Ambleside LA22 0HX
Tel: 015394 32277 • Fax: 015394 34344 • www.skelwith.com
The ideal getaway for families with children – adventure playground, mountain bike hire and a great selection of pubs and restaurants within walking distance. Open from March to November. 150 touring pitches. Caravans and motorhomes welcome.

APPLEBY-IN-WESTMORLAND. Wild Rose Park, Ormside, Appleby-in-Westmorland CA16 6EJ
Tel: 01768 351077 • Fax:017683 52551 • www.wildrose.co.uk
Cumbria Tourist and Holiday Park of the Year 2007. 5 star family park situated in Eden Valley, ideal for exploring the Lake District and Yorkshire Dales. Open all year round. 226 touring pitches. 100 motorhome pitches. 20 tent pitches.

Eden's caravanning paradise

Nestling in magnificent Eden - very close to the Lake District and the Pennines, Wild Rose Park is a multi-award winning park set in beautiful tranquil surroundings. This superb park includes over 230 designated camping and touring pitches, mini market, restaurant, laundrette, adventure playgrounds, outdoor pools, TV and Games Rooms ...paradise!

Wild Rose Park

Call or write for a FREE brochure:
Ormside, Appleby, Cumbria, CA16 6EJ.
017683 51077 reception@wildrose.co.uk

www.wildrose.co.uk

Three six-berth, modern, well-equipped caravans situated on a quiet family-run farm site with beautiful views over Coniston Water.

Showers, toilets, gas cookers, fires and water heaters; electric lighting, fridge, TV, kettle, toaster and microwave.

Pets are welcome, and pony trekking can be arranged from the farm. A good base for walking and touring the area. We have a good pub 200 yards down the road. Weekly terms on request.

Mrs E. Johnson, Spoon Hall, Coniston LA21 8AW
Telephone: 015394 41591

NORTH WEST ENGLAND — Cumbria

Flookburgh, Grange-over-Sands

FLOOKBURGH. Lakeland Leisure Park, Moor Lane, Flookburgh LA11 7LT
Tel: 01539 558 556 • Fax: 01539 559 352
Family-friendly park with plenty of activities and entertainment to amuse the kids and adults too! Ideal base for exploring the Lake District. Open from March to November. 100 touring pitches. 65 tent pitches. Caravans, motorhomes and tents welcome.

HOLIDAY PARKS & CENTRES

GRANGE-OVER-SANDS. Lakeland Leisure Park, Moor Lane, Flookburgh, near Grange-over-Sands.
Just ten miles from Lake Windermere, this picturesque Park offers the perfect family break. Set in fantastic surroundings on the edge of the Lake District, Lakeland Leisure Park combines a location of natural beauty with excellent activities, superb shows and awe-inspiring entertainment both during the day and night time. Add to all this Lakeland's first class Touring facilities and on-site amenities, and you can see all the ingredients for a great family holiday which bring its guests back year after year. **See also Colour Advertisement.**
Call our UK Central Team: 0871 230 1933 (open 7 days, 9am-9pm) or book on-line (quote: TO_FHG) www.touringholidays.co.uk
- Great for Groups! Just book 5 or more holiday homes for extra benefits and savings.
Visit www.havengroups.co.uk Or call 0871 230 1911.

Greaves Farm Caravan Park
Field Broughton, Grange-over-Sands

A small quiet grass site with luxury six-berth caravans.
Family owned and supervised. Beautifully situated in an old orchard. Two miles north of Cartmel, two miles south of foot of Lake Windermere. 30 minutes' from M6. Convenient base for touring Lake District,
Fully serviced. All sites have water, drainage and electricity. Colour TV, fridge. Equipped except for linen. Tourers and tents welcome. Small tented and touring site with electric hook ups if required.
Open March to October.

ENGLISH TOURISM COUNCIL ★★★★ HOLIDAY AND TOURING PARK

SAE for details to Mrs E. Rigg, Prospect House, Barber Green, Grange-over-Sands LA11 6HU
Tel: 015395 36329 or 36587

Electric hook-ups available		Facilities for disabled visitors	
Children's play area		Pets welcome	
Laundry facilities		Shop on site	
Licensed bar on site		Wifi access available	

Cumbria — NORTH WEST ENGLAND 135

Kendal

PATTON HALL FARM
kendal, the lake district

luxury static caravan accommodation

Two modern self-catering static caravans located on a 140 acre working sheep farm set in the Mint Valley and offers lovely panoramic views across Kendal and the Lake District fells beyond.

Easily accessible from the M6 motorway; just minutes from Kendal and yet this beautiful, rural location is both peaceful and tranquil.

Fully equipped with modern facilities. Kitchen with full sized cooker and oven, microwave and fridge with freezer box. TV and video. One twin and one double room and the lounge can also be converted to sleep two people. Bathroom with shower and mirrored vanity unit. Heated throughout with gas central heating.

**Patton Hall Farm,
Patton, Kendal,
Cumbria LA8 9DT
Tel: 01539 721590**
e-mail: stay@pattonhall.co.uk
www.pattonhallfarm.co.uk

Modern purpose-built park with top class amenities just three-quarters of a mile from M6 Exit 36. Within easy reach of the Lakes, Yorkshire Dales, West Coast and Morecambe Bay. With licensed lounge bar, off-licence, TV lounge, pool table, facilities for the disabled, shop, Calor gas, barbecues, picnic tables, fully tiled private showers, toilets and wash cubicles, laundry and washing up facilities all with free hot water. All hardstanding pitches with electric hook-ups. Many suitable for awnings. Please telephone or write for our free colour brochure. Call for bar opening times.

Waters Edge Caravan Park
**Crooklands, Near Kendal LA7 7NN
Tel: 015395 67708**

---

symbols

- ☀ Holiday Parks & Centres
- 🚐 Caravans for Hire
- Ⓢ Caravan Sites and Touring Parks
- ⛺ Camping Sites

CASTLERIGG HALL
CARAVAN & CAMPING PARK

In the heart of the English Lake District

"Deep down in the vallley, the lakes of Derwentwater and Bassenthwaite gleam blue or silver according to the hues of the weather. This fabulous view is visible from some of the fully serviced pitches which are arranged on hardstanding terraces."

Castlerigg Hall is one of Britain's most spectacularly scenic sites set in the heart of the English Lake District. Its elevated postion provides wonderful panoramic views. The facilities are of a high standard with underfloor heating to one of the toilet buildings, privacy cubicles, laundry and a bathroom to soak those weary legs after a days walking! The park's shop is well stocked with fresh bread, milk, papers and a wide range of other items. The park's restaurant is popular and open five days a week serving locally sourced food.

Castlerigg Hall's location is ideal for those who wish to leave their motorhome on the pitch as it is only a 25 minute woodland walk to the centre of Keswick. Another popular short walk is to the 400 year old Castlerigg Stone Cicle. Dog s are catered for too, in the form of an area where you can let your dog off the lead - supervised of course.

So why not click on the park's website and go the the live webcam and enjoy the view!

Caravans for hire • Camping
Touring Caravans • Motorhomes

Castlerigg Hall
Caravan & Camping Park,
Keswick CA12 4TE
Tel: 017687 74499
info@castlerigg.co.uk
www.castlerigg.co.uk

Burns Farm Caravan & Campsite
St Johns-in-the-Vale
Keswick CA12 4RR

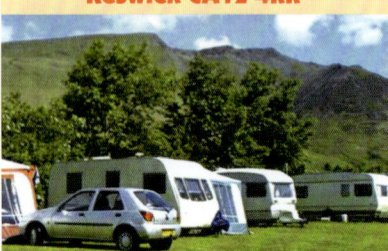

- Quiet family-run caravan and camping site, situated two-and-a-half miles east of Keswick-on-Derwentwater. Beautiful views of the surrounding fells.
- Ideal centre for walking and touring the Lake District.
- Touring caravans, motor caravans and tents are welcome. Electric hook-ups are available. Toilet block with hot showers etc.
- Prices from £10 per caravan inclusive of electric hook-up and from £8 per tent.

Enquiries with S.A.E. please to Mrs Linda Lamb.
Tel: 01768 779225
e-mail: linda@burns-farm.co.uk
www.burns-farm.co.uk

Two six-berth caravans in own private half-acre site, on quiet farm setting only 5 miles from Kirkby Stephen, 8 miles from Appleby, and 7 miles from Junction 38 of the M6 at Tebay. It is an ideal location for walking, relaxing or touring the Yorkshire Dales, Lake District and many local market towns.
Both caravans are Quality Cumbria inspected, and fully equipped with TV and DVD player, and all bedding is provided. All gas, water and electricity included in tariff.
Short Breaks available.

Whygill Head

Please phone or write for further information, brochure and tariff.

Little Asby, Appleby CA16 6QD • Tel: 07840 656532

Cumbria
Newby Bridge. Penrith

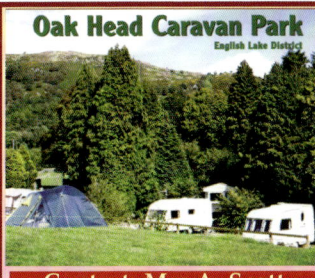

Oak Head Caravan Park
English Lake District

A well tended, uncrowded and wooded site set amidst picturesque fells between the Cartmel peninsula and the southern tip of Lake Windermere.

On-site facilities; flush toilets ✧ hot showers ✧ laundry facilities ✧ hair dryers ✧ deep freeze ✧ gas on sale

Tourers (30 pitches) £14 per night (incl. electricity & VAT). Tents (30 pitches) £12 - £14 per night. Auto homes £12 (£14 on electricity). All prices for outfit, plus 2 adults and 2 children. Open March 1st to October 31st.

Oak Head Caravan Park, Ayside, Grange-over-Sands LA11 6JA

Contact: Mrs A. Scott
Tel: 015395 31475

Park Foot Holiday Park combines an idyllic setting with so much to see and do

A family-run park catering for families and couples only, Park Foot offers touring caravan and camping pitches and self-catering cottages. All touring pitches have electricity and are close to a water point.

- Modern toilets with hot showers
- Laundry room • Shop
- Direct access to Lake Ullswater and Barton Fell
- Two children's playgrounds
- Games and amusements • Pony trekking
- Mountain bike hire • Dog walking areas
- Licensed club with bar, restaurant and takeaways, disco, live entertainment and children's club in the summer season.
- Static caravans and lodges for sale.

Parkfoot Caravan & Camping Park,
Howtown Road, Pooley Bridge, Penrith, Cumbria CA10 2NA
Tel: 017684 86309 • Fax: 017684 86041
holidays@parkfootullswater.co.uk • www.parkfootullswater.co.uk

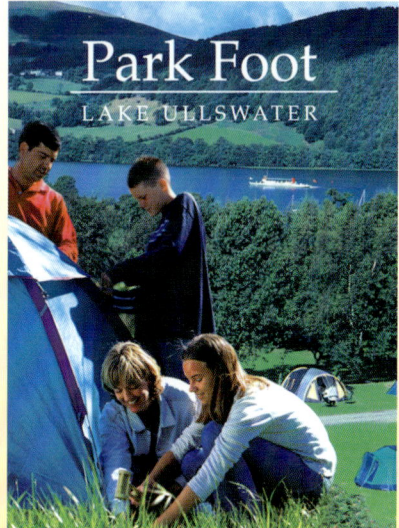

PENRITH. Lowther Holiday Park, Eamont Bridge, Penrith CA10 2JB
Tel: 01768 863231 • Fax: 01768 868126 • www.lowther-holidaypark.co.uk
The perfect base from which to explore the Northern Lakes, the Eden Valley and the North Pennines. Excellent facilities. Open from March to November. 221 touring pitches. Caravans, motorhomes and tents welcome

PENRITH. Waterfoot Caravan Park, Ullswater, Pooley Bridge, Penrith CA11 0JF
Tel: 017684 86302 • Fax:017684 86728 • www.waterfootpark.co.uk/
Prestigious five star family park situated in the grounds of a Georgian mansion. David Bellamy Gold Award. Excellent facilities and ideal for caravans and motorhomes. 34 touring pitches.

Cumbria

Penrith

Beckses Holiday Caravan Park

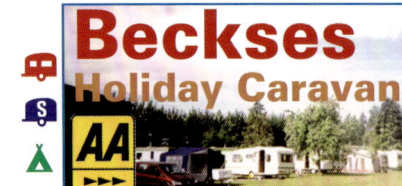

Conveniently situated within six miles of the M6 motorway, this caravan park offers a choice of holiday accommodation on the fringe of the Lake District National Park. Four and six-berth caravans for hire, with mains services, electric light and fridge, gas cooker and fire, toilet, separate double and bunk bedrooms, kitchen area and lounge. Fully equipped except linen. Alternatively those with touring caravans and tents will find excellent facilities on site; toilets, showers, chemical disposal points, stand pipes and laundry facilities. There is a play area with swings, etc, for children, also large recreation area. Within easy reach of outdoor heated swimming pool, pony trekking, fishing and fell walking. Some local pubs have restaurant facilities. Full details and terms on request.

Penruddock, Penrith, Cumbria CA11 0RX   Tel: 017684 83224

Side Farm, Patterdale, Penrith CA11 0NP

Camping on the shores of Lake Ullswater for tents and motor caravans (sorry, no towing caravans), surrounded by the beautiful scenery of the Lake District.
Activities on the lake include swimming, sailing, boating, canoeing and fishing; steamer cruises. Modern toilet block, showers, washing facilities, shaving, hair drying points, washing machines and dryers. Dogs allowed provided they are kept on a lead. Convenient for touring the Lake District National Park. Fresh milk and eggs are available at the farm, with shops and post office in nearby Patterdale; regular bus services.
Terms - Adults £4.50 per night; reductions for children; vehicles/motor bikes £1, boats/trailers 50p. Open Easter to November.

R & A Taylforth - 017684 82337

Gillside Caravan & Camping Site, Gillside Farm, Glenridding, Penrith CA11 0QQ
Tel: 017684 82346

Sited in an idyllic location above Ullswater, five minutes' walk from the village of Glenridding with shops, National Park Information Centre, cafés and restaurants. The path to Helvellyn passes the farm. Well-equipped six-berth holiday homes; bunkhouse, suitable for groups. Facilities include a constant supply of hot and cold water in the shower/toilet block, deep sinks for washing pots and pans and a laundry with washer/drier; electric hook-ups. Fresh milk and eggs available at the farmhouse. Activities include wind surfing, canoeing, sailing on the steamer, pony trekking and rock climbing. Open March to mid-November. Bunkhouse open all year.

e-mail: gillside@btconnect.com   www.gillsidecaravanandcampingsite.co.uk

Waterside House Campsite
Waterside House, Howtown Road, Pooley Bridge, Penrith, Cumbria CA10 2NA • Tel & Fax: 017684 86332

Farm and campsite situated about one mile from Pooley Bridge. Genuine Lakeside location with beautiful views of Lake Ullswater and Fells. Ideal for windsurfing, canoeing, boating, fell walking and fishing, table tennis, volleyball. Boat, canoe and mountain bike hire on site. Play area, shop and gas exchange also. SAE or telephone for brochure. Open March to October. Directions: M6 Junction 40, A66 follow signs for Ullswater, A592 to Pooley Bridge, one mile along Howtown Road on right - signposted.

e-mail: enquire@watersidefarm-campsite.co.uk
www.watersidefarm-campsite.co.uk

Stanwix Park Holiday Centre

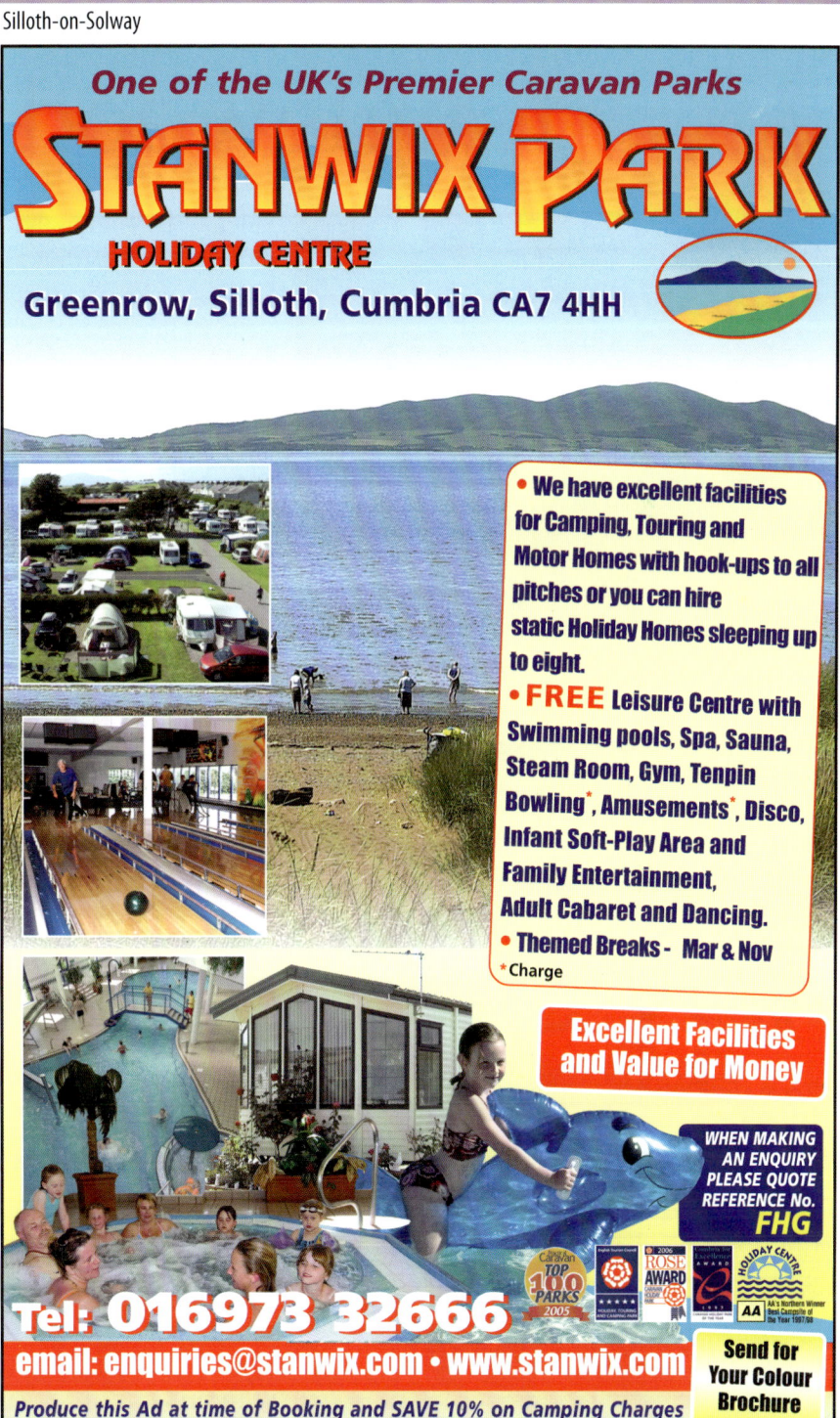

One of the UK's Premier Caravan Parks

HOLIDAY CENTRE
Greenrow, Silloth, Cumbria CA7 4HH

- We have excellent facilities for Camping, Touring and Motor Homes with hook-ups to all pitches or you can hire static Holiday Homes sleeping up to eight.
- **FREE** Leisure Centre with Swimming pools, Spa, Sauna, Steam Room, Gym, Tenpin Bowling*, Amusements*, Disco, Infant Soft-Play Area and Family Entertainment, Adult Cabaret and Dancing.
- Themed Breaks - Mar & Nov

*Charge

Excellent Facilities and Value for Money

WHEN MAKING AN ENQUIRY PLEASE QUOTE REFERENCE No. **FHG**

Tel: **016973 32666**
email: enquiries@stanwix.com • www.stanwix.com

Send for Your Colour Brochure

Produce this Ad at time of Booking and SAVE 10% on Camping Charges

Tanglewood Caravan Park

Tanglewood is a family-run park on the fringes of the Lake District National Park. It is tree-sheltered and situated one mile inland from the small port of Silloth on the Solway Firth, with a beautiful view of the Galloway Hills.

Large modern holiday homes are available from March to January, with car parking beside each home. Fully equipped except for bed linen, with end bedroom, panel heaters in both bedrooms and bathroom, electric lighting, hot and cold water, toilet, shower, gas fire, fridge and colour TV, all of which are included in the tariff. Touring pitches also available with electric hook-ups and water/drainage facilities, etc. Play area. Licensed lounge with adjoining children's play room. Pets welcome free but must be kept under control at all times. Full colour brochure available.

Mike and Jen Bowman
Tanglewood Caravan Park
Causewayhead
Silloth-on-Solway
Cumbria CA7 4PE
e-mail: tanglewoodcaravanpark@hotmail.com
www.tanglewoodcaravanpark.co.uk

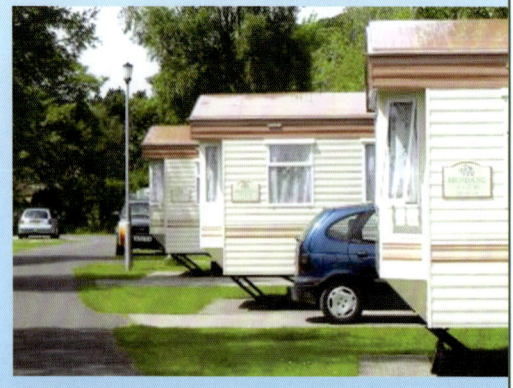

Cumbria
NORTH WEST ENGLAND 141

Silloth-on-Solway, Ullswater

Solway Holiday Village
HAGANS LEISURE GROUP

Located in the unspoiled seaside Victorian town of Silloth-on-Solway, this 120-acre family park has something for everyone. A truly idyllic location, the park enjoys breathtaking views out over the Solway Firth to Scotland and offers an ideal touring centre for the Scottish Borders and the English Lake District

- Indoor Leisure Pool
- Fitness Suite
- Tennis Courts
- 9-hole Golf Course
- Licensed Bars
- Live Entertainment
- Kids' Club
- Indoor Play Area
- Outdoor Play Area
- Ten-Pin Bowling
- Pool & Games Room
- Animal Farm
- NEW Italian-themed Courtyard Water Garden

Sale & Hiring from £19pppn
Touring Site from £5.50

Book Now on 016973 31236

solway@hagansleisure.co.uk
www.hagansleisure.co.uk

ULLSWATER. Ullswater Caravan, Camping & Marine Park, Watermillock, Ullswater CA11 0LR
Tel: 017684 86666 • www.uccmp.co.uk/
Set overlooking Lake Ullswater, this secluded park offers an excellent range of amenities, including a bar and entertainment area. Ideal base for walking, mountain biking and sailing. 58 touring pitches. Caravans, motorhomes and tents welcome.

Cove Park is a peaceful caravan & camping park overlooking Lake Ullswater, surrounded by Fells with beautiful views. The park is very well-maintained. We are ideally situated for walking, watersports and all of the Lake District tourist attractions in the North Lakes. Facilities include clean heated showers and washrooms with hand and hair dryers, washing and drying machines, iron & board, and a separate washing up area and a freezer for ice packs. We offer electric hook-ups with hardstandings, and plenty of sheltered grass for campers.

Cove Caravan & Camping Park
Watermillock, Penrith, Cumbria CA11 0LS
• Tel: 017684 86549 • www.cove-park.co.uk

FREE or REDUCED RATE entry to Holiday Visits and Attractions – see our
READERS' OFFER VOUCHERS on pages 205-234

Lancashire

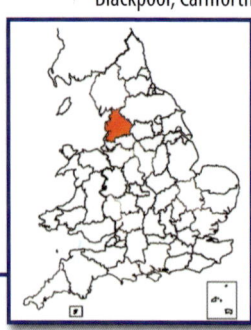

Blackpool, Carnforth

CLIFTON FIELDS CARAVAN PARK

Situated one mile from the M55, 3.5 miles to Blackpool and 4 miles to Lytham and St Annes. Clifton Fields is a family-owned and run caravan park with a warm welcome to families and couples, offering a touring caravan field with individual hard standing and electric hook-up points, secured by an automatic barrier. Facilities include toilets, showers, elsan disposal point and a launderette.

Directions: exit M55 at Junction 4, turn left, B&Q will be on your right hand side, at the roundabout go straight on then get into the right hand lane, at the traffic lights turn right then immediately left into Peel Road. We are the second caravan park on the right hand side.

CLIFTON FIELDS CARAVAN PARK
Peel Road, Peel, Blackpool FY4 5JU
Tel: 01253 761676

HOLIDAY PARKS & CENTRES

BLACKPOOL. Marton Mere Holiday Village, Mythop Road, Blackpool.
Located close to the bright lights of Blackpool, Marton Mere is a surprisingly green and rural Park complete with its own beautiful nature reserve. This Park caters for all tastes with a wide range of great sports activities, heated indoor pool with waterchute and excellent daytime and evening entertainment for the entire family. Try your hand at Family Park Rangers or Adventure Golf and feel the fun really come to life! With first class Touring facilities and on-site amenities you can be sure to want for nothing during your stay at Marton Mere. **See also Colour Advertisement.**
Call our UK Central Team: 0871 230 1933 (open 7 days, 9am-9pm) or book on-line (quote: TO_FHG) www.touringholidays.co.uk
• Great for Groups! Just book 5 or more holiday homes for extra benefits and savings.
Visit **www.havengroups.co.uk Or call 0871 230 1911.**

CARNFORTH. Holgates Caravan Park, Middlebarrow Plain Cove Road, Silverdale, Carnforth LA5 0SH
Tel: 01524 701508 • Fax: 01524 701580 • www.holgates.co.uk
Family-run countryside park with excellent activities and facilities. Situated between Silverdale and Arnside, with easy access to the coast. Open from December to November. 70 touring pitches. 5 tent pitches. 70 motorhome pitches.

Looking for holiday accommodation?
for details of hundreds of properties
throughout the UK including
comprehensive coverage of all areas of Scotland try:

www.holidayguides.com

Lancashire
NORTH WEST ENGLAND
Fleetwood, Lancaster, Lune Valley

FLEETWOOD. Cala Gran Holiday Park, Fleetwood Road, Fleetwood FY7 8JY
Tel: 01253 771288 • www.calagran-park.co.uk
Kids and grown ups will appreciate the wide variety of activities available at Cala Gran. Ideal for day trips to Blackpool. Seasonal and serviced pitches. Open from March to January.

Cockerham Sands Country Park

Unwind in the relaxed atmosphere whilst enjoying all the amenities of this idyllic holiday centre which include a licensed club, swimming and paddling pools, shop and launderette.

The superb family park situated in picturesque countryside on the estuary of the River Lune has immediate access to 15 miles of the Lancashire Coastal Walk.

Cockerham Sands Country Park offers you a perfect holiday choice. Luxury four and six-berth holiday homes for hire. All are double glazed and centrally heated. Pets welcome in special units.

Cockerham Sands Country Park, Cockerham, Lancaster LA2 0BB
Tel: 01524 751387 • www.cockerhamsandscountrypark.co.uk

Just 15 minutes from Junction 33 M6.
Ideally situated for visiting Blackpool or the Lake District.

Lune Valley

Well equipped, modern static caravan on Yorkshire/ Lancashire border, four miles from Ingleton. In quiet garden on working farm with panoramic views of Ingleborough and surrounding hills, central for dales, coast and the Lakes. Sleeps 4. Double and twin beds, TV, shower, fridge, microwave and garden furniture.

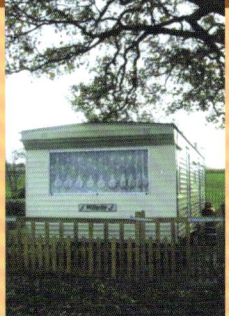

Nearest shop one mile, pub ¾ mile, and two miles from Bentham 18 hole golf course.
From £180 per week including gas, electricity and bed linen.

**Mrs B Mason,
Oxenforth Green,
Tatham, Lancaster
LA2 8PL
Tel: 01524 261784**

The FHG Directory of Website Addresses
on pages 235-250 is a useful quick reference guide for holiday accommodation with e-mail and/or website details

144 NORTH WEST ENGLAND — Lancashire
Poulton-le-Fylde, Preston, Rochdale

POULTON-LE-FYLDE. Windy Harbour Holiday Park, Poulton-le-Fylde, Blackpool FY6 8NB
Tel: 01253 883064 • Fax:01253 893101 • www.windyharbour.net
Situated by the banks of the River Wyre, only 6 miles from Blackpool. The park's pitches are level and the facilities are excellent. Open from March to November. 200 touring pitches. 40 tent pitches. 200 motorhome pitches.

Six Arches Caravan Park

Scorton, Garstang,
Near Preston PR3 1AL
Tel: 01524 791683
www.sixarchescaravanpark.co.uk

A friendly welcome awaits you at this established Holiday Park where holiday home owners and visitors can enjoy the modern facilities on offer.

Modern, fully equipped four and six-berth caravans for hire, spacious two-bedroom apartments, touring van pitches. Pets welcome in special units.

Just five minutes from Junction 33 M6, ideally located for visiting the Lake District, Trough of Bowland and Blackpool

On site facilities include:
- licensed club with two bars • shop
- fish & chip shop • modern amusements
- launderette
- heated swimming and paddling pool
- children's playground
- salmon & trout fishing • dog exercise area.

ROCHDALE. Gelder Wood Country Park, Ashworth Road, Rochdale OL11 5UP
Tel: 01706 364858 • e-mail gelderwood@aol.com
Adults-only park set in 10 acres of well maintained parkland. Within walking distance of a variety of restaurants for a special night out. Open from March to November. 34 touring pitches, 4 tent pitches. Caravans, motorhomes and tents welcome.

---

symbols

- ☼ Holiday Parks & Centres
- 🚐 Caravans for Hire
- Ⓢ Caravan Sites and Touring Parks
- ▲ Camping Sites

SCOTLAND 145

Scotland

Speyside Leisure Park, Aviemore, Inverness-shire, p167

Braidhaugh Holiday Park, Crieff, Perthshire, p176

Loch Lomond Holiday Park, p152

Scotland · Regions

SHETLAND ISLANDS

WESTERN ISLES
HIGHLAND
MORAY
ABERDEENSHIRE
14
PERTH AND KINROSS
ANGUS
ARGYLL AND BUTE
STIRLING
FIFE
13
9
NORTH AYRSHIRE
2 6 8 11 EAST LOTHIAN
1 3 5 7 10
4 12
S. LANARKSHIRE
EAST AYRSHIRE
SCOTTISH BORDERS
SOUTH AYRSHIRE
DUMFRIES AND GALLOWAY

1. Inverclyde
2. West Dunbartonshire
3. Renfrewshire
4. East Renfrewshire
5. City of Glasgow
6. East Dunbartonshire
7. North Lanarkshire
8. Falkirk
9. Clackmannanshire
10. West Lothian
11. City of Edinburgh
12. Midlothian
13. Dundee City
14. Aberdeen City

Aberdeenshire, Banff & Moray

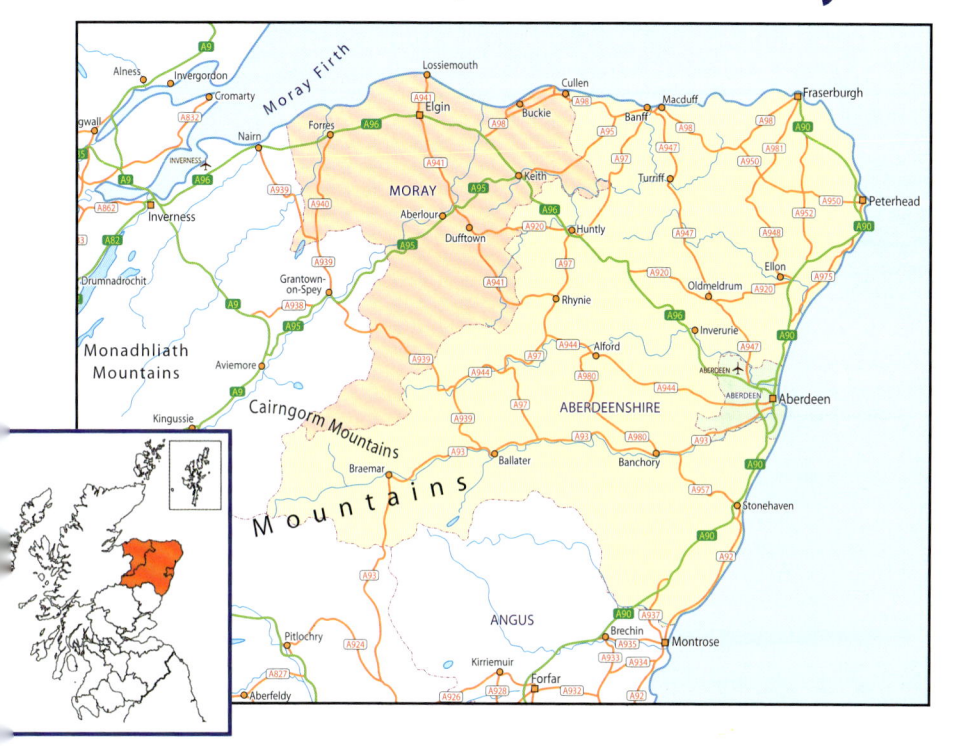

Aberdeenshire, Banff & Moray - one of the easiest ways to explore the area is by following one of the signposted tourist routes and theme trails. Perhaps the most famous of these is the Malt Whisky Trail around magnificent Speyside which links the award winning Speyside Cooperage and eight famous distilleries. Aberdeenshire is very much Scotland's "Castle Country" and 13 of the region's finest castles and great houses are located along Scotland's only Castle Trail. A lesser known feature of Scotland's North East is the fact that 10% of Scotland's Standing Stones are to be found here. Archaeolink, Scotland's prehistory park, interprets the early history of Grampian and promotes a journey through time for all ages. Royal Deeside has many attractions associated with Queen Victoria and a succession of British monarchs. There are many well known sites in this part of the region along the Victorian Heritage Trail including Balmoral Castle, home to royalty for 150 years, Crathie Church, Royal Lochnagar Distillery and Loch Muick. Around the Coastal Trail you will find some of Europe's best coastline, visually stunning, clean air and clear seawater. There are delightful villages such as the "Local Hero" village of Pennan, picturesque harbours, spectacular cliff formations, 150 miles of unspoilt beaches and fabulous golf courses such as Cruden Bay, Royal Tarlair, Duff House Royal and many more along the Moray Firth, as well as the company of the area's wildlife from dolphins to seals and seabirds.

SCOTLAND

Aberdeenshire, Banff & Moray
Aberlour, Ballater, Banchory, Elgin, Macduff

ABERLOUR. Aberlour Gardens Caravan and Camping Park, Aberlour AB38 9LD
Tel: 01340 871216 • www.aberlourgardens.co.uk

Beautiful 5-acre site within a Victorian walled garden, just 500m from the River Spey, where magnificent salmon fishing can be enjoyed. 73 pitches include 34 level touring pitches and 16 all-weather pitches. There is a wooded area for camping. Open March to end December.

BALLATER. Ballater Caravan Park, Anderson Road, Ballater AB35 5QW
01339 755727

Set beside the River Dee in the heart of Royal Deeside, this friendly park is within easy reach of major tourist attractions. Aberdeen 43 miles, Braemar 17 miles. Tourers, motorhomes and tents welcome.

BANCHORY. Silverbank Caravan Site, North Deeside Road, Banchory AB31 5PY
Tel: 01330 822477

Banchory is an attractive little town which provides the perfect base for exploring all that this scenic area has to offer. Take a walk along to Bridge of Feugh where you may spot salmon leaping, or venture further afield to the city of Aberdeen, with its busy harbour and sandy beach. Open March to January.

Station Caravan Park boasts terrific views of the Moray Firth where we often sight the Moray Firth dolphins, and is an ideal place to relax and have a good holiday. As well as the beach, there are caves, rockpools and fossils within walking distance. The village itself has all the shops you will need including a chemist, post office, takeaway food, ice cream, convenience store and pubs. We have luxury caravan holiday homes for hire, many with sea views, plus there are usually a few for sale. For the touring units there are electric hook-ups, water points, modern toilet/shower blocks and a launderette. Open from 28th March till 31st October. For full price information please contact the park direct.

Station Caravan Park • West Beach, Hopeman • Near Elgin IV30 5RU
Tel & Fax: 01343 830880

e-mail: enquiries@stationcaravanpark.co.uk   www.stationcaravanpark.co.uk

---

MACDUFF. Myrus Holiday Park, Macduff AB45 3TP
Tel: 01261 812845 • www.myruscaravanpark.co.uk/

Quiet, privately owned park, a superb base for exploring the many attractions of this beautiful area. This is an adults-only site and offers spacious grass and hardstanding pitches, plus super pitches with satellite TV hook-up. Tourers, and motorhomes welcome.

Electric hook-ups available	Facilities for disabled visitors
Children's play area	Pets welcome
Laundry facilities	Shop on site
Licensed bar on site	Wifi access available

Angus & Dundee

Arbroath, Brechin, Forfar, Glamis, Monifieth

Angus & Dundee

SCOTLAND 149

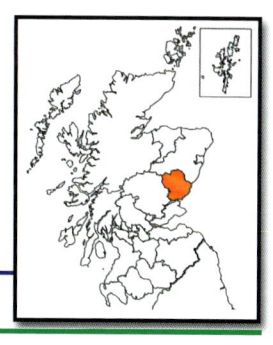

ARBROATH. Seaton Estate Holiday Village, Seaton Road, Arbroath DD11 5SE
Tel: 01241 874721 • Fax: 01241 877044 • www.seatonestate.com
In a picturesque setting known as "Scotland's secret garden", this family park has 75 touring pitches and is located just 10 minutes' walk from the seashore. Adults can relax, and hildren will love the play areas. Open March to October.

Eastmill Caravan Park
Brechin, Angus DD9 7EL

Beautifully situated on flat grassy site along the River South Esk, within easy access of scenic Angus Glens, local walks and 10 miles from sandy east coast beaches; midway between Dundee and Aberdeen.
Shop, gas supplies, shower block, laundry and hook-ups on site; licensed premises nearby.
Six-berth caravans with mains services available to rent.
Facilities for tourers, caravanettes and tents.
Dogs welcome. Open April to October.

Telephone: 01356 625206
(out of season 01356 622487)
Fax: 01356 623356)

FORFAR. Foresterseat Caravan Park, Arbroath Road, Forfar DD8 2RY
Tel: 01307 818880 • www.foresterseat.co.uk
Set amidst the beautiful Angus glens, this modern site is ideal for a relaxing break, with Murton Nature Reserve just across the road. Hardstanding pitches are available, and a well kept grassed area for tents. Open March to November.

FORFAR. Lochlands Caravan Site, Dundee Road, Forfar DD8 1XE
Tel: 01307 463621 • Fax: 01307 469665
Small site, a good base for exploring the east coast of Scotland, and recently upgraded to provide excellent facilities for caravans, motorhomes and tents. A local bus service provides links to Forfar and Dundee. Open April to October.

GLAMIS. Drumshademuir Caravan Park, Roundyhill, By Glamis DD8 1QT
Tel: 01575 573284 • 01575 570130 • www.drumshademuir.com
Just 3 miles from Glamis Castle, family home of the late Queen Mother, this friendly park provides 60 touring pitches, all close to the immaculate facilities. Tent pitches also available (adults only). Open March to October.

MONIFIETH. Riverview Caravan Park, Marine Drive, Monifieth DD5 4NN
Tel: 01382 535471 • Fax: 01382 535375 • www.riverview.co.uk
With magnificent views across the River Tay, Riverview is just a five minute walk from the village and shopping, and provides a peaceful base for relaxing and touring. Dundee 3 miles. No tents. Open April to October.

Argyll & Bute

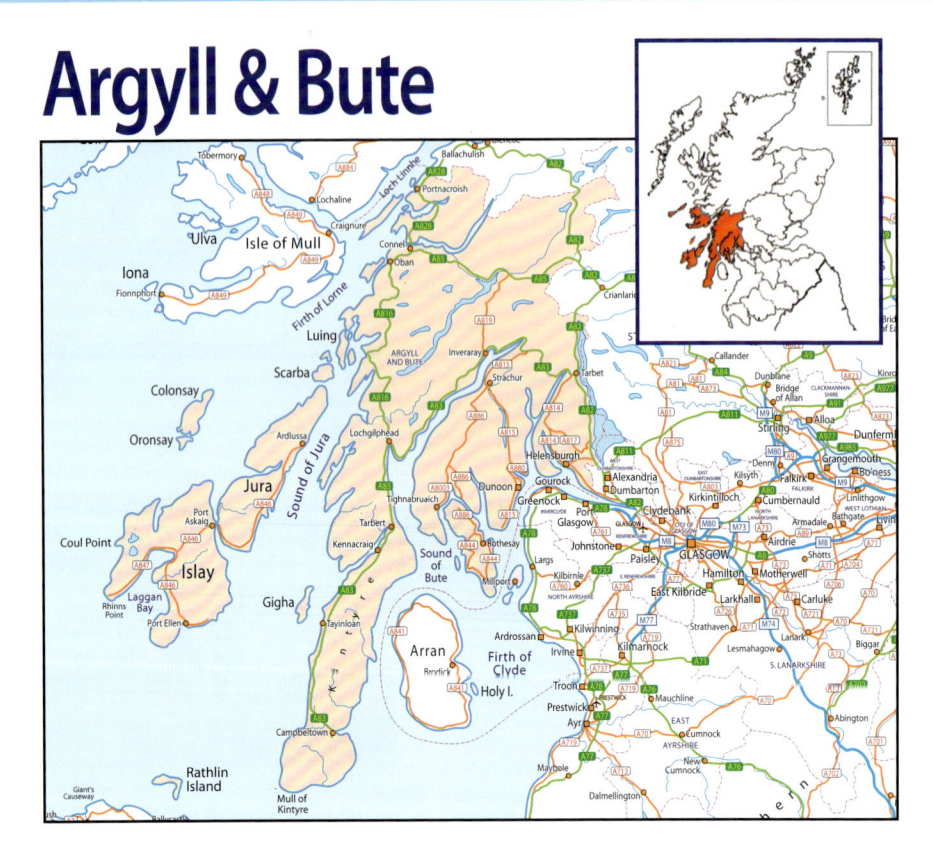

ARGYLL & BUTE is a wonderfully unspoilt area, historically the heartland of Scotland and home to a wealth of fascinating wildlife. Here you may be lucky enough to catch a glimpse of an eagle, a wildcat or an osprey, or even a fine antlered stag. At every step the sea fringed landscape is steeped in history, from prehistoric sculpture at Kilmartin, to the elegant ducal home of the once feared Clan Campbell. There are also reminders of pre-historic times with Bronze Age cup-and-ring engravings, and standing stone circles. On the upper reaches of Loch Caolisport can be found St Columba's Cave, and more recent times are illustrated at the Auchindrain Highland Township south of Inveraray, a friendly little town with plenty to see, including the Jail, Wildlife Park and Maritime Museum.

Bute is the most accessible of the west coast islands, and Rothesay is its main town. Explore the dungeons and grand hall of Rothesay Castle, or visit the fascinating Bute Museum. The town offers a full range of leisure facilities, including a fine swimming pool and superb golf course, and there are vast areas of parkland where youngsters can safely play.

FREE or REDUCED RATE entry to Holiday Visits and Attractions – see our
READERS' OFFER VOUCHERS on pages 205-234

Argyll & Bute

SCOTLAND 151

Carradale, Glencoe, Inveraray

CARRADALE. Carradale Bay Caravan Site, Carradale, Kintyre PA28 6QG
Tel: 01583 431665 • www.carradalebay.com
Ideal for a quiet, relaxing holiday, this award-winning park is set on a southerly corner of the Carradale Estate, adjoining a mile of golden sands. Popular activities in the area inlcude walking, cycling, golf, fishing and horse riding. Open April to September.

INVERCOE HIGHLAND HOLIDAYS

Invercoe, Glencoe, Argyll PH49 4HP • TEL: *01855 811210* • FAX: *01855 811210*
www.invercoe.co.uk • e-mail: holidays@invercoe.co.uk

At Invercoe Highland Holidays we offer you quiet, get-away-from-it-all vacations, in what is one of the most picturesque of the Scottish glens. You can have a relaxing break in a stone cottage, luxury timber lodge, mobile holiday homes or bring your own caravan, tent or tourer for the holiday of your choice.

We have been providing holidays for over thirty years and are confident our high standard of accommodation will provide an excellent base to explore the West Highlands.

Self Catering   ★ OPEN ALL YEAR ★

INVERARAY. Argyll Caravan Park, Inveraray PA32 8XT
Tel: 01499 302285 • www.argyllcaravanpark.com
Just 2½ miles south of the historic town of Inveraray, this park is ideal for relaxing or as a base for exploring this scenic area. 30 serviced pitches are available, 9 with grass for awning. Please note tents are not allowed. Open April to October.

💬	Electric hook-ups available	♿	Facilities for disabled visitors
⚠	Children's play area	🐕	Pets welcome
◻	Laundry facilities	🛒	Shop on site
🍷	Licensed bar on site	W	Wifi access available

Other specialised holiday guides from FHG

PUBS & INNS OF BRITAIN • **COUNTRY HOTELS** OF BRITAIN
WEEKEND & SHORT BREAK HOLIDAYS IN BRITAIN
THE GOLF GUIDE WHERE TO PLAY, WHERE TO STAY
500 GREAT PLACES TO STAY • **SELF-CATERING HOLIDAYS** IN BRITAIN
BED & BREAKFAST STOPS • **PETS WELCOME!**
FAMILY BREAKS IN BRITAIN

Published annually: available in all good bookshops or direct from the publisher:
FHG Guides, Abbey Mill Business Centre, Seedhill, Paisley PA1 1TJ
Tel: 0141 887 0428 • Fax: 0141 889 7204
e-mail: admin@fhguides.co.uk • www.holidayguides.com

152 SCOTLAND — Argyll & Bute
Kinlochleven, Loch Lomond

There are 20 static six-berth caravans for holiday hire on this lovely site with breathtaking mountain scenery on the edge of Loch Leven — an ideal touring centre.

Caravans have electric lighting, Calor gas cookers and heaters, toilet, shower, fridge and colour TV. There are two toilet blocks with hot water and showers and laundry facilities. Children are welcome and pets allowed. Open from April to October. Milk, gas, soft drinks available on site; shops three miles. Sea loch fishing, hill walking and boating; boats and rods for hire, fishing tackle for sale.

CAOLASNACON
Caravan & Camping Park, Kinlochleven PH50 4RJ

For details contact Mrs Patsy Cameron
Tel: 01855 831279
E-mail: caolasnacon@hotmail.co.uk
www.kinlochlevencaravans.com

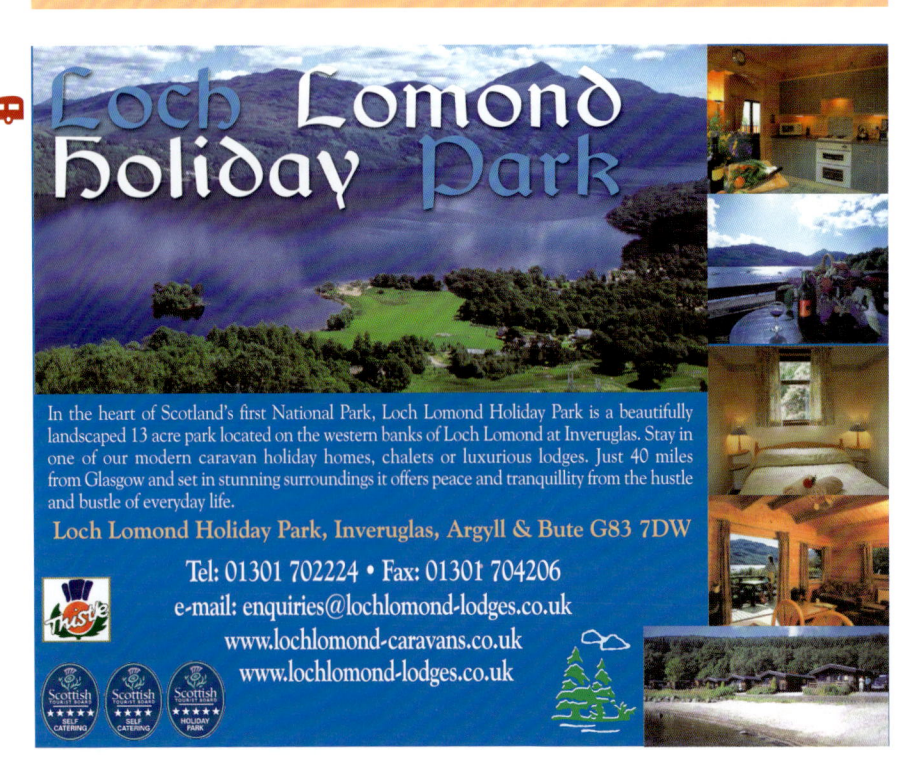

Loch Lomond Holiday Park

In the heart of Scotland's first National Park, Loch Lomond Holiday Park is a beautifully landscaped 13 acre park located on the western banks of Loch Lomond at Inveruglas. Stay in one of our modern caravan holiday homes, chalets or luxurious lodges. Just 40 miles from Glasgow and set in stunning surroundings it offers peace and tranquillity from the hustle and bustle of everyday life.

Loch Lomond Holiday Park, Inveruglas, Argyll & Bute G83 7DW

Tel: 01301 702224 • Fax: 01301 704206
e-mail: enquiries@lochlomond-lodges.co.uk
www.lochlomond-caravans.co.uk
www.lochlomond-lodges.co.uk

Argyll & Bute
Oban

SCOTLAND 153

Tralee Bay Holidays

Top Graded 5 Star, Tralee Bay Holidays has been a David Bellamy Gold Award Park for the last 5 years.

Located on the West Coast of Scotland near Oban, overlooking Ardmucknish Bay, the wooded surroundings and sandy beach make Tralee the ideal destination for a self-catering lodge or caravan holiday at any time of the year.

The Park offers something for everyone with play area, mini golf, fly fishing, nature walks and boat slipway. Set in breathtaking Highland countryside, the gateway to the Isles.

The choice of self-catering accommodation ranges from 2003 model 2 and 3 bedroom caravans to brand new lavishly furnished lodges. Pets welcome.

Tralee Bay Holidays, Benderloch, by Oban, Argyll PA37 1QR
Tel: 01631 720255/217
E-mail: tralee@easynet.co.uk
Website: www.tralee.com

154 **SCOTLAND** — Argyll & Bute
Oban, Tarbert, Tayinloan

In an area of outstanding scenic beauty and graded as "Very Good", Gallanachmore Farm is situated on the seafront overlooking the Island of Kerrera. The Park provides excellent toilet and shower facilities, a well-stocked shop, launderette, children's play area and lends itself superbly for boating, fishing, windsurfing and scuba diving holidays. Also our static park has modern caravans for hire, all with sea views. Situated two-and-a-half miles south of Oban; from roundabout in the centre of the town, follow signs to Gallanach. Terms from £10.50 to £13.50 per night (two persons in touring van, tent or motorhome). *Howard and Judy Jones.*

Oban Caravan and Camping Park, Gallanachmore Farm, Oban PA34 4QH
Tel: 01631 562425
e-mail: info@obancaravanpark.com • www.obancaravanpark.com

Port Ban Holiday Park
Kilberry, Tarbert, Argyll PA29 6YD

Tel: 01880 770224

www.portban.com
e-mail: portban@aol.com

Beautiful, remote, secluded, coastal park enjoying fantastic sunsets over the Paps of Jura. Many sports facilities including Games Hall, Putting Green, Football Pitch, Tennis Court, Crazy Golf, Bowling Green and also Bikes for Hire. Sandy Beaches and rock pools. Organised events during school holidays including children's club, sports competitions and ceilidhs.
Ideal for wildlife enthusiasts – dolphins, seals, birds of prey, wildflowers etc.
Shop selling gifts and basic groceries.
Cafe selling snacks, homemade cakes and freshly ground coffees.
Standard and Luxury caravans for hire from £200 -£455 per week.
Pitches available for tourers and Tents from £8/night.
Reduced rates for Senior Citizens outside school holidays.
Christian Fellowship available and Services held during School Holidays.

TARBERT. Muasdale Holiday Park, Muasdale, Tarbert PA29 6XD
Tel: 01583 421207 • Fax: 01583 421137 • www.muasdaleholidays.com
Situated alongside the beach, with unobstructed views of the Atlantic and the islands of Gigha, Islay and Jura, this small touring park is ideal for a relaxing holiday - and for surfers, who make for the long sandy beach at Machrihanish. 10 touring pitches; tents welcome. Open March to October.

TAYINLOAN. Point Sands Holiday Park, Tayinloan, Kintyre PA29 6XG
Tel & Fax: 01583 441263 • www.pointsands.co.uk
Amidst magnificent coastal scenery, this tranquil touring park offers a real 'get away from it all' break. Local wildlife includes otters, seals, ducks and deer. Open April to October. Tourers, motorhomes and tents welcome.

Ayrshire & Arran

Ayrshire and Arran has always held a special affinity with families and this is reflected in the many fun attractions and activities geared towards children. These include farm parks, theme parks with daring funfair rides, and many sports and leisure centres. There's plenty to see and do with features like the Vikingar Viking Centre at Largs and The Scottish Industrial Railway Centre at Dalmellington adding to established attractions like Culzean Castle and the thriving business built on the life, loves and works of Scotland's best-loved poet, Robert Burns. A visit to the Secret Forest at Kelburn Country Centre is a must – its canopy of trees hides a multitude of surprises, the green man, the spirit of the forest, a Chinese garden with pagoda, and a crocodile swamp. Older visitors may enjoy a visit to Ayr Racecourse, enjoy a shopping spree, or treat themselves to a round on one the area's 44 golf courses. Whether the pace is leisurely or frantic, it's got to be Ayrshire and the Isle of Arran.

FHG Guides

publish a large range of well-known accommodation guides.
We will be happy to send you details or you can use the order form
at the back of this book.

Ayrshire & Arran
Ayr

AYR. Craigie Gardens Caravan Club Site, Craigie Road, Ayr KA8 0SS
Tel: 01292 264909
7-acre site set in a beautiful park just a short walk from the centre of Ayr, which has excellent shopping amenities and attractions such as a theatre, racecourse, golf courses and long, sandy beach. Open all year round.

AYR. Heads of Ayr Caravan Park, Dunure Road, Ayr KA7 4LD
Tel: 01292 442269 • Fax: 01292 500298 • www.headsofayr.com
5 miles south of Ayr, this family-owned park (mainly static) has 36 pitches for tourers and also caters for tents. Facilities are excellent, with entertainment in high season, and the beach is just a 15-minute walk away. Open March to October.

HOLIDAY PARKS & CENTRES

AYR. Craig Tara Holiday Park, Dunure Road, Ayr KA7 4LB (01292 265 141).
Set on Scotland's west coast, this impressive Park looks out across to the Heads of Ayr. Craig Tara is the Park to go to if you want big views and even bigger family holiday action. With brilliant outdoor and indoor fun to be had – from the All-Weather Multi Sports Court and new 9-hole golf course to the great Tonix Soft Play Area for the little ones, Craig Tara really does offer something for the whole family. Craig Tara also boasts great Touring facilities and on-site amenities – it's designed to make your stay effortless. See also Colour Advertisement.
Call our UK Central Team: 0871 230 1933 (open 7 days, 9am-9pm) or book on-line (quote: TO_FHG) www.touringholidays.co.uk
• Great for Groups! Just book 5 or more holiday homes for extra benefits and savings.
Visit www.havengroups.co.uk Or call 0871 230 1911.

Crofthead
Holiday Park, Ayr

One of Ayrshire's premier 4- Star parks, Crofthead is peacefully situated amidst beautiful Ayrshire countryside, yet just two miles from the fabulous amenities of bustling Ayr. This friendly and relaxing park offers a perfect base for exploring Scotland's glorious south west.

Our family-run ten acre park nestles in a sheltered, tranquil hollow in rolling farmland, with the Annfield burn flowing alongside.

Shop, launderette and snooker facilities available. Pets welcome. Touring sites and tenting pitches, mainly on grass, some hardstanding available. Electric hook-ups.

Local activities include golf, riding, fishing, swimming pool and many sites of historic interest.

Contact: Mr & Mrs McCormack
Crofthead Holiday Park, McNairston, Ayr KA6 6EN
Tel: 01292 263516 • Fax: 01292 263675
e-mail: holidays@croftheadholidaypark.co.uk • www.croftheadholidaypark.co.uk

---

The FHG Directory of Website Addresses
on pages 235-250 is a useful quick reference guide for holiday accommodation with e-mail and/or website details

Ayrshire & Arran
SCOTLAND 157
Barrhill, Girvan, Skelmorlie

Tel & Fax: 01465 821355

Barrhill
HOLIDAY PARK

A family park set in six acres of south west Scotland, ten miles from the coast. All caravans are privately owned, well spaced and connected to mains services. The park has a shop, launderette and children's play area, while surrounded by beautiful countryside which offers scenic walks, fishing, bird watching, mountain biking and golf courses in any direction. New facilities for touring and camping with electricity and water to each pitch. Opens 1st March to 31st January. New and used caravans for sale with choice of pitches. Please telephone, write or visit for further information.

Barrhill Holiday Park, Barrhill, Girvan, Ayrshire KA26 0PZ

www.barrhillholidaypark.com

GIRVAN. Ardmillan Castle Holiday Park, Girvan KA26 0HP
Tel: 01465 714891 • Fax: 01465 714714
Enjoy the quiet country surroundings and spectacular sunsets over Ailsa Craig from this friendly site situated on the A77, two miles south of Girvan. Tourers, motorhomes and tents welcome. Open March to October.

SKELMORLIE. Skelmorlie Mains Caravan Park, Skelmorlie PA17 5EU
Tel & Fax: 01475 520794 • www.skelmorliemainscaravanpark.co.uk
With panoramic views over the Firth of Clyde to Arran, this friendly park is situated off the A78, just 4 miles from Largs. Sailing, golf and water sports are available locally, and there are good transport links for exploring all of the West of Scotland. Tourers and motorhomes welcome. Open March to October.

Other specialised holiday guides from FHG
PUBS & INNS OF BRITAIN
COUNTRY HOTELS OF BRITAIN
WEEKEND & SHORT BREAKS IN BRITAIN & IRELAND
THE GOLF GUIDE WHERE TO PLAY, WHERE TO STAY
500 GREAT PLACES TO STAY
SELF-CATERING HOLIDAYS IN BRITAIN
BED & BREAKFAST STOPS IN BRITAIN
PETS WELCOME!
FAMILY BREAKS IN BRITAIN

Published annually: available in all good bookshops or direct from the publisher:
FHG Guides, Abbey Mill Business Centre, Seedhill, Paisley PA1 1TJ
Tel: 0141 887 0428 • Fax: 0141 889 7204
e-mail: admin@fhgguides.co.uk • www.holidayguides.com

Borders

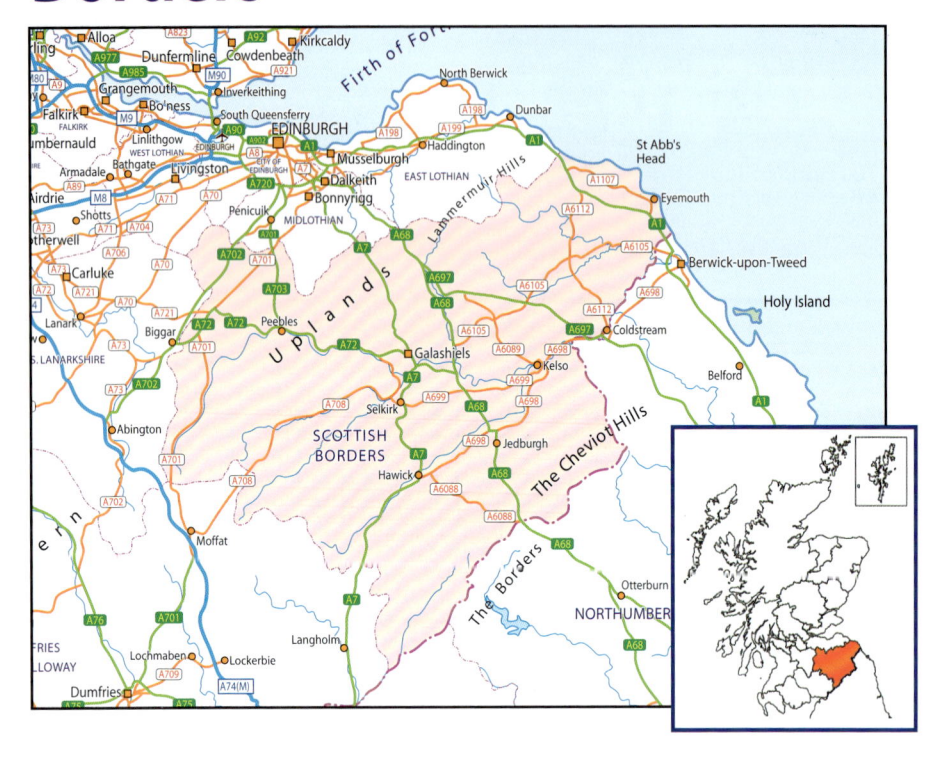

Covering about eighteen hundred miles, **The Scottish Borders** stretch from the rolling hills and moorland in the west, through gentler valleys to the rich agricultural plains of the east, and the rocky Berwickshire coastline with its secluded coves and picturesque fishing villages. Through the centre, tracing a silvery course from the hills to the sea, runs the River Tweed which provides some of the best fishing in Scotland. As well as fishing there is golf – 18 courses in all, riding or cycling and some of the best modern sports centres and swimming pools in the country. Friendly towns and charming villages are there to be discovered, while castles, abbeys, stately homes and museums illustrate the exciting and often bloody history of the area. It's this history which is commemorated in the Common Ridings and other local festivals, creating a colourful pageant much enjoyed by visitors and native Borderers alike.

One of the delights of travelling is finding gifts and keepsakes with a genuine local flavour, and dedicated souvenir hunters will find a plentiful supply of traditional delicacies, from drinks to baking and handmade sweets. Handcrafted jewellery, pottery, glass and woodwork, as well as beautiful tweeds and high quality knitwear can be found in the many interesting little shops throughout the area.

Scottish Borders eating establishments take pride in providing particularly good food and service and the choice of hotels, inns restaurants and cafes make eating out a real pleasure.

Borders

SCOTLAND 159

Coldingham, Greenlaw, Ettrick Valley, Jedburgh, Peebles

COLDINGHAM. Crosslaw Caravan Park, School Road, Coldingham TD14 5NT
Tel: 01890 771316 • www.crosslaw.co.uk
22-acre site set in the beautiful Borders and ideal for exploring this historic area. Excellent facilities include a games room and licensed bar, and there is regular live entertainment in season. Standard and super pitches available. Open February to January.

COLDINGHAM. Scoutscroft Holiday Centre, St Abbs Road, Coldingham TD14 5NB
Tel: 01890 771338 • Fax: 01890 771746 • www.scoutscroft.co.uk
Situated in the picturesque Borders village of Coldingham, just a few minutes' walk from a safe, sandy beach. Excellent facilities include regular entertainment in high season, lounge bars, restaurant and takeaway. Tourers and motorhomes welcome. Open March to November.

Greenlaw Caravan Park,
Bank Street, Greenlaw, Duns TD10 6XX
01361 884075 • www.greenlawcaravanpark.com

Picturesque riverside park attached to a friendly country village offering shops, hotels and inns with regular functions; ideal for bowling, fishing, golf, walking or simply relaxing.

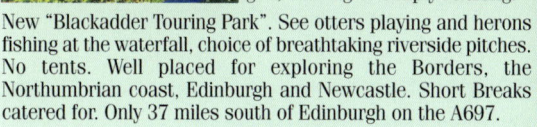

New "Blackadder Touring Park". See otters playing and herons fishing at the waterfall, choice of breathtaking riverside pitches. No tents. Well placed for exploring the Borders, the Northumbrian coast, Edinburgh and Newcastle. Short Breaks catered for. Only 37 miles south of Edinburgh on the A697.

Winner/Runner up - Most Improved Park in Scotland 2001.

ETTRICK VALLEY. Honey Cottage Caravan Park, Hope House, Ettrick Valley TD7 5HU
Tel: 01750 62246 www.honeycottagecaravanpark.co.uk
On the banks of Ettrick Water, this level, 7-acre park has a 3-acre touring park with grass and hardstanding pitches. Great walks locally include the Southern Upland Way, and it is a pleasant stroll along to the nearby inn which serves meals. Open all year.

JEDBURGH. Jedwater Caravan Park, Jedburgh TD8 6PJ
Tel: 01835 840219 • Fax: 01835 869510 • www.jedwater.co.uk
This peaceful country park nestles in a wooded ravine just 4 miles south of Jedburgh, off the A68. A warm welcome is assured from the resident owners and from the friendly animals on the family farm. Open April to October.

PEEBLES. Crossburn Caravan Park, Edinburgh Road, Peebles EH45 8ED
Tel: 01721 720501 • Fax 01721 720501
Secluded and friendly park, well located for a range of activities and within walking distance of the charming market town of Peebles. Tourers, motorhomes and tents welcome. Open April to October.

Electric hook-ups available		Facilities for disabled visitors	
Children's play area		Pets welcome	
Laundry facilities		Shop on site	
Licensed bar on site		Wifi access available	

Dumfries & Galloway

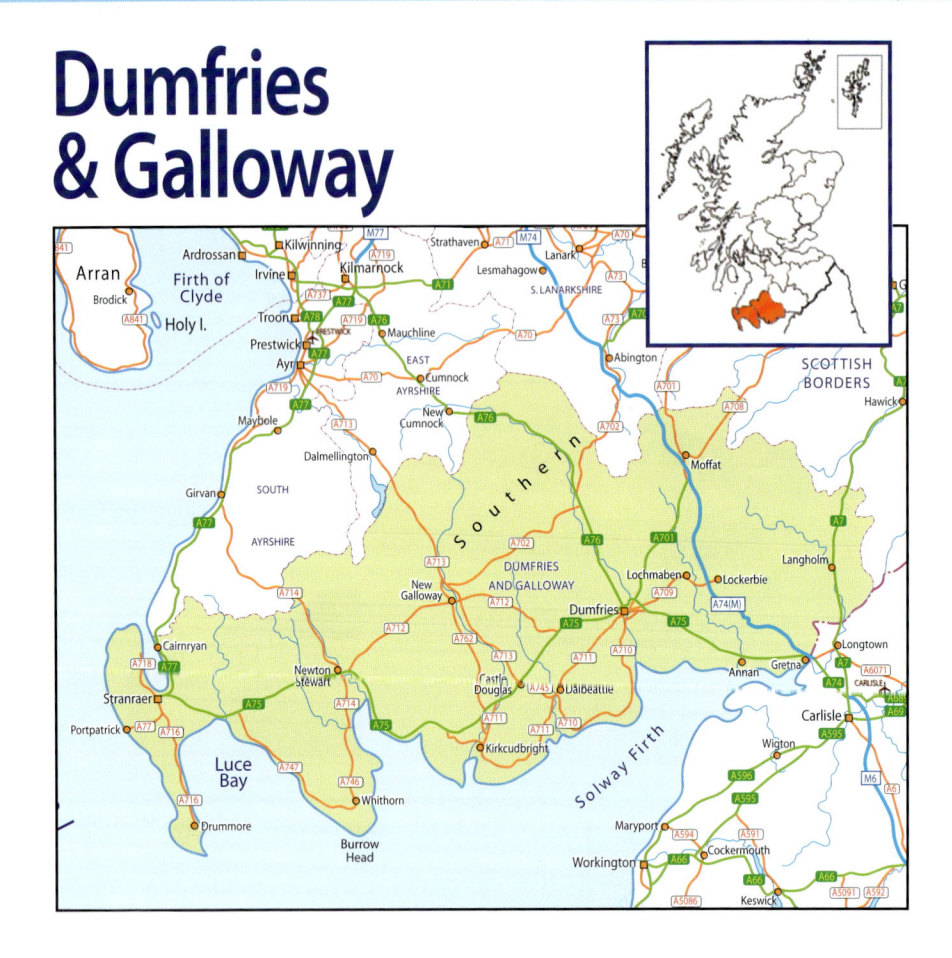

DUMFRIES & GALLOWAY is a mixture of high moorland and sheltered glens, and presents abundant opportunities for hill walking, rambling, fishing for salmon and sea trout, cycling, bird watching and field sports. There are at least 32 golf courses, ranging from the challenging Stranraer course at Creachmore to the scenic, clifftop course at Port Patrick. The Stranraer course has the distinction of being the last course designed by James Braid. The warming influence of the Gulf Stream ensures a mild climate which makes touring a pleasure, and many visitors come here to visit the dozens of interesting castles, gardens, museums and historic sites. In addition, pony trekking and riding plus a never-ending succession of ceilidhs, village fairs, country dances, classical music concerts and children's entertainment guarantee plenty of scope for enjoyment. Discover the many hidden secrets of this lovely and unspoilt landscape such as the pretty little villages along the coast or visit some of the interesting towns in the area including Stranraer, the principal town and ferry port with its busy shopping streets, park and leisure centre. Those who love 'the written word' must surely visit the book town of Wigtown, and the gourmet amongst us will love the new concept of Castle Douglas, the recently designated 'Food Town'.

Dumfries & Galloway

SCOTLAND 161

Castle Douglas, Dalbeattie, Dumfries

CASTLE DOUGLAS. Barlochan Caravan Park, Palnackie, Castle Douglas DG7 1PF
Tel: 01557 870267 • www.gillespie-leisure.co.uk
Peaceful, relaxing and tranquil, this popular site offers sheltered pitches for tourers and tents, and a good range of play equipment for children. Nearby Barwhinnie Loch provides fishing, and there is a spacious games room. Open April to October.

DALBEATTIE. Kippford Holiday Park, Kippford, Dalbeattie DG5 4LF
Tel: 01556 620636 • Fax: 01556 620607 • www.kippfordholidaypark.co.uk
Dumfries and Galloway has been described as "Scotland in miniature", and this friendly park is superbly positioned for exploring the many attractions of the area. Children are well catered for, with a play area and assault course. Fishing available on private loch. Tourers, motorhomes and tents welcome. Open all year.

DUMFRIES. Halleaths Caravan And Camping Park, Lochmaben, Dumfries DG11 1NA
Tel: 01387 810630 • Fax: 01387 810005 • www.halleaths.co.uk
Family-owned site conveniently situated off the M74 and ideal as an overnight break travelling north or south. Set in 8 acres of gently sloping meadow, the park has 7 touring pitches and 81 tent pitches. Open March to January.

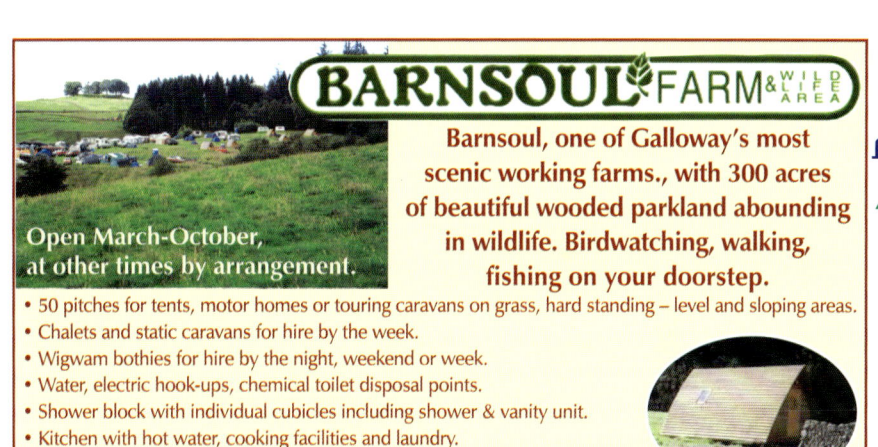

BARNSOUL FARM & WILDLIFE AREA

Barnsoul, one of Galloway's most scenic working farms., with 300 acres of beautiful wooded parkland abounding in wildlife. Birdwatching, walking, fishing on your doorstep.

Open March-October, at other times by arrangement.

- 50 pitches for tents, motor homes or touring caravans on grass, hard standing – level and sloping areas.
- Chalets and static caravans for hire by the week.
- Wigwam bothies for hire by the night, weekend or week.
- Water, electric hook-ups, chemical toilet disposal points.
- Shower block with individual cubicles including shower & vanity unit.
- Kitchen with hot water, cooking facilities and laundry.
- On site barbecues.

Our latest accommodation Scandinavian Wigwam Bothies

Terms: Car/Caravan £12-£18
Car/Tent £12-£18
Cycle/Motorcycle/Tent £12-£14

Irongray, Shawhead, Dumfries DG2 9SQ
Tel: 01387 730249
Tel/Fax: 01387 730453
e-mail: barnsouldg@aol.com
www.barnsoulfarm.co.uk

The FHG Directory of Website Addresses

on pages 235-250 is a useful quick reference guide for holiday accommodation with e-mail and/or website details

Dumfries & Galloway
Newton Stewart, Stranraer

Drumroamin Farm Camping and Caravan Site

A family-run, private site in the heart of Wigtownshire, overlooking Wigtown Bay and the Galloway hills. Level, well-drained field with electric hook-ups. Modern, well equipped heated shower/toilet block with separate family/disabled shower room. Indoor TV/playroom with sitting area.
Dogs welcome, woodland walks close by.
Two static caravans for holiday letting, screened from main campsite. Open all year.

**1 South Balfern, Kirkinner,
Newton Stewart, Wigtownshire DG8 9DB
Tel: 01988 840613 • mobile: 07752 471456
e-mail: enquiry@drumroamin.co.uk
www.drumroamin.co.uk**

NEWTON STEWART. Burrowhead Holiday Village, Isle of Whithorn, Newton Stewart DG8 8JB
Tel: 01988 500252 • 01988 500855 • www.burrowheadholidayvillage.co.uk
A spacious 100-acre site with excellent facilities to ensure a relaxing break for all the family. Local attractions include walking, fishing, golf and sailing. Tourers, motorhomes and tents welcome. Open March to January.

STRANRAER. Aird Donald Caravan Park, London Road, Stranraer DG9 8RN
Tel: 01776 702025 • www.aird-donald.com
With easy access to all the attractions of South West Scotland, and close to the ferry to Ireland, this small site has level pitches, mainly grass, but with some hardstanding. Shower and toilet facilities are excellent. Rallies catered for.

- Electric hook-ups available
- Facilities for disabled visitors
- Children's play area
- Pets welcome
- Laundry facilities
- Shop on site
- Licensed bar on site
- Wifi access available

Looking for holiday accommodation?
for details of hundreds of properties
throughout the UK including
comprehensive coverage of all areas of Scotland try:

www.holidayguides.com

Edinburgh & Lothians

SCOTLAND 163

EDINBURGH & LOTHIANS - Scotland's Capital is home to a wide range of attractions offering something for visitors of all ages. The Royal Mile holds many of the most historic sights, but within a short distance there are fine gardens to visit or the chance to sample the latest in interactive technology. A network of signposted paths allow walkers of all abilities to enjoy the contrasts of the area, whether for a leisurely stroll or at a more energetic pace. The annual Festival in August is part of the city's tradition and visitors flock to enjoy the performing arts, theatre, ballet, cinema and music, and of course "The Tattoo" itself. At the Festival Fringe there are free shows and impromptu acts, a jazz festival and book festivals. Other events take place throughout the year, including children's festivals, science festivals, the famous Royal Highland Show and the Hogmanay street party. East Lothian has beautiful countryside and dramatic coastline, all only a short distance from Edinburgh. Once thriving fishing villages, North Berwick and Dunbar now cater for visitors who delight in their traditional seaside charm. In Midlothian you can step back in time with a visit to Rosslyn Chapel or Borthwick and Crichton Castles, or seize the chance to brush up on your swing at one of the excellent courses in the area. The Almond Valley Heritage Centre in Livingston has a museum, friendly farmyard animals and children's activities, while the Butterfly and Insect World at Lasswade offers a fabulous tropical display.

Edinburgh & Lothians
Dunbar, Linlithgow, Longniddry

DUNBAR. Thurston Manor Holiday Home Park, Innerwick, Dunbar EH42 1SA
Tel: 01368 840643 • Fax: 01368 840261 • www.thurstonmanor.co.uk
Set in the grounds of a former country estate, Thurston Manor Park provides the highest standards combined with a peaceful, friendly atmosphere. Standard and super pitches are available and there is a clean, fully heated shower block. Tourers, motorhomes and tents welcome. Open March to January.

DUNBAR. Belhaven Bay Caravan Park, Edinburgh Road, Dunbar EH42 1TU
Tel: 01368 865956 • www.meadowhead.co.uk/belhaven
Award-winning park adjoining the John Muir Country Park and close to the beach, Belhaven is just two minutes off the A1 north of Dunbar, with convenient rail links to Edinburgh. on an 18-acre site, pitches range from fully serviced hard standings to traditional grass. Open March to October.

LINLITHGOW. Beecraigs Caravan and Camping Site, Linlithgow EH49 6PL
Tel: 01506 844516 • www.beecraigs.com
Popular site in a country park just 2 miles from the historic town of Linlithgow, midway between Glasgow and Edinburgh. Spread over 100 acres, the site offers hardstanding pitches and is open to caravans, motorhomes and tents. Open all year.

HOLIDAY PARKS & CENTRES
LONGNIDDRY. Seton Sands Holiday Village, Longniddry.
Just 30 minutes outside Edinburgh, Seton Sands Holiday Village is set in a wonderfully scenic location opposite a gloriously sandy beach. From heated indoor pool and multi sports court to fantastic daytime and evening entertainment and children's clubs for all ages, this Park definitely has it all. In addition to this, Seton Sands has excellent Touring facilities and on-site amenities to cater for all your Touring needs. With all this to offer, you can be sure of a first class family holiday at Seton Sands Holiday Village. **See also Colour Advertisement.**
Call our UK Central Team: 0871 230 1933 (open 7 days, 9am-9pm) or book on-line (quote: TO_FHG) www.touringholidays.co.uk
• Great for Groups! Just book 5 or more holiday homes for extra benefits and savings.
Visit www.havengroups.co.uk Or call 0871 230 1911.

Other specialised holiday guides from FHG

PUBS & INNS OF BRITAIN • **COUNTRY HOTELS** OF BRITAIN
WEEKEND & SHORT BREAK HOLIDAYS IN BRITAIN
THE GOLF GUIDE WHERE TO PLAY, WHERE TO STAY
500 GREAT PLACES TO STAY • **SELF-CATERING HOLIDAYS** IN BRITAIN
BED & BREAKFAST STOPS • **PETS WELCOME!**
FAMILY BREAKS IN BRITAIN

Published annually: available in all good bookshops or direct from the publisher:
FHG Guides, Abbey Mill Business Centre, Seedhill, Paisley PA1 1TJ
Tel: 0141 887 0428 • Fax: 0141 889 7204
e-mail: admin@fhguides.co.uk • www.holidayguides.com

Fife

Crail, Glenrothes, Kinghorn, Leven, St Andrews

Fife - whether as 'County', 'Region' or more traditionally 'Kingdom', Fife has always been a prosperous and self-contained part of Scotland. The coast, with small ports such as Crail, Anstruther, Pittenweem, St Monance, Elie and the more commercial Methil, Burntisland and Kirkcaldy, has always been interesting and important. St Andrews with its university, castle, cathedral and golf, is the best known and most visited town. Dunfermline has a historic past with many royal associations and was the birthplace of the philanthropist, Andrew Carnegie. Medieval buildings have been restored by the National Trust in nearby Culross. Cupar, Falkland, Kinross (for Loch Leven), Auchtermuchty and Leuchars are amongst the many other historic sites in Fife, and at North Queensferry is one of Fife's newest and most popular attractions, Deep Sea World. The picturesque seaside village of Aberdour with its own castle is nearby.

CRAIL. Sauchope Links Caravan Park, Near Crail KY10 3XL
Tel: 01333 450460 • Fax: 01333 450246 • www.largoleisure.co.uk
Well laid out and landscaped park with superb sea views to the Isle of May. Close to many fine golf courses and other tourist attractions, and ideal for a relaxing holiday. Facilities include a heated outdoor pool and indoor recreation room. Tourers welcome. Open March to November.

GLENROTHES. Kingdom Caravan Park, Overstenton Farm, Glenrothes KY6 2NG
Tel & Fax: 01592 772226 • www.kingdomcaravanpark.com
A modern site with good amenities for visitors to this popular area. Glenrothes has good shopping and leisure amenities, and all the attractions of St Andrews and the East Neuk are just a short drive away. Open March to October.

KINGHORN. Pettycur Bay Holiday Park, Burntisland Road, Kinghorn KY3 9YE
Tel: 01592 892200 • Fax: 01592 892206 • www.pettycur.co.uk
Overlooking miles of golden sands, this is an ideal base for enjoying the wealth of leisure facilities in the area. Facilities are excellent, with a Leisure Centre with a swimming pool and entertainment. Open from March to October.

LEVEN. Leven Beach Caravan Site, North Promenade, Leven KY8 4HY
Tel: 01333 426008 • www.pettycur.co.uk
Located on the promenade with direct access to the beach, the park's location makes it an ideal base for exploring the Kingdom of Fife; Edinburgh only 35 minutes by road or rail. Hardstanding and grassed pitches are well laid out, and there is a modern utility block.

ST ANDREWS. Clayton Caravan Park, Near St Andrews KY16 9YE
Tel: 01334 870242 • Fax: 01334 870357 • www.clayton-caravan-park.co.uk
All touring pitches at this popular site just outside St Andrews are super pitches and are sheltered by trees, within a short distance of the main facilities. Tents not accepted. Open April to October.

Highlands

Highlands
Aviemore

SCOTLAND 167

SPEYSIDE LEISURE PARK
Self-Catering Holidays in he Heart of the Highlands

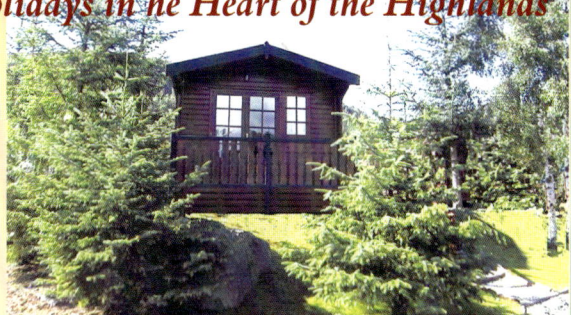

The park is situated in a quiet riverside setting with mountain views, only a short walk from Aviemore centre and shops. We offer a range of warm, well equipped chalets, cabins and caravans, including a caravan for the disabled. Prices include electricity, gas, linen, towels and use of our heated indoor pool and sauna. There are swings, a climbing frame and low level balance beams for the children. Permit fishing is available on the river. Discounts are given on some local attractions.

Families, couples or groups will find this an ideal location for a wide range of activities including:

- Horse riding • Golf • Fishing • Hillwalking
- RSPB Reserves • Mountain and Watersports • Reindeer herd
- Steam railway and the Whisky Trail

Only slightly further afield you will find Culloden Moor, the Moray Firth dolphins and of course, the not to be missed, Loch Ness.
Accommodation sleeps from 1-8, and we offer a reduced rate for a couple or one single person. Short Breaks are available.
Sorry, no pets, except guide and hearing dogs. No tents or camper vans.

Speyside Leisure Park
Dalfaber Road, Aviemore,
Inverness-shire PH22 1PX
Tel: 01479 810236
Fax: 01479 811688
e-mail:
fhg@speysideleisure.com
www.speysideleisure.com

SCOTLAND — Highlands

Aviemore, Beauly, Dingwall

AVIEMORE. Dalraddy Holiday Park, Aviemore PH22 1QB
Tel: 01479 810330 • www.alvie-estate.co.uk/dalraddy_holiday_park.htm
Quiet family park in 25 acres of woodland, just 3 miles south of Aviemore, with spectacular views of the Cairngorms. Tourers, motorhomes and tents welcome. Open all year.

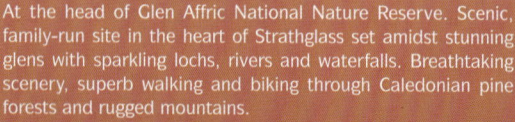

Cannich
Caravan & Camping Park
Cannich, Strathglass
Inverness-shire IV4 7LN

At the head of Glen Affric National Nature Reserve. Scenic, family-run site in the heart of Strathglass set amidst stunning glens with sparkling lochs, rivers and waterfalls. Breathtaking scenery, superb walking and biking through Caledonian pine forests and rugged mountains.

We welcome touring caravans, motorhomes and tents. Choose from our open grassy pitches or the shelter of the Scots pines, and enjoy free HOT showers, indoor washing up, TV room, laundry and playpark. Comfortable, luxury fully equipped static caravans are available for weekly or nightly hire. Visit our cafe serving drinks and snacks all day. Central heating, double glazing. Ideal for a winter getaway. ON SITE BIKE HIRE.

Tel & Fax: 01456 415364 • www.highlandcamping.co.uk

DINGWALL. Black Rock Caravan and Camping Park, Evanton, Dingwall IV16 9UN
Tel & Fax. 01349 030917 • www.blackrockscotland.co.uk
In the shadow of Ben Wyvis, this is an ideal base for a relaxing break, or to explore the local area which takes in some of the most spectacular and unspoiled scenery in the Highlands. Dingwall is 4 miles away and Inverness 15 miles. Touring caravans and tents welcome. Open April to October.

Electric hook-ups available		Facilities for disabled visitors
Children's play area		Pets welcome
Laundry facilities		Shop on site
Licensed bar on site		Wifi access available

FHG Guides

publish a large range of well-known accommodation guides.
We will be happy to send you details or you can use the order form
at the back of this book.

Linnhe
LOCHSIDE HOLIDAYS

Almost a botanical garden, Linnhe is recognised as one of the best and most beautful Lochside parks in Britain. Magnificent gardens contrast with the wild, dramatic scenery of Loch Eil and the mountains beyond. Superb amenities, launderette, shop & bakery, and free fishing on private shoreline with its own jetty all help give Linnhe its Five Star grading. Linnhe Lochside Holidays is ideally situated for day trips with Oban, Skye, Mull, Inverness and the Cairngorms all within easy driving distance.

- ◆ Holiday Caravans from £240 per week
- ◆ Touring pitches from £16 per night
- ◆ Tent pitches from £12 per night
- ◆ Pets welcome
- ◆ Tourer playground, pet exercise area
- ◆ Motorhome waste and water facilities
- ◆ Recycling on park
- ◆ Colour brochure sent with pleasure.

Linnhe
LOCHSIDE HOLIDAYS

www.linnhe-lochside-holidays.co.uk/brochure
Tel: 01397 772 376 to check availability

SCOTLAND — Highlands

Gairloch, Grantown-on-Spey, Inverness, John O' Groats, Laide

GAIRLOCH. Gairloch Holiday Park, Strath, Gairloch IV21 2BX
Tel: 01445 712373
Family-owned park situated just 6 miles from the world renowned Inverewe Gardens. The village of Strath is within walking distance, and other local activities include fishing, pony trekking and golf.

GRANTOWN-ON-SPEY. Grantown-on-Spey Caravan Park, Grantown-on-Spey PH26 3JQ
Tel: 01479 872474 • www.caravanscotland.com
Explore the Whisky Trail and Speyside Railway from this landscaped park which offers spacious pitches and a friendly welcome. Superb toilet and laundry facilities; grass and hardstanding pitches available.

HOLIDAY PARKS & CENTRES

INVERNESS near. Auchnahillin Caravan & Camping Park, Daviot East, Inverness IV2 5XQ (01463 772286).
Friendly, informal family-run ten-acre park, set in tranquil glen, yet conveniently located just off the A9, only eight miles south of Inverness with several other popular destinations being within an easy drive. Informative reception area, small shop, children's play area, laundry and dishwashing facilities, showers, toilets and hairdryers.
Rates: 11 fully equipped, self-contained static caravan/chalet holiday homes for hire, £35 to £65 per night/£170 to £320 per week. 45 pitches for touring units, £9 to £15 per night. Camping ground for up to 30 tents, £8 to £10 per night.
• Disabled/baby changing facilities. • Dogs welcome. • Open April until October.
STB ★★★★ HOLIDAY PARK
e-mail: info@auchnahillin.co.uk
www.auchnahillin.co.uk

CARAVAN SITES & TOURING PARKS

JOHN O'GROATS. John O'Groats Caravan and Camping Site, John O'Groats KW1 4YR (01955 611329/744). At end of A99 on seafront beside "last house in Scotland", caravan and camping site with showers, launderette, electric hook-ups and disabled toilet. Internet access. Caravans, caravanettes and tents welcome. Booking office for day trips to Orkney Islands on site. Hotel, restaurant, cafe, harbour 150 metres. Magnificent cliff scenery with sea birds galore including puffins, guillemots, skuas within one-and-a-half-miles. Seals are often seen swimming to and fro and there is a seal colony only four miles away. From the site you can see the wide panorama of the Orkney Islands, the nearest of which is only seven miles away. Public telephone 150 metres.
Rates: from £13 per night.
STB ★★★ HOLIDAY PARK
e-mail: info@johnogroatscampsite.co.uk
www.johnogroatscampsite.co.uk

Gruinard Bay Caravan Park

Situated just a stone's throw from the beach, Gruinard Bay Caravan Park offers the perfect setting for a holiday or a stopover on the West Coast of Scotland. Family-owned and personally operated, the park boasts magnificent views across Gruinard Bay.
• Sea front Touring Pitches • Electric Hook-ups • No charge for Awnings
• Camping Pitches • Free Toilet and Shower facilities • Shop Gas available on site • Laundry facilities • Static Holiday Homes available
• Pets Welcome (not in Holiday Homes)

**Tony & Ann Davis, Gruinard Bay Caravan Park,
Laide, Wester Ross IV22 2ND
Tel/Fax: 01445 73122 • www.highlandbreaks.net**

CALOR Gas

Hillhead Caravans
Achmelvich

Excellent self-catering accommodation at the beautiful white, safe, sandy beach of Achmelvich, near Lochinver in North West Scotland, one of the country's beauty spots. Ideal for family holidays.

Clean, modern, 6-berth, fully serviced caravans to let, 150 metres from the beach.

Our accommodation and area are perfect for country lovers and a good centre for hillwalking, photography, cycling, climbing, caving, geology, swimming, bird-watching, touring, fishing, sailing – or just relaxing with a good book! Open late March to late October.

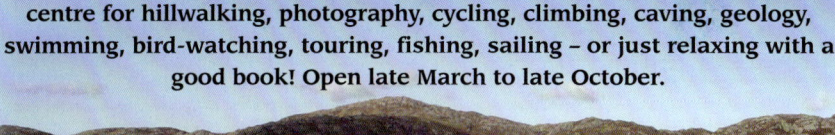

Details from Durrant and Maysie Macleod
Hillhead Caravans, Lochinver IV27 4JA
Tel & Fax: 01571 844454
e-mail:info@lochinverholidays.co.uk

Highlands

Lairg, Nairn, Scourie, Shielbridge

Dunroamin Caravan Park
Main Street, Lairg
Sutherland IV27 4AR

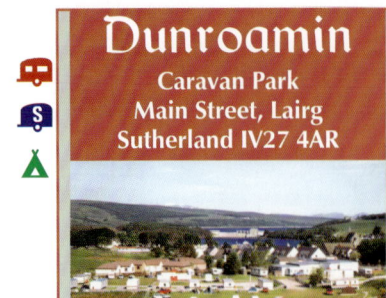

Lew Hudson, his wife Margaret and their family welcome you to Dunroamin Caravan Park. A small family-run park situated in the picturesque village of Lairg by Loch Shin, this is the ideal base for touring the whole of Sutherland and Caithness. Fishing and walking nearby, with golf just 15 miles away. Outstandingly well maintained grounds with Crofters licensed restaurant on site. Electric hook-ups. 200 yards from pub, bank, shops, post office, etc. Holiday caravans for hire, tourers and tents welcome.

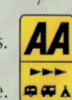

Tel: 01549 402447
enquiries@lairgcaravanpark.co.uk
www.lairgcaravanpark.co.uk

NAIRN. Nairn Camping and Caravanning Club Site, Delnies Wood, Nairn IV12 5NX
Tel: 01667 455281
Level, sheltered site near the Moray Firth, where you may be lucky enough to spot dolphins. Nairn with it sandy beach is well worth a visit, and the surrounding countryside is home to many species of birds and other wildlife.

Bayview, Badcall, Scourie IV27 4TH

Contact: Florence or Bert Macleod
01349 864072

Six-berth caravan with gas cooking, heating, shower and mains electricity. Situated in the beautiful North West Highlands of Scotland, two hours driving time from the city of Inverness. Ideal centre for touring Northern Scotland and the Western Isles (vehicle ferry sails from Ullapool to Stornoway). There are ample opportunities for climbing and hillwalking. Visit the Handa Island bird sanctuary, also local boat trips. Permits available for trout fishing. The scenery around the caravan is breathtaking, and there are many beautiful beaches within a short drive.

CAMPING SITES

SHIELBRIDGE (Glen Shiel). Shiel Caravan Site, Shielbridge, By Kyle (01599 511221).
Touring site situated at the west end of the spectacular Glen Shiel on the A87 Fort William to Kyle of Lochalsh road (access by shop at Shielbridge). This is an ideal centre from which to explore the beautiful West Coast and is 15 miles from the Isle of Skye bridge at Kyle. There is space for 16 caravans and 50 tents; all usual facilities including showers. Shop adjacent, gas and petrol available. New toilet and shower block opened 2005. Electric hook-ups available.
Rates: from £5 per person per night.
• Pets welcome. • Children welcome. • Open from March 16th to October 16th.

	Electric hook-ups available			Facilities for disabled visitors
	Children's play area			Pets welcome
	Laundry facilities			Shop on site
	Licensed bar on site			Wifi access available

Lanarkshire

Abington, Motherwell. Stepps

Lanarkshire

Mount View Caravan Park

Luxury holiday homes for hire on caravan park set in peaceful, unspoilt countryside with beautiful views of the Clyde valley. Good for walking, cycling, fishing, golf and touring the area. Near to Moffat, Biggar, Edinburgh, Glasgow and Scottish Borders.
Fully equipped holiday home including microwave, TV/DVD and with double glazing and central heating.
En suite shower room, lounge, dining area, kitchen, twin and double bedrooms. Bedding and towels can be provided at an extra cost. Easy access, just five minutes from J13 of the M74 and a short walk from the village shop.
£170 to £350 per week.

Abington, South Lanarkshire ML12 6RW   Tel: 01864 502808
e-mail: info@mountviewcaravanpark.co.uk • www.mountviewcaravanpark.co.uk

---

MOTHERWELL. Strathclyde Country Park Caravan Site, Hamilton Road, Motherwell ML1 3ED
Tel: 01698 402060 • Fax: 01698 252925
Open from April to October, the site can accommodate up to 100 caravans and 50 tents. Facilities are excellent and it is an excellent base for visiting Glasgow, Edinburgh and the whole of Central Scotland. Strathclyde Country Park has ample opportunities for outdoor activities of every kind, plus a large funfair.

STEPPS. Craigendmuir Park, Stepps, Glasgow G33 6AF
Tel: 0141 779 2973 • Fax: 0141 779 4057 • www.craigendmuir.co.uk
Conveniently situated just off the A80, this friendly park enjoys good public transport links to Glasgow and further afield, making it an ideal base for touring. Hardstanding and grassed pitches are available, and facilities on site are well maintained. Open all year. Tents, caravans and motorhomes welcome.

---

symbols

- Holiday Parks & Centres
- Caravans for Hire
- Caravan Sites and Touring Parks
- Camping Sites

Perth & Kinross

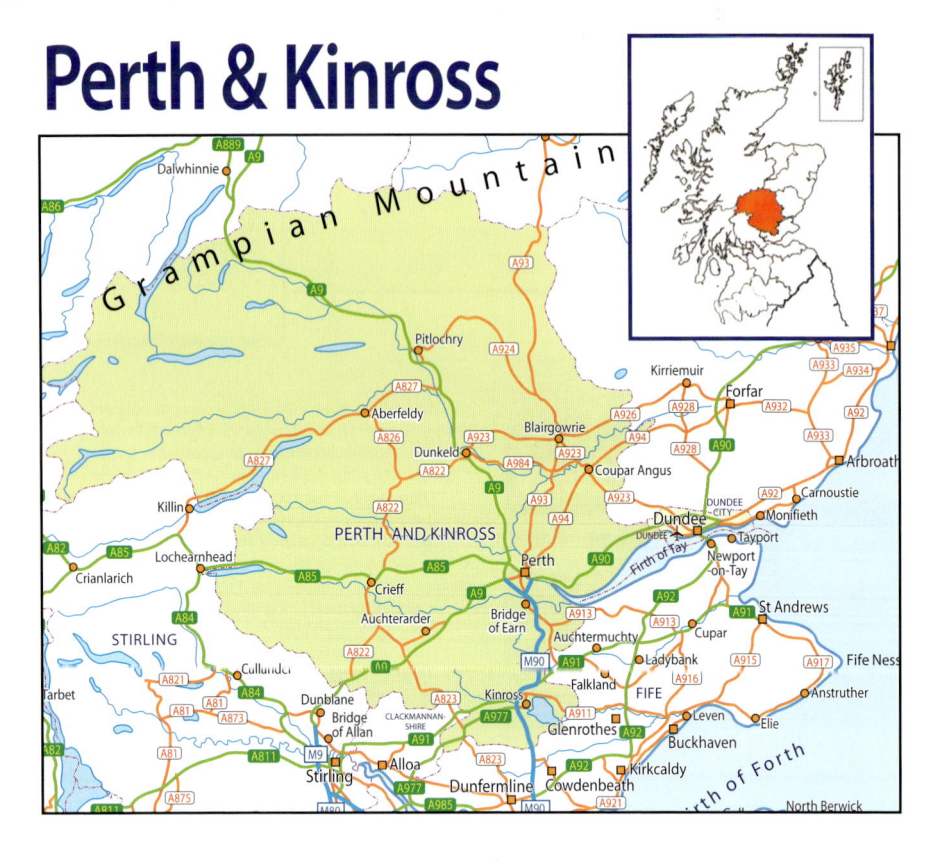

Perth & Kinross embraces both Highland and Lowland. Close to where the two Scotlands meet, a cluster of little resort towns has grown up: Crieff, Comrie, Dunkeld, Aberfeldy, and Pitlochry, set, some say, right in the very centre of Scotland. Perthshire touring is a special delight, as north-south hill roads drop into long loch-filled glens - Loch Rannoch, Loch Tay or Loch Earn, for example. No matter where you base yourself, from Kinross by Loch Leven to the south to Blairgowrie by the berryfields on the edge of Strathmore, you can be sure to find a string of interesting places to visit. If your tastes run to nature wild, rather than tamed in gardens, then Perthshire offers not only the delights of Caledonian pinewoods by Rannoch and the alpine flowers of the Lawers range, but also wildlife spectacle such as nesting ospreys at Loch of the Lowes by Dunkeld. There are viewing facilities by way of hides and telescopes by the lochside. Water is an important element in the Perthshire landscape, and it also plays a part in the activities choice. Angling and sailing are two of the 'mainstream' activities on offer, though if you are looking for a new experience, then canyoning is a Perthshire speciality on offer from a number of activity operators. Enjoy a round of golf on any of Perthshire's 40 courses, including those at Gleneagles by Auchterarder.

The main town of Perth has plenty of shops with High Street names as well as specialist outlets selling everything from Scottish crafts to local pearls. With attractions including an excellent repertory theatre and a great choice of eating places, this is an ideal base to explore the true heartland of Scotland.

Perth & Kinross

SCOTLAND 175

Aberfeldy, Alyth, Auchterarder, Blair Atholl, Blairgowrie

ABERFELDY. Aberfeldy Caravan Park, Dunkeld Road, Aberfeldy PH15 2AQ
Tel: 01887 820662
Within walking distance of the delightful little town of Aberfeldy, this friendly site is deservedly popular with regular visitors. Golfers and fishermen find it particularly attractive, as do all who want a convenient base for exploring this scenic area.

For a peaceful break in the Perthshire countryside, Five Roads is the perfect location. It is situated on the outskirts of Alyth, a small, historic town offering a wide variety of attractions in close proximity. The park is open all year and welcomes tourers and tents. Each pitch has an electric hook-up. There are two Thistle Award holiday homes for hire; each has central heating, double glazing, shower, microwave, TV and is fully furnished. Bed linen is provided. Play area for small children. Pets not permitted in holiday homes. There are three golf courses within a one mile radius.

FIVE ROADS CARAVAN PARK, Alyth, Blairgowrie PH11 8NB
Tel: 01828 632555
steven.ewart@openworld.com • www.fiveroads-caravan-park.co.uk

---

AUCHTERARDER. Auchterarder Caravan park, Auchterarder PH3 1ET
Tel & Fax: 01764 663119 • www.prestonpark.co.uk/caravan.htm
Family-run park with modern facilities, in a secluded location two miles from Auchterarder and 12 miles from Perth. Pitches are generously spaced, with level hardstandings and a separate area for tents. Open all year.

BLAIR ATHOLL. River Tilt Park, Bridge of Tilt, Blair Atholl, Pitlochry PH18 5TE
Tel: 01796 481467 • Fax: 01796 481511 • www.rivertiltpark.co.uk
Family-owned and run park which has been awarded the highest gradings for the quality of its facilities. The touring park has a separate area for dog owners and for tents, and offers hardstanding or grassed pitches. Tourers, motorhomes and tents welcome. Open March to November.

BLAIRGOWRIE. Five Roads Caravan Park, By Alyth, Blairgowrie PH11 8NB
Tel: 01828 632555 • Fax: 01828 633324 • www.fiveroads-caravan-park.co.uk
With three golf courses within a one mile radius, and pony trekking, fishing and walking in the area, as well as beautiful scenery, this site is very popular with those seeking a base for an active or leisurely holiday. Caravans, motorhomes and tents welcome. Open all year.

🚐	Electric hook-ups available	♿	Facilities for disabled visitors
⛺	Children's play area	🐕	Pets welcome
🍴	Laundry facilities	🛒	Shop on site
🍷	Licensed bar on site	W	Wifi access available

FREE or REDUCED RATE entry to Holiday Visits and Attractions – see our READERS' OFFER VOUCHERS on pages 205-234

… 176 SCOTLAND — Perth & Kinross — Crieff, Loch Rannoch, Lochearnhead

Braidhaugh Holiday Park

South Bridgend, Crieff PH7 4DH

Peaceful, picturesque, riverside park, a few minutes' walk from the centre of this popular holiday destination, at the foot of the Highlands. Surrounded by stunning scenery, with leisure pursuits, family fun and many craft and gift centres on offer, Crieff sits in the heart of Perthshire, providing an excellent base for exploring this beautiful part of Scotland.

Braidhaugh offers both touring and hire accommodation at competitive rates, is open all year round and now has Luxury Holiday Lodges for sale.

Largo Leisure Parks

Tel: 01764 652951
www.braidhaugh.co.uk
e-mail: info@braidhaugh.co.uk

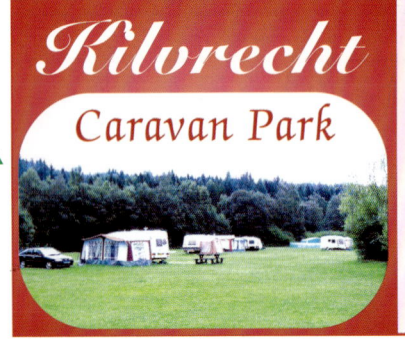

Kilvrecht Caravan Park

Secluded campsite on a level open area in quiet and secluded woodland setting. There is fishing available for brown trout on Loch Rannoch. Several trails begin from the campsite.

Please write, fax or telephone for further information.

Loch Rannoch, Perthshire PH8 0JR
Tel: 01350 727284
Fax: 01350 727811
e-mail: hamish.murray@forestry.gsi.gov.uk

LOCHEARNHEAD. Balquhidder Braes Caravan and Camping Park, Near Lochearnhead FK19 8NX
Tel & Fax: 01567 830293 • www.balquhidderbraes.co.uk
Centrally located for touring and sightseeing, this small, family-run park offers modern self-catering holiday homes, as well as touring caravan and tent pitches. Set within the Trossachs National Park, a great location for outdoor pursuits. Open March to October.

The FHG Directory of Website Addresses

on pages 235-250 is a useful quick reference guide for holiday accommodation with e-mail and/or website details

Perth & Kinross
Pitlochry

SCOTLAND 177

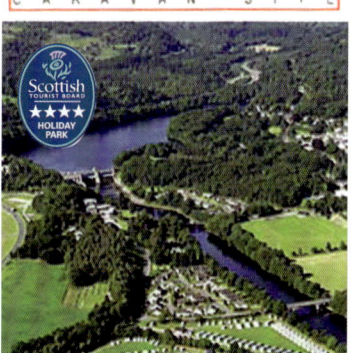

A 16 acre site with 154 touring pitches (last arrival 9pm) with electricity and awnings extra and 36 caravans to let, sleep six (minimum let two nights) with mains water, shower, toilet, TV, etc. Site facilities include showers, electric hook-ups, chemical disposal point, telephone, shop, etc. Shops and eating out places one mile. We also take tents. Fishing available. Children and pets welcome. Caravans from £250 to £400 per week; pitches from £15.00 per night. Open March to October.

Milton of Fonab Caravan Site
Pitlochry PH16 5NA • 01796 472882 • Fax: 01796 474363
e-mail: info@fonab.co.uk • www.fonab.co.uk

Other specialised holiday guides from FHG

PUBS & INNS OF BRITAIN
COUNTRY HOTELS OF BRITAIN
WEEKEND & SHORT BREAKS IN BRITAIN & IRELAND
THE GOLF GUIDE WHERE TO PLAY, WHERE TO STAY
500 GREAT PLACES TO STAY
SELF-CATERING HOLIDAYS IN BRITAIN
BED & BREAKFAST STOPS IN BRITAIN
PETS WELCOME!
FAMILY BREAKS IN BRITAIN

Published annually: available in all good bookshops or direct from the publisher:
FHG Guides, Abbey Mill Business Centre, Seedhill, Paisley PA1 1TJ
Tel: 0141 887 0428 • Fax: 0141 889 7204
e-mail: admin@fhguides.co.uk • www.holidayguides.com

Stirling & The Trossachs

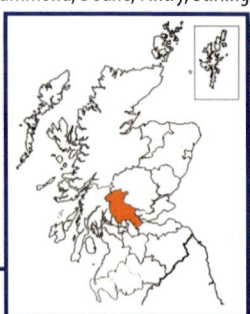

Blair Drummond, Doune, Fintry, Stirling

BLAIR DRUMMOND. Blair Drummond Caravan Park, Cuthil Brae, Blair Drummond FK9 4UP
Tel: 01786 841208 • Fax: 01786 842407 • www.blairdrummondcaravanpark.co.uk
A delightful sheltered site set around a walled garden, with mature trees and shrubs. Good access to Doune Castle and the Safari Park (preferential rates for caravan visitors). Tents not allowed. Open March to January.

DOUNE. Ashmill Caravan Park, Doune FK16 6AA
Tel: 01786 842608
This new site offers facilities fro touring caravans, campervans and tents. It is conveniently located for walking and for exploring Loch Lomond and The Trossachs. Just off the A84, there is also easy access to Stirling and all its amenities. Open April to October.

FINTRY. Balgair Castle Caravan Park, Fintry G63 0LP
Tel: 01360 860283/349 • www.balgaircastle.com
Located off the B822, this friendly site has its own club and entertainment, and fishing is available on site. 63 touring pitches are ideal if you are looking for a base for exploring Central Scotland - please note that tents are not allowed. Open from March to October.

STIRLING. Witches Craig Caravan & Camping Park, Blairlogie, Stirling FK9 5PX
Tel: 01786 474947 • Fax: 01786 447286 • www.witchescraig.co.uk
Attractive, well maintained site at the foot of the Ochil Hills, ideal for relaxing and centrally located for exploring Central Scotland. Winner of many awards including Gold David Bellamy Award and National Loo of the Year. Tourers, motorhomes and tents welcome. Open April to October.

STIRLING. Auchenbowie Caravan Site, Auchenbowie, Stirling FK7 8HE
Tel: 01324 823999/822141
Touring and tent pitches are available on this well kept site located off the M80/M9, just four miles from historic Stirling. Rates for overnight stays are very reasonable, and visitors will appreciate the peaceful surroundings. Open April to October.

Electric hook-ups available		Facilities for disabled visitors	
Children's play area		Pets welcome	
Laundry facilities		Shop on site	
Licensed bar on site		Wifi access available	

Scottish Islands

Kirkwall, Westray

Scottish Islands
Orkney

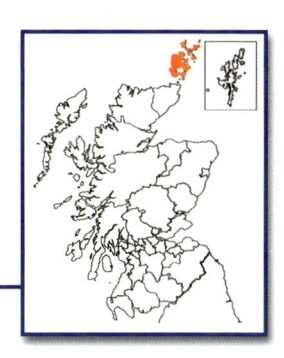

The Pickaquoy Centre Caravan & Camping Park • Kirkwall, Orkney
Tel: 01856 879900 • www.pickaquoy.co.uk • e-mail: enquiries@pickaquoy.com
The St Magnus Cathedral is the central feature of Kirkwall, Orkney's main town, a relaxing and interesting centre from which to explore the surrounding areas. The site is situated within The Pickaquoy Centre complex, an impressive modern leisure facility offering a range of activities for all the family.

Birsay Outdoor Centre/ Caravan & Camping Site
A new site located in the picturesque north west of Orkney

Point of Ness Caravan & Camping Site • Stromness, Orkney.
Stromness is a small, picturesque town with impressive views of the hills of Hoy. The site is one mile from the harbour in a quiet, shoreline location. Many leisure activities are available close by, including fishing, sea angling, golf and a swimming & fitness centre.

For Birsay and Point of Ness contact: Department of Education & Recreation Services, Orkney Islands Council, Kirkwall, Orkney KW15 1NY • Tel: 01856 873535 ext. 2404

Mount Pleasant

Westray, Isle of Orkney

Caravans to let
from £10 per night

Long or short lets available.
Special prices for students. All linen provided.
Lovely sandy beaches, shops and swimming pool nearby.
Pets welcome. Children welcome.

Relax on this beautiful island.

Westray and Papa Westray are two of the Orkney's Northern Isles. Both are easy to get to by foot or car with good air and sea links.

There is plenty to do in the islands, whether you're interested in walking, crafts, nature watching, sailing, or just relaxing, there is something here for everyone whatever the season and whatever the weather.

Please contact for further details.
Mount Pleasant. Westray, Orkney Isands KW17 2DH • Tel: 01857 677229

Ratings & Awards

For the first time ever the AA, VisitBritain, VisitScotland, and the Wales Tourist Board will use a single method of assessing and rating serviced accommodation. Irrespective of which organisation inspects an establishment the rating awarded will be the same, using a common set of standards, giving a clear guide of what to expect. The RAC is no longer operating an Hotel inspection and accreditation business.

Accommodation Standards: Star Grading Scheme

Using a scale of 1-5 stars the objective quality ratings give a clear indication of accommodation standard, cleanliness, ambience, hospitality, service and food, This shows the full range of standards suitable for every budget and preference, and allows visitors to distinguish between the quality of accommodation and facilities on offer in different establishments. All types of board and self-catering accommodation are covered, including hotels, B&Bs, holiday parks, campus accommodation, hostels, caravans and camping, and boats.

VisitBritain and the regional tourist boards, enjoyEngland.com, VisitScotland and VisitWales, and the AA have full details of the grading system on their websites

The more stars, the higher level of quality

★★★★★
exceptional quality, with a degree of luxury

★★★★
excellent standard throughout

★★★
very good level of quality and comfort

★★
good quality, well presented and well run

★
acceptable quality; simple, practical, no frills

National Accessible Scheme

If you have particular mobility, visual or hearing needs, look out for the National Accessible Scheme. You can be confident of finding accommodation or attractions that meet your needs by looking for the following symbols.

- Typically suitable for a person with sufficient mobility to climb a flight of steps but would benefit from fixtures and fittings to aid balance

- Typically suitable for a person with restricted walking ability and for those that may need to use a wheelchair some of the time and can negotiate a maximum of three steps

- Typically suitable for a person who depends on the use of a wheelchair and transfers unaided to and from the wheelchair in a seated position. This person may be an independent traveller

- Typically suitable for a person who depends on the use of a wheelchair in a seated position. This person also requires personal or mechanical assistance (eg carer, hoist).

Wales

Bryn Gloch Caravan & Camping Park, Snowdonia, p188

The Pines Caravan Park, Rhayader, Powys, p197

Grawen Caravan & Camping Park, Merthyr Tydfil, p199

Anglesey & Gwynedd

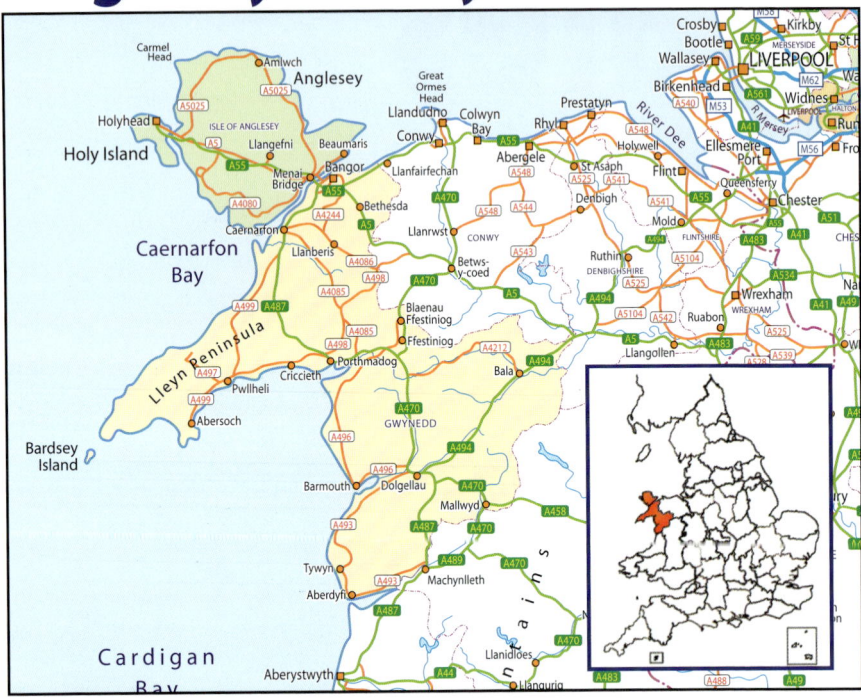

ANGLESEY & GWYNEDD, the northernmost area of Wales, bordered by the Irish sea, has something for everyone. Its beautiful coastline has glorious sandy beaches which offer safe bathing, and there are quaint coastal resorts with attractive harbours and maritime activities, The stunning Snowdonia National Park, right at its centre, covers 823 miles of beautiful, unspoilt countryside and a wide range of leisure activities can be enjoyed. Natural attractions abound throughout the area - mountains, forests, lakes, rivers and waterfalls all wait to be explored, and man-made attractions include castles, railways and industrial archaeology.

symbols

- Holiday Parks & Centres
- Caravans for Hire
- Caravan Sites and Touring Parks
- Camping Sites

Anglesey & Gwynedd
Anglesey, Bala

WALES 183

Tyddyn Isaf
Camping and Caravan Park

Lligwy Bay, Dulas, Anglesey LL70 9PQ
Tel: 01248 410203 • Fax: 01248 410667

Award-winning superior park which has been described as a 'wild life wonderland' by David Bellamy. Touring caravans and tents are catered for by the high standard of facilities – "Loo of the Year" award. The site facilities include sanitation, water, electricity, gas, shop, swings, licensed club, take-away food and laundry facilities. Safe, sandy beach reached directly from the site. Golf, tennis, fishing, riding and bathing all within easy reach. Open from 1st March to 31st October.

Children welcome. Pets by arrangement. Tourers from £18.
Six acres for campers from £15 per tent.
CALOR GAS 'FINALIST' BEST TOURING PARK IN WALES

www.tyddynisaf.co.uk

Minffordd Caravan Park, Minffordd,
Lligwy, Dulas, Isle of Anglesey LL70 9HJ
01248 410678 • Fax: 01248 410378

Modern caravans to let on small 5★ garden park near the safe sandy beach of Lligwy (approx half a mile). Surrounded by flowers and lawns, each caravan is a recent model, complete with shower, W.C., wash basin, colour TV, fridge, microwave, and are fully equipped with the exception of personal linen.
TWO CARAVANS HAVE BEEN SPECIALLY DESIGNED AND EQUIPPED FOR ACCOMPANIED PHYSICALLY DISABLED GUESTS.

Nearby, in their own separate gardens, are a luxury four-bedroom detached house, a superb two-bedroom cottage, and two new semi-detached cottages - all 5★. Please contact us for availability and brochure. Telephone, fax, e-mail or send SAE. Personally managed by the owners.
WALES IN BLOOM AWARD WINNERS 2002/3/4/5/6/7.

e-mail: enq@minffordd-holidays.com • www.minffordd-holidays.com

---

❖ Ty Gwyn ❖
Tel: 01678 521267 or 520234

• **TY GWYN** • Static six-berth luxury caravan with two bedrooms, shower, bathroom, colour TV, microwave, etc. on private grounds.

Situated two miles from Bala in beautiful country area. Ideal for walking, sailing, fishing and canoeing. 30 miles from nearest beach. Pets welcome

Contact: **MRS A. SKINNER, TY GWYN, RHYDUCHAF, BALA LL23 7SD**

Islawrffordd
Caravan Park

Situated on the Snowdonia coastline, just north of Barmouth, our park offers a limited number of caravans for hire, most of which come with double glazing and central heating along with laundered bedding.

Our touring caravan field has been modernised to super pitch quality including hard standing with each plot being reservable.

Camping is also available on a first-come, first-served basis.

Park facilities include
- shop • bar • laundry
- indoor heated pool
- jacuzzi • sauna
- amusements
- food bars

Enquiries regarding any of the above to John or Jane.

Tel: 01341 247269
Fax: 01341 242639
e-mail: info@islawrffordd.co.uk
www.islawrffordd.co.uk

Tal-y-Bont, Gwynedd LL43 2BQ

Anglesey & Gwynedd
Benllech

WALES

Sports and Leisure

We have horse riding facilities on the site together with beach donkeys that work regularly depending on the tide and weather. Immediately adjacent to the site there are tennis courts and a bowling green. There is also a golf course within two miles.
A particular feature of the site is that whilst having the benefits of the village on one side, it has an attractive cliff path for walkers between the site and sea that stretches for miles. It is the intention of the local council to extend this walk right around the island.

The Site.....

There are a number of flush toilet blocks together with two shower blocks. Mains water is laid in all fields, and dustbins and skips are regularly serviced. There are electric hook-ups to numerous marked-out touring caravan pitches, and hook-ups are available for tents. We have a designated family field, and one of the most popular features of the camping site is that it is split up into numerous hedged enclosures.

We do not take advanced bookings for tents and touring caravans in the main designated area, as there is usually plenty of room, although electric hook-ups cannot be guaranteed. However we do take advanced bookings for touring caravans, only a small number of which are situated within the main caravan park. During the peak season and Bank Holidays, bookings will only be taken for a minimum of a week. Seasonal tourers are welcome, and reservations can be made for these.

Organised Camps

Organised camps for schools, scouts, guides etc are welcome, and we give quotations on enquiry. Each organised camp can have its own separate field with mains water and full facilities.

GOLDEN SUNSET HOLIDAYS
BENLLECH
ANGLESEY LL74 8SW
TEL: 01248 852345
www.goldensunsetholidays.com

Coastal Snowdonia
300 YARDS FROM LONG SANDY BEACH

ENJOY THE BEST OF BOTH WORLDS, BETWEEN SEA AND MOUNTAINS

LUXURY HOLIDAY HOMES FOR SALE AND HIRE

- Licensed Club House
- Pets Welcome
- Heated Swimming Pool
- Games Room
- Electrical Hook-ups available
- Super Pitches available
- Two Shower Blocks
- Two Children's Play Areas
- Touring & Camping on level grassland
- Washing-up and Laundry facilities

To request a brochure please contact:
Dinlle Caravan Park, Dinas Dinlle, Caernarfon LL54 5TS
Tel: 01286 830324
www.thornleyleisure.co.uk

Anglesey & Gwynedd

Caernarfon, Criccieth, Dolgellau, Llanuwchllyn

Plas-Y-Bryn Chalet Park
Bontnewydd, Near Caernarfon LL54 7YE
Tel: 01286 672811

Our small park is situated two miles from the historic town of Caernarfon. Set into a walled garden it offers safety, seclusion and beautiful views of Snowdonia. It is ideally positioned for touring the area. Shop and village pub nearby.

A selection of chalets and caravans available at prices from £195 (low season) to £445 (high season) per week for the caravans and £140 (low season) to £580 (high season) per week for the chalets. Well behaved pets always welcome.

e-mail: philplasybryn@aol.com • www.plasybrynholidayscaernarfon.co.uk

---

CRICCIETH. Eisteddfa Caravan and Camping Site, Criccieth LL52 0PT
Tel & Fax: 01766 522696 • www.eisteddfapark.co.uk
Ideal for caravan, camping and touring holidays in North Wales, the park has an excellent range of amenities and enjoys spectacular views over Cardigan Bay. It is on the A497, convenient for Porthmadog and Criccieth (don't miss the famous Cadwalladers ice cream!). Open Easter to end October.

DOLGELLAU. Torrent Walk Campsite, Dolgun Uchaf, Dolgellau LL40 2AB
Tel: 01341 422269 • Fax: 01341 422481
Large sheltered site in an area popular for walking, mountain biking, pony trekking and fishing. The town of Dolgellau is just 1½ miles away, and has a good range of shops and other amenities. Open all year.

DOLGELLAU. Llwyn-yr-helm Caravan and Camping Park, Brithdir, Dolgellau LL40 2SA
Tel & Fax: 01341 450254
Small family-run park on working farm set in the beautiful Snowdonia National Park. The park is mainly grass, with some hardstandings for caravans and motorhomes; tents also welcome. Open Easter to October.

Llwyn-Yr-Helm Farm

Situated on a minor road half a mile off B4416 which is a loop road between A470 and A494, this is a quiet, small working farm site, four miles from Dolgellau in beautiful countryside, ideal for walking and mountain biking. Many places of interest in the area including slate mines, narrow gauge railways, lakes and mountains and nine miles from sandy beaches.
• Toilet block • Laundry
• Caravans, Dormobiles and tents; electric hook-ups.
• Pets welcome. • Facilities for the disabled.
• Self-catering accommodation also available.

Mrs Helen Rowlands, Llwyn-Yr-Helm Farm, Brithdir, Dolgellau LL40 2SA • 01341 450254

e-mail: info@llwynyrhelmcaravanpark.co.uk
www.llwynyrhelmcaravanpark.co.uk

LLANUWCHLLYN. Bwch Yn Uchaf Camping And Caravanning Park, Llanuwchllyn, Bala LL23 7DD
Tel: 01978 812179 • www.bwch-yn-uchaf.co.uk
Small, one-acre site on the outskirts of the village, and ideal base for enjoying the many scenic walks in the area, and for birdwatching and fishing. Tourers, motorhomes and tents welcome. Open all year.

WALES

Anglesey & Gwynedd
Porthmadog, Pwllheli, Snowdonia

HOLIDAY PARKS & CENTRES

PORTHMADOG. Greenacres Holiday Park, Black Rock Sands, Morfa Bychan, Porthmadog.
Greenacres Holiday Park offers everything with wonderfully sandy beaches, picturesque mountains and its very own nature reserve. But that's not all - with fantastic sports and leisure activities and facilities including 9-Hole Pitch 'n' Putt, SplashZone heated indoor pool and children's clubs for all ages, the whole family will be spoilt for choice. With fantastic Touring facilities and on-site amenities, you'll have all you need to make your stay at Greenacres spectacular. **See also Colour Advertisement.**
Call our UK Central Team: 0871 230 1933 (open 7 days, 9am-9pm) or book on-line (quote: TO_FHG)
www.touringholidays.co.uk
• Great for Groups! Just book 5 or more holiday homes for extra benefits and savings.
Visit **www.havengroups.co.uk** Or call **0871 230 1911.**

PWLLHELI. Bolmynydd Touring And Camping Park, Bolmynydd, Llanbedrog, Pwllheli LL53 7UP
Tel: 07882 850 820 • www.bolmynydd.co.uk
In an idyllic, peaceful setting, this family-run site is within easy walking distance of glorious beaches, a well stocked grocery shop and a pub. Facilities for tourers and campers are excellent, with four camping fields to choose from. Open April to October.

HOLIDAY PARKS & CENTRES

PWLLHELI. Hafan y Môr Holiday Park, Pwllheli, Gwynedd, North Wales.
Set around its own sandy bay, with a breathtaking backdrop of Snowdonia, Hafan y Môr offers the perfect family base for stunning scenery, fantastic facilities and masses of activities. From a large heated indoor pool complete with flumes and slides to a relaxing boating lake for all to enjoy. From first class children's clubs for all ages to magnificent cabaret and other fabulous daytime and evening entertainment. Hafan y Môr is everything you want it to be and much much more. Hafan y Môr offers electric pitches and well maintained Touring facilities. What more could you ask for **See also Colour Advertisement.**
Call our UK Central Team: 0871 230 1933 (open 7 days, 9am-9pm) or book on-line (quote: TO_FHG)
www.touringholidays.co.uk
• Great for Groups! Just book 5 or more holiday homes for extra benefits and savings.
Visit **www.havengroups.co.uk** Or call **0871 230 1911.**

Bryn Gloch
Caravan and Camping Park
Betws Garmon
Near Caernarfon LL54 7YY

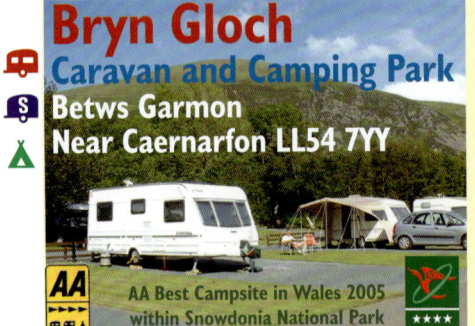

AA Best Campsite in Wales 2005 within Snowdonia National Park

Nestled between Snowdonia mountain ranges and on the banks of the River Gwyrfai with breathtaking views. Clean, peaceful site, electric hook-ups, luxury toilet/showers and launderette, mother and baby changing room, shop and off-licence, games room, spacious play area, fishing and mini-golf. Footpath to Snowdon two-and-a-half miles, a pub and restaurant within one mile. Many local attractions close by, plus watersports, climbing, walking, horseriding and much more. Modern Caravans, Touring Pitches, Tent Pitches and Self-catering Accommodation. Open all year.

Tel: 01286 650216 • Fax: 01286 650591
e-mail: eurig@bryngloch.co.uk
www.bryngloch.co.uk

	Electric hook-ups available		Facilities for disabled visitors
	Children's play area		Pets welcome
	Laundry facilities		Shop on site
	Licensed bar on site	W	Wifi access available

Anglesey & Gwynedd

Tal-y-Llyn, Trearddur Bay

CAMPING SITES

TYWYN. Marian Rees, Dôl-Einion Camp Site, Tal-y-Llyn, Tywyn LL36 9AJ (01654 761312).
Dôl-Einion is perhaps the prettiest campsite in the Snowdonia National Park. It is a flat three-acre meadow bordered by colourful rhododendrons in season and there is an attractive trout stream. The site nestles at the foot of mighty Cader Idris, at the start of the main path to the summit. Easy access on B4405 for caravans, camping vans. Hard standing area useful in bad weather. Hook - ups available. Good centre for walking or touring. Castle, narrow gauge railway and lake fishing nearby. On a bus route. Pub and restaurant five minute walk. Toilets and showers. Managed by resident owners. Terms on application.
e-mail: marianrees@tiscali.co.uk

TYN RHÔS CAMPING SITE

Ravenspoint Road,
Trearddur Bay, Holyhead,
Isle of Anglesey LL65 2AX
Tel: 01407 860369

Clean facilities, hot showers, toilets, chemical disposal, electric hook-ups etc. Couples and families welcome; separate rally field available. Bookings for electric pitches advisable, some disabled access – access statement/further information on request.

Rocky coves and sandy bays, Blue Flag beaches and public slipway, horse riding, golf. Spectacular coastal views all on the doorstep. Discover this diverse island steeped in history with its many attractions. The Royal town of Caernarfon and Snowdonia all within easy reach. Ferries to Ireland 3 miles.

Access from the A55. Junction 2 for Trearddur Bay on the B4545, turn right onto Ravenspoint Road, (after Spar shop), one mile to shared entrance, bear left.

Wales Cymru ★★★

symbols

- ☀ Holiday Parks & Centres
- 🚐 Caravans for Hire
- Ⓢ Caravan Sites and Touring Parks
- ▲ Camping Sites

North Wales

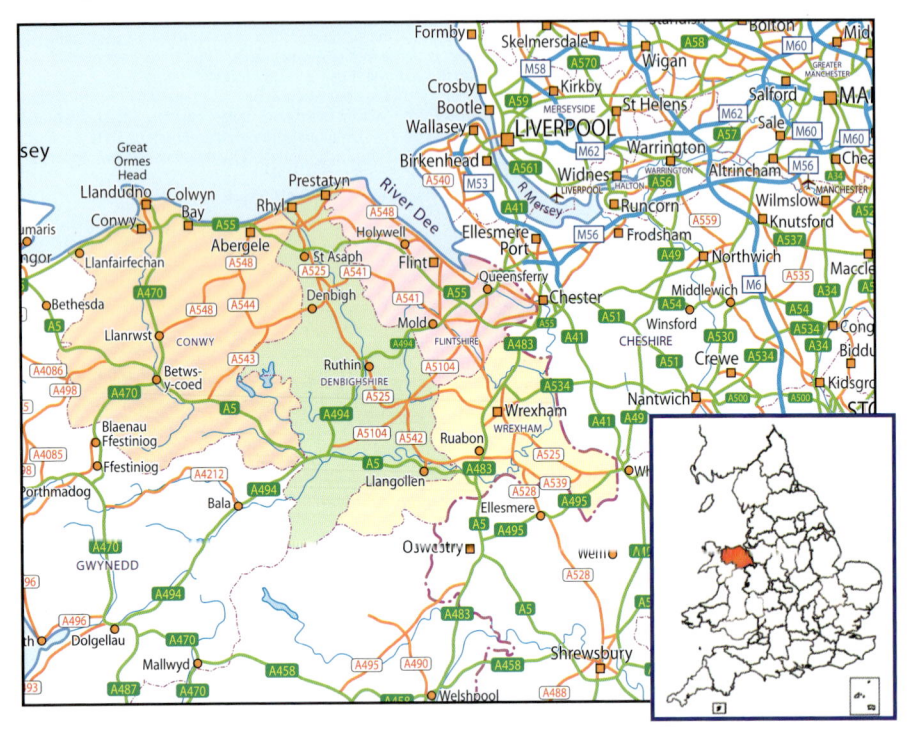

Static Caravan Park in peaceful location in North Wales

This small caravan site is situated in beautiful unspoilt countryside, 10 miles from the coast and 12 miles from Betws-y-coed, ideal for touring North Wales. The six-berth caravans are fully equipped except for linen and towels and have shower, flush toilets, hot and cold water, Calor gas cooker, electric light and fridge. Children especially will enjoy a holiday here, there being ample play space and facilities for fishing and pony riding. Pets are allowed but must be kept under control. Terms on application. SAE please. Open March- Oct.

Pen Isaf Farm Caravan Park
Llangernyw, Abergele LL22 8RN
Tel: 01745 860276
Mr and Mrs T.P. Williams,

www.caravan-park-wales.co.uk

FHG Guides

publish a large range of well-known accommodation guides.
We will be happy to send you details or you can use the order form at the back of this book.

North Wales   WALES 191
Abergele, Bangor-on-Dee, Betws-y-Coed, Mold, Prestatyn

ABERGELE. Plas Farm Caravan Park, Plas Yn Betws, Betws Yn Rhos, Abergele LL22 8AU
Tel: 01492 680254 • www.plasfarmcaravanpark.co.uk
For those who enjoy walking and other country pursuits, or are simply looking for a peaceful break, this small site on a working farm is an ideal location. Multiserviced pitches are available for tourers, and the site is within walking distance of the local pub and restaurant. Open March to October.

ABERGELE. Hunters Hamlet Caravan Park, Sirior Goch Farm, Betws yn Rhos, Abergele LL22 8PL
Tel: 01745 832237 • www.huntershamlet.co.uk
A quiet, peaceful site set among country lanes which can cater for 23 touring units (8 pitches have full services). Just a little further afield are the lively resorts of the North Wales coast. Open March to October.

BANGOR-ON-DEE. Emral Gardens Caravan Park, Holly Bush, Bangor-on-Dee, Wrexham LL13 0BG
Tel: 01948 770401 • www.emralgardens.co.uk
An adults-only site, partly surrounded by woodland, and with views across the fields. Level grass pitches have basic or luxury hook-ups, and there is a washing up area and TV room. Open March to October.

BETWS-Y-COED. Rynys Farm Camping Site, Llanrwst, Betws-y- Coed LL26 0RU
Tel: 01690 710218 • www.rynys-camping.co.uk
The views from this from this small, friendly site are simply breathtaking, and it lies within easy reach of many attractions and superb walking country. It caters mainly for tents and camper vans, plus a few touring caravans.

MOLD. Fron Farm Caravan and Camping Park, Rhes y Cae Road, Hendre, Mold CH7 5QW
Tel: 01352 741482 • www.fronfarmcaravanpark.co.uk
A spacious 5-acre site with stunning views of the Clwydian Mountains, with modern purpose-built facilities. It is very popular with children, who love the friendly farm animals and well equipped play area. Open April to October.

HOLIDAY PARKS & CENTRES
PRESTATYN. Presthaven Sands Holiday Park, Gronant, Prestatyn.
Located in Prestatyn, North Wales, Presthaven Sands really knows how to party! Just like the broad sandy beach, the fun is almost endless. With no less than three pools, three entertainment venues and a non-stop programme of events to keep the fun-loving atmosphere in full swing, Presthaven Sands really is the place to be for that great family holiday. From fantastic activities for the whole family to excellent Touring facilities and on-site amenities to make your stay totally stress free, you can't possibly ask for more! **See also Colour Advertisement.**
Call our UK Central Team: 0871 230 1933 (open 7 days, 9am-9pm) or book on-line (quote: TO_FHG) www.touringholidays.co.uk
• Great for Groups! Just book 5 or more holiday homes for extra benefits and savings.
Visit www.havengroups.co.uk Or call 0871 230 1911.

Electric hook-ups available   Facilities for disabled visitors

Children's play area   Pets welcome

Laundry facilities   Shop on site

Licensed bar on site   Wifi access available

Carmarthenshire

Llandovery, Llangadog, Newcastle Emlyn

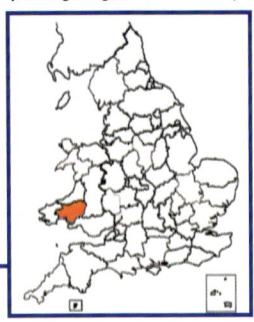

LLANDOVERY. Erwlon Caravan & Camping Park, Brecon Road, Llandovery SA20 0RD
Tel: 01550 721021 • Fax: 01550 720943 • www.erwlon.co.uk
Erwlon is a family-run park with excellent award-winning facilities, within easy walking distance of the ancient borough of Llandovery and at the foothills of the Brecon Beacons. It is an ideal base for touring, walking or cycling in South West Wales. Open all year.

LLANGADOG. Black Mountain Caravan and Camping Park, Llanddeusant, Llangadog SA19 9YG
Tel: 01550 740217 • www.blackmountainholidays.co.uk
This small, family-run caravan and camping park is located in the Brecon Beacons National Park on the border between Carmarthenshire and Powys. The 6.5 acre site accommodates tourers and tents and is an ideal base for exploring this scenic area. Open all year.

NEWCASTLE EMLYN. Dolbryn Caravan & Camping, Capel Iwan Road, Newcastle Emlyn SA38 9LP
Tel: 01239 710683 • www.dolbryn.co.uk
A quiet site set in a secluded valley with an abundance of wildlife. There are two spacious camping fields, and a small licensed bar is open at weekends and high season evenings. Fishing is permitted in a small pond on site. Open March to November.

Other specialised holiday guides from FHG

PUBS & INNS OF BRITAIN • **COUNTRY HOTELS** OF BRITAIN
WEEKEND & SHORT BREAK HOLIDAYS IN BRITAIN
THE GOLF GUIDE WHERE TO PLAY, WHERE TO STAY
500 GREAT PLACES TO STAY • **SELF-CATERING HOLIDAYS** IN BRITAIN
BED & BREAKFAST STOPS • **PETS WELCOME!**
FAMILY BREAKS IN BRITAIN

Published annually: available in all good bookshops or direct from the publisher:
FHG Guides, Abbey Mill Business Centre, Seedhill, Paisley PA1 1TJ
Tel: 0141 887 0428 • Fax: 0141 889 7204
e-mail: admin@fhguides.co.uk • www.holidayguides.com

Ceredigion
Aberystwyth, Llanarth, Llandysul

Ceredigion

ABERYSTWYTH. Aberystwyth Holiday Village, Penparcau Road, Aberystwyth SY23 1TH
Tel: 01970 624211 • Fax: 01970 611536 • www.aberystwythholidays.co.uk
Set in 30 acres, just a few minutes' walk from the town centre and beach, this is an ideal location for a family holiday. The excellent facilities include an indoor pool, fitness centre, bars and entertainment. Open March to October.

LLANARTH. Llanina Caravan Park, Llanarth, New Quay SA47 0NP
Tel & Fax: 01545 580947 • www.llanina-caravan-park.co.uk
Situated close to Cardigan Bay, this sheltered site is within easy walking distance of local amenities. Wildlife lovers will delight in spotting Red Kites, seals and dolphins, and there are many attractions in the area to interest all the family. 30 pitches for tourers/motorhomes and 20 for tents. Open April to October.

This family-owned park is situated in the unspoilt valley leading down to Penbryn Beach. The Park is sheltered yet has views out to sea. We have modern holiday homes for hire. Tents and tourers welcome. Located in an Area of Outstanding Natural Beauty, Maes Glas is an ideal location for family holidays and also walking holidays; short breaks available early and late season.

A warm welcome awaits you.
Mr and Mrs T. Hill,
Maes Glas Caravan Park, Penbryn, Sarnau,
Llandysul, Ceredigion SA44 6QE
Tel & Fax: 01239 654268
e-mail: enquiries@maesglascaravanpark.co.uk • www.maesglascaravanpark.co.uk

---

Treddafydd Farm Caravan Site

Treddafydd, being a small site, offers a peaceful and restful holiday overlooking the beautiful Hoffnant and Penbryn valley. All caravans have inside toilet and shower, fridge and Calor gas cookers, spacious lounge with gas heater and TV; dining area. Hot and cold water. All are fully equipped with electricity and mains water. Linen not supplied. Launderette on site, also a toilet block with two shower rooms. Safe beach at Penbryn, one mile away, cliff walks, sea and river fishing, pony rides available locally. Children are most welcome, with plenty of room for them to play. Treddafydd is a working dairy farm: cows, young calves. Children are welcome to see life on the farm. Pitches also available for tents and touring vans.

Sarnau, Llandysul SA44 6PZ • Tel: 01239 654551

Pembrokeshire

Pembrokeshire — Haverfordwest

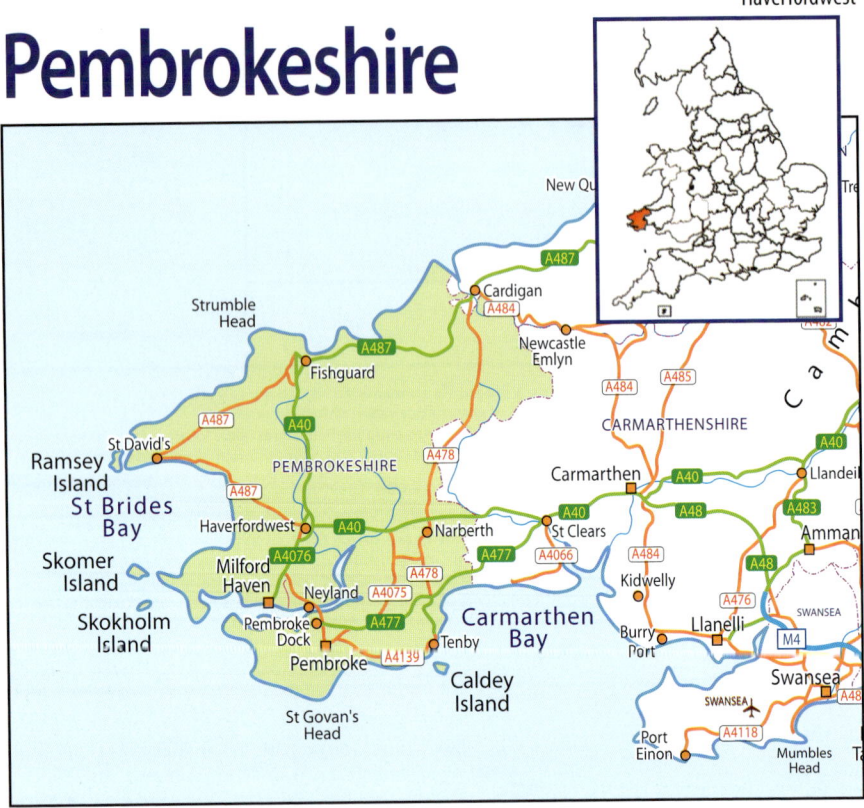

PEMBROKESHIRE'S entire coastline is a designated National Park, with its sheltered coves and wooded estuaries, fine sandy beaches and some of the most dramatic cliffs in Britain. The islands of Skomer, Stokholm and Grasholm are home to thousands of seabirds, and Ramsey Island, as well as being an RSPB Reserve boasts the second largest grey seal colony in Britain. Pembrokeshire's mild climate and the many delightful towns and villages, family attractions and outdoor facilities such as surfing, water skiing, diving, pony trekking and fishing make this a favourite holiday destination.

❖ Brandy Brook ❖
Caravan and Camping Site
Rhyndaston, Hayscastle, Haverfordwest SA62 5PT

This is a small, secluded site in very attractive surroundings, a quiet valley with a trout stream. The ideal situation for the true country lover. Campers welcome. Hot water/showers on site.
Car essential to get the most from your holiday. Take A487 from Haverfordwest, turn right at Roch Motel, signposted from turning. Pets accepted at £1.50 per night per pet. Children welcome.

Rates: £10.40 per night for 2 adults with one tent and a car.

Tel: 01348 840272 ❖ **e-mail: f.m.rowe@btopenworld.com**

Pembrokeshire

Manorbier, St Davids, Saundersfoot, Tenby

MANORBIER. Buttyland Touring & Tent Park, Station Road, Manorbier, Tenby SA70 7SX
Tel: 01834 871278 • www.arreton.net
With its wonderful scenery and unspoilt beaches within a mile, Buttyland is the perfect location for a relaxing holiday. Tenby and Pembroke are only a few miles away, and nearby Manorbier Bay has a lovely beach and good bathing.

ST DAVIDS. Porthclais Farm Campsite, Porthclais, St Davids SA62 6RR
Tel: 01437 720616 • www.porthclais-farm-campsite.co.uk
This spacious, flat site caters for tents and up to 12 touring vans. Near the Coastal Path, it is ideally located for enjoying the spectacular scenery and tranquil coastal surroundings (small boats can be launched). Open Easter to October.

ST DAVIDS. Tretio Caravan and Camping, Tretio, St Davids SA62 6DE
Tel: 01437 781600
Set against a stunning backdrop of the Pembrokeshire National Park this site is just 3 miles from some of the most beautiful beaches in Britain. Touring caravans, tents and campervans welcome. Open March to October.

SAUNDERSFOOT. Trevayne Farm Caravan & Camping Park, Monkstone, Saundersfoot SA69 9DL
Tel: 01834 813402 • www.camping-pembrokeshire.co.uk
Whether you are looking for a quiet short break away or a great base for a family holiday. Trevayne is the perfect rustic getaway, with access to a clean bathing beach. Open Easter to October.

TENBY. Rowston Holiday Park, New Hedges, Tenby SA70 8TL
Tel: 01834 842178 • Fax: 01834 842177 • www.rowston-holiday-park.co.uk
With easy access to the Pembrokshire Coast National Park, this beautifully landscaped park is ideal for a peaceful and relaxing holiday. An on-site diner offers a wide range of meals and snacks, and there is a games room (peak season). Open March to October for touring vans, motorhomes and tents.

HOLIDAY PARKS & CENTRES

TENBY. Kiln Park Holiday Centre, Marsh Road, Tenby.
With direct access to Tenby's beautiful, sandy South Beach, Kiln Park boasts a whole host of attractions for a great family holiday. With fantastic surroundings and non-stop entertainment and fun, there's something for the whole family. Set on the Pembrokeshire Coast National Park, Kiln Park offers top-notch Touring facilities and on-site amenities as well as first class activities, superb swimming pools and the very best daytime and evening entertainment. With all this to pick from you will be spoilt for choice! **See also Colour Advertisement.**
Call our UK Central Team: 0871 230 1933 (open 7 days, 9am-9pm) or book on-line (quote: TO_FHG) www.touringholidays.co.uk
• Great for Groups! Just book 5 or more holiday homes for extra benefits and savings.
Visit **www.havengroups.co.uk Or call 0871 230 1911.**

---

symbols

- Holiday Parks & Centres
- Caravans for Hire
- Caravan Sites and Touring Parks
- Camping Sites

Powys

Brecon

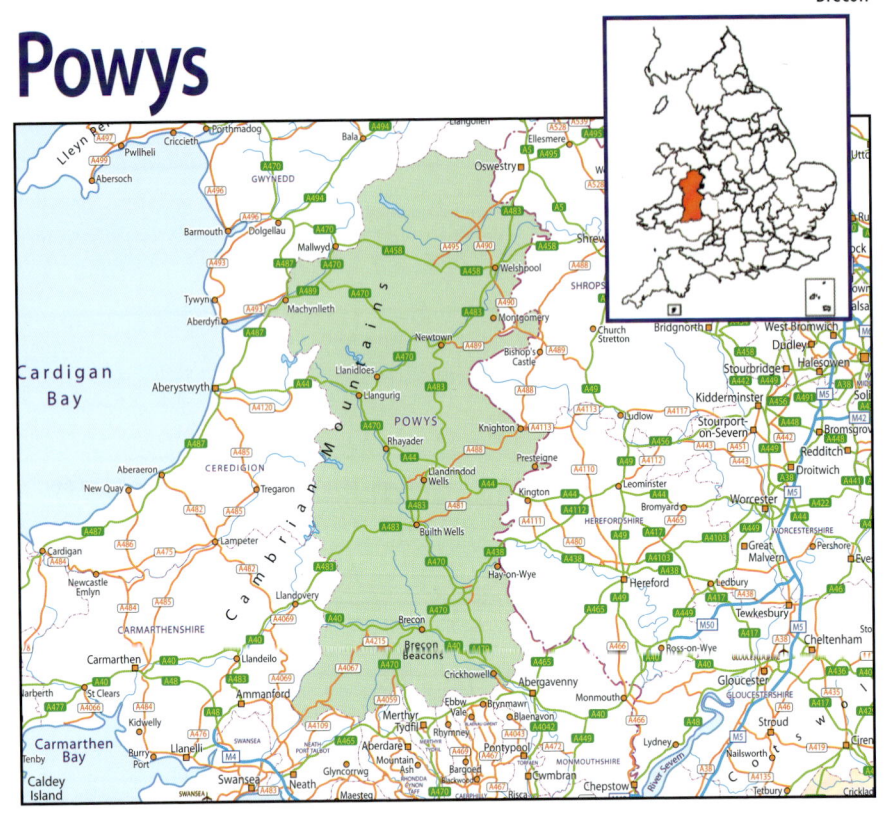

POWYS is situated right on England's doorstep and boasts some of the most spectacular scenery in Europe. Ideal for an action packed holiday with fishing, golfing, pony trekking, sailing and canal cruising readily available, and walkers have a choice of everything from riverside trails to mountain hikes. Offa's Dyke Path and Glyndwr's Way pass through the region. Offa's Dyke Path runs for 177 miles through Border country, often following the ancient earthworks, while Glyndwr's Way takes in some of the finest landscape features in Wales on its journey from Knighton to Machynlleth and back to the borders at Welshpool.
There are border towns with Georgian architecture and half-timbered black and white houses to visit, or wander round the wonderful shops in the book town of Hay, famous for its Literary Festival each May. There are Victorian spa towns too, with even the smallest of places holding festivals and events throughout the year.

BRECON. Aberbran Caravan Club Site, Aberbran, Brecon LD3 9NH
Tel: 01874 622424
A small peaceful site on the edge of the Brecon Beacons National Park, with breathtaking views and ample opportunities for walking and birdwatching. Tourers, motorhomes and tents welcome. Open March to October.

Powys
WALES 197
Brecon, Builth Wells, Rhayader, Welshpool

BRECON. Pencelli Castle Caravan & Camping Park, Pencelli, Brecon LD3 7LX
Tel: 01874 665451 • www.pencelli-castle.com
A multi-award winning family-run park in the heart of the Brecon Beacons National Park, ideal for walking, cycling, pony trekking and canoeing, as well as simply relaxing. The historic town of Brecon is 4 miles away. Closed December.

BUILTH WELLS. Fforest Fields Caravan & Camping Park, Hundred House, Builth Wells LD1 5RT
Tel: 01982 570406 • www.fforestfields.co.uk
A secluded 7-acre rural site a few miles from the market town of Builth Wells. It is landscaped with lots of trees to provide shelter and screening, and there is no traffic noise, so a relaxing stay is guaranteed. Open Easter to November.

The Pines Caravan Park

Small, peaceful, family-run park, with views in glorious mid-Wales. Situated on A470 four miles south of Rhayader – a good central position for exploring the Elan and Wye Valleys. A bird watchers' paradise, with many varieties of birds including the Red Kite.

Luxury modern holiday homes for hire and for sale. Fully equipped with shower, flush toilet, hot and cold water, cooker, fridge, microwave, colour TV. Weekly hire terms from £220 per week.

Mid-week bookings accepted. Inn, restaurant and shop adjacent. Pets welcome. Wheelchair accessible caravan available for hire. Please send for brochure. Philip and Sally Tolson.

**Doldowlod,
Llandrindod Wells LD1 6NN
Tel/Fax: 01597 810068**
www.pinescaravanpark.co.uk
email: info@pinescaravanpark.co.uk

WELSHPOOL. Riverbend Caravan Park, Welshpool SY21 0PP
Tel & Fax: 01938 820356 • www.hillandale.co.uk
Touring caravans are welcome at this tranquil park which is located in a curve of the meandering River Banwy, within easy reach of all the attractions of this scenic area. It is more suited to adults and older children. Open all year.

WELSHPOOL. Rhyd Y Groes Touring & Camping Park, Pont Rhyd-y-groes, Marton, Welshpool SY21 8JJ
Tel: 01938 561228 • www.rhyd-y-groes.co.uk
Set in 12 acres of tranquillity and natural beauty, this family-run site is set on the Wales/Shropshire border near the delightful market town of Welshpool. Hardstanding and grassed pitches are available. Open all year.

South Wales

Abergavenny, Blackwood, Gower, Llantwit Major, Monmouth

ABERGAVENNY. Pont Kemys Caravan Park, Chainbridge, Abergavenny NP7 9DS
Tel: 01873 880688 • Fax: 01873 880270 • www.pontkemys.co.uk
Lying adjacent to the River Usk, this family-run park has been popular for many years with caravanners and campers. There is an adults-only area with 20 fully serviced pitches. Open March to October.

BLACKWOOD. Pen Y Fan Caravan Park, Manmoel Road, Oakdale, Blackwood NP12 0HY
Tel: 01495 226636 • Fax: 01495 227778 • www.penyfancaravanpark.co.uk
Providing excellent value for money, this friendly park offers good amenities including an on-site public house serving meals and snacks. All-weather touring pitches have lovely views of the surrounding countryside. Open all year.

GOWER. Nicholaston Farm Caravan & Camping, Nicholaston, Gower, Swansea SA3 2HL
Tel: 01792 371209 • www.nicholastonfarm.co.uk
On a working family farm, this peaceful site provides 23 level hardstanding pitches for motorhomes and caravans; tents are also catered for. There is a cafe on site, and a shop selling delicious farm produce. Open March to October.

LLANTWIT MAJOR. Acorn Camping and Caravanning, Ham Lane South, Llantwit Major CF61 1RP
Tel: 01446 794024 • www.acorncamping.co.uk
In the beautiful Vale of Glamorgan, this friendly site enjoys easy access to all the attractions of Cardiff and South Wales. Children will love the trampoline and adventure play area, and there is a games room and snooker table. Open February to December.

MONMOUTH. Glen Trothy Caravan & Camping, Mitchel Troy, Monmouth NP25 4BD
Tel: 01600 712295 • www.glentrothy.co.uk
A 6½ acre site offering 74 touring pitches (all with electric hook-ups) and two fields for tents. Amenities are good, and there is a well equipped children's play area. Open March to October.

🚐	Electric hook-ups available	♿	Facilities for disabled visitors
/⊓\	Children's play area	🐕	Pets welcome
🧺	Laundry facilities	🛒	Shop on site
🍷	Licensed bar on site	W	Wifi access available

South Wales
Merthyr Tydfil

WALES 199

GRAWEN
Caravan and Camping Park, Grawen Farm, Cwm-Taff, Cefn Coed, Merthyr Tydfil CF48 2HS

Clean modern facilities
* Picturesque surroundings with forest, mountain, reservoir walks from site
* Reservoir trout fishing
* Ideally located for touring, visiting places of historic interest and enjoying scenic views
* Easy access A470 Brecon Beacons road, 1½ miles Cefn Coed, 3½ miles Merthyr Tydfil, 2 miles from A456 (known as the Heads of the Valleys)
* Dogs on leads
* Open April to end October.

Car, tent, two persons from £10-£12.
Caravan, car, two persons from £12-£15.
Electric hook-ups available.

Tel: 01685 723740

e-mail: grawen.touring@virgin.net • www.walescaravanandcamping.com

---

Other specialised holiday guides from FHG

PUBS & INNS OF BRITAIN

COUNTRY HOTELS OF BRITAIN

WEEKEND & SHORT BREAKS IN BRITAIN & IRELAND

THE GOLF GUIDE WHERE TO PLAY, WHERE TO STAY

500 GREAT PLACES TO STAY

SELF-CATERING HOLIDAYS IN BRITAIN

BED & BREAKFAST STOPS IN BRITAIN

PETS WELCOME!

FAMILY BREAKS IN BRITAIN

Published annually: available in all good bookshops or direct from the publisher:
FHG Guides, Abbey Mill Business Centre, Seedhill, Paisley PA1 1TJ
Tel: 0141 887 0428 • Fax: 0141 889 7204
e-mail: admin@fhguides.co.uk • www.holidayguides.com

Looking for Holiday Accommodation?

for details of hundreds of properties throughout the UK, visit our website

www.holidayguides.com

Northern Ireland

Antrim, Ballycastle, Bushmills

Antrim

Six Mile Water Caravan Park

**Lough Road,
Antrim BT41 4DG**

The Six Mile Water Caravan and Camping Park is situated on the beautiful shores of Lough Neagh, an area steeped in history and natural beauty, with many attractions and activities to enjoy. On-site facilities include a modern toilet and shower block, fully equipped laundry room, hard stands with 20 electric hook-up caravan pitches, 24 tent pitches and visitor information services. There is also a TV lounge, games room and reception.
The park's central location, coupled with its close proximity to the ports of Larne and Belfast, make it an ideal base for touring not only the Borough of Antrim, but all of Northern Ireland. The park accommodates touring caravans, motor caravans and tents.

**Tel: 028 9446 4963
e-mail: sixmilewater@antrim.gov.uk
www.antrim.gov.uk/caravanpark**

NITB ★★★★★

Open from March to October.

BALLYCASTLE. Watertop Farm, 188 Cushendall Road, Ballycastle BT54 6RN
Tel: 028 2076 2576 • Fax: 028 2076 2175 • www.watertopfarm.co.uk
Children will love a holiday at this friendly farm, where the fun is guaranteed. Open all year round. 14 touring pitches. 4 tent pitches. Caravans, motorhomes and tents welcome.

BUSHMILLS. Ballyness Caravan Park, 40 Castlecatt Road, Bushmills BT57 8TN
Tel: 028 2073 2393 • Fax: 028 2073 2713 • www.ballynesscaravanpark.com
Multi-award winning park set in Northern Ireland's breathtaking Ballyness countryside. Dogs welcome. Open from March to November. 46 touring pitches. 6 tent pitches. Caravans, motorhomes and tents welcome.

Co. Down

Ballywalter, Hillsborough, Kilkeel, Killyleagh, Newcastle

BALLYWALTER. Sandycove Holiday Park, 191 Whitechurch Road, Ballywalter BT22 2JZ
Tel: 07801 228814 • Fax: 028 4275 8379
Excellent facilities including a tennis court and direct access to beach. Ideal for day trips to Newtownards and Bangor. Open from March to November. No tents. 40 touring pitches. Caravans and motorhomes welcome.

HILLSBOROUGH. Lakeside View, 71 Magheraconluce Road, Annahilt, Hillsborough BT26 6PR
Tel: 028 92 682098
Idyllic getaway situated near Lough Aghery Lake where visitors can enjoy watching summer water sports and the surrounding natural wildlife. Open from March to October. 25 touring pitches. 15 tent pitches. Caravans, motorhomes and tents welcome.

KILKEEL. Cranfield Caravan Park, 123 Cranfield Road, Kilkeel BT34 4LJ
Tel: 028 417 62572 • Fax: 028 417 69642 • www.cranfieldcaravanpark.co.uk
Enjoy the glorious sea views at this family-run park situated on the most southerly point of Northern Ireland. High standard facilities and direct access to the beach. Open from March to October. 45 touring pitches. Caravans, motorhomes and tents welcome.

KILLYLEAGH. Delamont Country Park, Downpatrick Road, Killyleagh BT30 9TZ
Tel: 028 4482 1833 • www.delamontcountrypark.com
Located close to the beautiful Strangford Lough, an ideal location to get away from it all. Children will love the miniature railway. Open all year round. 60 touring pitches. Caravans, motorhomes and tents welcome.

NEWCASTLE. Murlough Cottage Caravan Park, 180-182 Dundrum Road, Newcastle BT33 0LN
Tel: 028 437 23184 • Fax: 028 437 26436 • www.murloughcottage.com
With an outstanding selection of activities and facilities, this site makes a fun yet relaxing base from which to explore the area. Ideal for all the family. Open all year round. 25 touring pitches. Caravans and motorhomes welcome.

NEWCASTLE. Sunnyholme Caravan Park, 33 Caslewellan Road, Newcastle BT33 0JY
Tel: 028 437 22739
Charming park situated just on the border of the town. Touring guests can expect top of the range facilities for a relaxing and peaceful holiday. Open from March-November. 20 touring pitches. Caravans, motorhomes and tents welcome.

🚐	Electric hook-ups available
♿	Facilities for disabled visitors
/Ⅱ\	Children's play area
🐕	Pets welcome
📻	Laundry facilities
🧺	Shop on site
🍷	Licensed bar on site
W	Wifi access available

Enniskillen, Kesh
Fermanagh

ENNISKILLEN. Blaney Caravan Park, Blaney, Enniskillen BT93 7ER
Tel: 028 6864 1634 • www.blaneycaravanpark.com/
Beautiful fishing location, central for a number of rural activities in and around this delightful area. Open all year round. 20 touring pitches. 10 tent pitches. Caravans, motorhomes and tents welcome.

KESH. Loaneden Caravan Park, Muckross Bay, Kesh BT93 1TZ
Tel: 028 68 631603
Relax with the family on Lower Lough Erne. With modern facilities and numerous attractions including superb countryside. Waterskiing/wakeboarding, jet skiing and banana boating nearby. Open from March to November.

Londonderry

Coleraine, Portstewart

COLERAINE. Tullans Park Caravan Park, 46 Newmills Road, Coleraine BT52 2JB
Tel: 028 7034 2309
A working farm where visitors can watch activities such as sheep shearing and see delightful new lambs in Spring. Portrush and Portstewart are just a short distance from the site. Open from March to September. 35 touring pitches. 5 tent pitches. Caravans, motorhomes and tents welcome

COLERAINE. Castlerock Holiday Park, 24 Sea Road Castlerock, Coleraine BT51 4TN
Tel: 028 7084 8381 • Fax: 028 70848381
Set on Northern Ireland's celebrated Causeway Coast, with a delightful beach nearby and great facilities including golf and a children's play park. Open from March to October. Touring pitches. Caravans and motorhomes welcome.

PORTSTEWART. Millfield Holiday Village, 80 Mill Road, Portstewart BT55 7SW
Tel: 028 70 833308 • Fax: 028 70 833308
Modern park offering unparalleled cliff-top views. Promenade, beach and local shops/restaurants nearby. Open from March to October. 16 touring pitches. Caravans and motorhomes welcome.

Please note

All the information in this book is given in good faith in the belief that it is correct. However, the publishers cannot guarantee the facts given in these pages, neither are they responsible for changes in policy, ownership or terms that may take place after the date of going to press. Readers should always satisfy themselves that the facilities they require are available and that the terms, if quoted, still apply.

Republic of Ireland

Kerry

"Where relaxing comes as naturally as the surrounding beauty"

West's Caravan Park
Killarney Road, Killorglin, Ring of Kerry, SW Ireland
Tel: 00 353 66 9761240

Mobile Homes for hire on family-run park situated on banks of River Laune overlooking Ireland's highest mountain. Ideal touring centre for Ring of Kerry, Dingle Peninsula, Cork, Blarney Stone, Killarney National Park and Tralee.

Ferry and mobile home price available.

Pool table, tennis, table-tennis, laundry. Town one mile.

Open Easter to end October

e-mail: enquiries@westcaravans.com

Creveen Lodge — *Immaculately run small hill farm overlooking Kenmare Bay in a striking area of County Kerry.* Reception is found at the Lodge, which also offers guests a comfortable sitting room, while a separate block has well-equipped and immaculately maintained toilets and showers, plus a communal room with a large fridge, freezer and ironing facilities. The park is carefully tended, with bins and picnic tables informally placed, plus a children's play area with slides and swings.

There are 20 pitches in total, 16 for tents and 4 for caravans, with an area of hardstanding for motor caravans. Electrical connections are available. Fishing, bicycle hire, water sports and horse riding available nearby. SAE please, for replies.

Mrs M. Moriarty, Creveen Lodge, Healy Pass Road, Lauragh
00 35364 83131 • 00 353 64 66 83131 from June 2009
e-mail: info@creveenlodge.com • www.creveenlodge.com

MUSEUM OF LONDON DOCKLANDS
No1 Warehouse, West India Quay, London E14 4AL
Tel: 0870 444 3855 • e-mail: info@museumoflondon.org.uk
www.museumoflondon.org.uk

FHG · K·U·P·E·R·A·R·D · READERS' OFFER 2009

This voucher entitles the bearer to TWO full price adult tickets for the price of ONE on presentation at the Museum of London Docklands admission desk. A max. of one person goes free per voucher. Offer valid until 31 Dec. 2009. Only one voucher per transaction. Non-transferable and non-exchangeable. No cash alternative. Subject to availability. Tickets allow unlimited entry for one year. Children enter free as standard all year round.

NOT TO BE USED IN CONJUNCTION WITH ANY OTHER OFFER

LEIGHTON BUZZARD RAILWAY
Page's Park Station, Billington Road,
Leighton Buzzard, Bedfordshire LU7 4TN
Tel: 01525 373888
e-mail: station@lbngrs.org.uk
www.buzzrail.co.uk

FHG · K·U·P·E·R·A·R·D · READERS' OFFER 2009

One FREE adult/child with full-fare adult ticket
Valid 15/3/2009 - 8/11/2009

NOT TO BE USED IN CONJUNCTION WITH ANY OTHER OFFER

BUCKINGHAMSHIRE RAILWAY CENTRE
Quainton Road Station, Quainton,
Aylesbury HP22 4BY
Tel & Fax: 01296 655720
e-mail: bucksrailcentre@btconnect.com
www.bucksrailcentre.org

FHG · K·U·P·E·R·A·R·D · READERS' OFFER 2009

One child FREE with each full-paying adult
Not valid for Special Events

NOT TO BE USED IN CONJUNCTION WITH ANY OTHER OFFER

BEKONSCOT MODEL VILLAGE & RAILWAY
Warwick Road, Beaconsfield,
Buckinghamshire HP9 2PL
Tel: 01494 672919
e-mail: info@bekonscot.co.uk
www.bekonscot.com

FHG · K·U·P·E·R·A·R·D · READERS' OFFER 2009

One child FREE when accompanied by full-paying adult
Valid February to October 2009

NOT TO BE USED IN CONJUNCTION WITH ANY OTHER OFFER

From Roman settlement to Dockland's regeneration, unlock the history of London's river, port and people in this historic West India Quay warehouse. Discover a wealth of objects, from whalebones to WWII gas masks, in state-of-the-art galleries, including Mudlarks, an interactive area for children; Sailortown, an atmospheric re-creation of 19thC riverside Wapping; and London, Sugar & Slavery, which reveals the city's involvement in the transatlantic slave trade.	**Open:** daily 10am-6pm. Closed 24-26 December. **Directions:** 2 minutes' walk from West India Quay. Nearest Tube Canary Wharf.

FHG GUIDES, ABBEY MILL BUSINESS CENTRE, PAISLEY PA1 1TJ • www.holidayguides.com

A 70-minute journey into the lost world of the English narrow gauge light railway. Features historic steam locomotives from many countries. **PETS MUST BE KEPT UNDER CONTROL AND NOT ALLOWED ON TRACKS**	**Open:** Sundays and Bank Holiday weekends 22 March to 25 October. Additional days in summer. **Directions:** on south side of Leighton Buzzard. Follow brown signs from town centre or A505/A4146 bypass.

FHG GUIDES, ABBEY MILL BUSINESS CENTRE, PAISLEY PA1 1TJ • www.holidayguides.com

A working steam railway centre. Steam train rides, miniature railway rides, large collection of historic preserved steam locomotives, carriages and wagons.	**Open:** daily April to October 10.30am to 4.30pm. Variable programme - check website or call. **Directions:** off A41 Aylesbury to Bicester Road, 6 miles north west of Aylesbury.

FHG GUIDES, ABBEY MILL BUSINESS CENTRE, PAISLEY PA1 1TJ • www.holidayguides.com

Be a giant in a magical miniature world of make-believe depicting rural England in the 1930s. "A little piece of history that is forever England."	**Open:** 10am-5pm daily mid February to end October. **Directions:** Junction 16 M25, Junction 2 M40.

FHG GUIDES, ABBEY MILL BUSINESS CENTRE, PAISLEY PA1 1TJ • www.holidayguides.com

207

FHG
·K·U·P·E·R·A·R·D·
READERS' OFFER 2009

THE RAPTOR FOUNDATION
The Heath, St Ives Road,
Woodhurst, Huntingdon, Cambs PE28 3BT
Tel: 01487 741140 • Fax: 01487 841140
e-mail: heleowl@aol.com
www.raptorfoundation.org.uk

TWO for the price of ONE
Valid until end 2009 (not Bank Holidays)

NOT TO BE USED IN CONJUNCTION WITH ANY OTHER OFFER

FHG
·K·U·P·E·R·A·R·D·
READERS' OFFER 2009

FLAG FEN ARCHAEOLOGY PARK
The Droveway, Northey Road,
Peterborough, Cambs PE6 7QJ
Tel: 0844 414 0646 • Fax: 0844 414 0647
e-mail: info@flagfen.org
www.flagfen.org

20% off normal entry price. Valid 1st March-31st Oct 2009
Not for special events or ticketed events.

NOT TO BE USED IN CONJUNCTION WITH ANY OTHER OFFER

FHG
·K·U·P·E·R·A·R·D·
READERS' OFFER 2009

ANSON ENGINE MUSEUM
Anson Road, Poynton,
Cheshire SK12 1TD
Tel: 01625 874426
e-mail: enquiry@enginemuseum.org
www.enginemuseum.org

Saturdays - 2 for 1 entry (when one of equal or greater
value is purchased). Valid 12 April-30 Sept 2009

NOT TO BE USED IN CONJUNCTION WITH ANY OTHER OFFER

FHG
·K·U·P·E·R·A·R·D·
READERS' OFFER 2009

BRITISH CYCLING MUSEUM
The Old Station,
Camelford,
Cornwall PL32 9TZ
Tel: 01840 212811
www.camelford.org

Child FREE with one paying adult
Valid during 2009

NOT TO BE USED IN CONJUNCTION WITH ANY OTHER OFFER

Birds of Prey Centre offering audience participation in flying displays which are held 3 times daily. Tours, picnic area, gift shop, tearoom, craft shop.	**Open:** 10am-5pm all year except Christmas and New Year. **Directions:** follow brown tourist signs from B1040.

FHG GUIDES, ABBEY MILL BUSINESS CENTRE, PAISLEY PA1 1TJ • www.holidayguides.com

Home to a unique ancient wooden monument, a km long causeway and platform, perfectly preserved in the wetland. Originally built from 60,000 upright timbers and 250,000 horizontal timbers. Also visit roundhouses, fields and museum.	**Open:** March to October 10am to 5pm Tuesday to Sunday. Last entry 4pm. **Directions:** by bicycle or on foot from the Green Wheel. By car from J5 of A1139, Peterborough ring road, then follow the brown signs.

FHG GUIDES, ABBEY MILL BUSINESS CENTRE, PAISLEY PA1 1TJ • www.holidayguides.com

As seen on TV, this multi award-winning attraction has a great deal to offer visitors. It houses the largest collection of engines in Europe, local history area, craft centre (bodging and smithy work), with changing exhibitions throughout the season.	**Open:** Easter Sunday until end October, Friday to Sunday and Bank Holidays, 10am to 5pm. **Directions:** approx 7 miles from J1 M60 and 9 miles J3 M60. Follow brown tourist signs from Poynton traffic lights.

FHG GUIDES, ABBEY MILL BUSINESS CENTRE, PAISLEY PA1 1TJ • www.holidayguides.com

The nation's foremost and largest museum of historic cycling, with over 400 examples of cycles, and 1000s of items of cycling memorabilia.	**Open:** all year, Sunday to Thursday, 10am to 5pm. **Directions:** one mile north of Camelford, B3266/B3314 crossroads.

FHG GUIDES, ABBEY MILL BUSINESS CENTRE, PAISLEY PA1 1TJ • www.holidayguides.com

FHG
·K·U·P·E·R·A·R·D·
READERS' OFFER 2009

CHINA CLAY COUNTRY PARK
Wheal Martyn, Carthew, St Austell,
Cornwall PL26 8XG
Tel & Fax: 01726 850362
e-mail: info@chinaclaycountry.co.uk
www.chinaclaycountry.co.uk

*TWO for ONE adult entry, saving £7.50.
One voucher per person. Valid until July 2009.*

NOT TO BE USED IN CONJUNCTION WITH ANY OTHER OFFER

FHG
·K·U·P·E·R·A·R·D·
READERS' OFFER 2009

NATIONAL LOBSTER HATCHERY
South Quay, Padstow,
Cornwall PL28 8BL
Tel: 01841 533877 • Fax: 0870 7060299
e-mail: info@nationallobsterhatchery.co.uk
www.nationallobsterhatchery.co.uk

*TWO for the price of ONE
Valid November 2008 to March 2009*

NOT TO BE USED IN CONJUNCTION WITH ANY OTHER OFFER

FHG
·K·U·P·E·R·A·R·D·
READERS' OFFER 2009

NATIONAL SEAL SANCTUARY
Gweek, Helston,
Cornwall TR12 6UG
Tel: 01326 221361
e-mail: seals@sealsanctuary.co.uk
www.sealsanctuary.co.uk

*TWO for ONE - on purchase of another ticket of
equal or greater value. Valid until December 2009.*

NOT TO BE USED IN CONJUNCTION WITH ANY OTHER OFFER

FHG
·K·U·P·E·R·A·R·D·
READERS' OFFER 2009

PORFELL WILDLIFE PARK & SANCTUARY
Trecangate, Near Llanreath,
Liskeard,
Cornwall PL14 4RE
Tel: 01503 220211
www.porfellanimalland.co.uk

*One child FREE with one paying adult per voucher
Valid 1st April-31st October 2009.*

NOT TO BE USED IN CONJUNCTION WITH ANY OTHER OFFER

The Country Park covers 26 acres and includes woodland and historic trails, picnic sites, children's adventure trail and award-winning cycle trail. Remains of a Victorian clay works complete with the largest working water wheel in Cornwall. Shop, cafe, exhibitions, museum.

Open: 10am-6pm daily (closed Christmas Day)

Directions: two miles north of St Austell on the B3274. Follow brown tourist signs. 5 minutes from Eden Project.

FHG GUIDES, ABBEY MILL BUSINESS CENTRE, PAISLEY PA1 1TJ • www.holidayguides.com

---

A unique conservation programme - see our fisheries at work and find out everything there is to know about the European lobster.

Open: from 10am seven days a week.

Directions: right on the water's edge, in the South Quay car park, right opposite Rick Stein's fish & chip shop.

FHG GUIDES, ABBEY MILL BUSINESS CENTRE, PAISLEY PA1 1TJ • www.holidayguides.com

---

Britain's leading grey seal rescue centre

Open: daily (except Christmas Day) from 10am

Directions: from A30 follow signs to Helston, then brown tourist signs to Seal Sanctuary.

FHG GUIDES, ABBEY MILL BUSINESS CENTRE, PAISLEY PA1 1TJ • www.holidayguides.com

---

Porfell is home to wild and exotic animals from around the world. Idyllically situated amongst the rolling hills of south east Cornwall. It has a beautiful woodland with raised boardwalks over marsh areas, and a children's farm.

Open: 10am-6pm daily from April 1st to October 31st.

Directions: A38 Liskeard, A390 for St Austell. Turn off at East Taphouse on to B3359, follow brown tourist signs.

FHG GUIDES, ABBEY MILL BUSINESS CENTRE, PAISLEY PA1 1TJ • www.holidayguides.com

FHG READERS' OFFER 2009

TAMAR VALLEY DONKEY PARK
St Ann's Chapel, Gunnislake,
Cornwall PL18 9HW
Tel: 01822 834072
e-mail: info@donkeypark.com
www.donkeypark.com

50p OFF per person, up to 6 persons
Valid from Easter until end October 2009

NOT TO BE USED IN CONJUNCTION WITH ANY OTHER OFFER

FHG READERS' OFFER 2009

CARS OF THE STARS MOTOR MUSEUM
Standish Street, Keswick,
Cumbria CA12 5HH
Tel: 017687 73757
e-mail: cotsmm@aol.com
www.carsofthestars.com

One child free with two paying adults
Valid during 2009

NOT TO BE USED IN CONJUNCTION WITH ANY OTHER OFFER

FHG READERS' OFFER 2009

THE BEACON
West Strand, Whitehaven,
Cumbria CA28 7LY
Tel: 01946 592302 • Fax: 01946 598150
e-mail: thebeacon@copelandbc.gov.uk
www.thebeacon-whitehaven.co.uk

One FREE adult/concesssion when accompanied by one full paying
adult/concession. Under 16s free. Valid from Oct 08 to end 09.
Not valid for special events. Day tickets only.

NOT TO BE USED IN CONJUNCTION WITH ANY OTHER OFFER

FHG READERS' OFFER 2009

CRICH TRAMWAY VILLAGE
Crich, Matlock
Derbyshire DE4 5DP
Tel: 01773 854321 • Fax: 01773 854320
e-mail: enquiry@tramway.co.uk
www.tramway.co.uk

One child FREE with every full-paying adult
Valid during 2009

NOT TO BE USED IN CONJUNCTION WITH ANY OTHER OFFER

Cornwall's only Donkey Sanctuary set in 14 acres overlooking the beautiful Tamar Valley. Donkey rides, goat hill, children's playgrounds, cafe and picnic area. New all-weather play barn.

Open: Easter to end Oct: daily 10am to 5pm. Nov to March: weekends and all school holidays 10.30am to 4.30pm

Directions: just off A390 between Callington and Gunnislake at St Ann's Chapel.

FHG GUIDES, ABBEY MILL BUSINESS CENTRE, PAISLEY PA1 1TJ • www.holidayguides.com

---

A collection of cars from film and TV, including Chitty Chitty Bang Bang, James Bond's Aston Martin, Del Boy's van, Fab1 and many more.

PETS MUST BE KEPT ON LEAD

Open: daily 10am-5pm. Open February half term, 1st April to end November, also weekends in December.

Directions: in centre of Keswick close to car park.

FHG GUIDES, ABBEY MILL BUSINESS CENTRE, PAISLEY PA1 1TJ • www.holidayguides.com

---

The Beacon is the Copeland area's interactive museum, tracing the area's rich history, from as far back as prehistoric times to the modern day. Enjoy panoramic views of the Georgian town and harbour from the 4th floor viewing gallery. Art gallery, gift shop, restaurant. Fully accessible.

Open: open all year (excl. 24-26 Dec) Tuesday to Sunday, plus Monday Bank Holidays.

Directions: enter Whitehaven from north or south on A595. Follow the town centre and brown museum signs; located on harbourside.

FHG GUIDES, ABBEY MILL BUSINESS CENTRE, PAISLEY PA1 1TJ • www.holidayguides.com

---

A superb family day out in the atmosphere of a bygone era. Explore the recreated period street and fascinating exhibitions. Unlimited tram rides are free with entry. Play areas, woodland walk and sculpture trail, shops, tea rooms, pub, restaurant and lots more.

Open: daily April to October 10 am to 5.30pm.

Directions: eight miles from M1 Junction 28, follow brown and white signs for "Tramway Museum".

FHG GUIDES, ABBEY MILL BUSINESS CENTRE, PAISLEY PA1 1TJ • www.holidayguides.com

FHG KUPERARD READERS' OFFER 2009

POOLE'S CAVERN & BUXTON COUNTRY PARK
Green Lane, Buxton,
Derbyshire Sk17 9DH
Tel: 01298 26978 • Fax: 01298 73563
e-mail: info@poolescavern.co.uk
www.poolescavern.co.uk

*20% off standard entry price to Poole's Cavern.
Not valid for special events. Valid during 2009.*

NOT TO BE USED IN CONJUNCTION WITH ANY OTHER OFFER

FHG KUPERARD READERS' OFFER 2009

WOODLANDS
Blackawton, Dartmouth,
Devon TQ9 7DQ
Tel: 01803 712598 • Fax: 01803 712680
e-mail: fun@woodlandspark.com
www.woodlandspark.com

*12% discount off individual entry price for up to 4
persons. No photocopies. Valid 4/4/09 – 1/11/09*

NOT TO BE USED IN CONJUNCTION WITH ANY OTHER OFFER

FHG KUPERARD READERS' OFFER 2009

DEVONSHIRE COLLECTION OF PERIOD COSTUME
Totnes Costume Museum,
Bogan House, 43 High Street,
Totnes,
Devon TQ9 5NP

*FREE child with a paying adult with voucher
Valid from Spring Bank Holiday to end of Sept 2009*

NOT TO BE USED IN CONJUNCTION WITH ANY OTHER OFFER

FHG KUPERARD READERS' OFFER 2009

TWEDDLE CHILDREN'S ANIMAL FARM
Fillpoke Lane, Blackhall Colliery,
Co. Durham TS27 4BT
Tel: 0191 586 3311
e-mail: info@tweddle-farm.co.uk
www.tweddle-farm.co.uk

*FREE bag of animal food to every paying customer.
Valid until end 2009*

NOT TO BE USED IN CONJUNCTION WITH ANY OTHER OFFER

A spectacular natural cavern set in beautiful woodlands. Explore the crystal-lined chambers with expert guides, deep into the Peak District underground world. Climb to Solomon's Temple viewpoint at the summit of Grin Low.	**Open:** daily March to November 9.30am to 5pm; winter weekends. **Directions:** one mile from Buxton town centre, off A515.

FHG GUIDES, ABBEY MILL BUSINESS CENTRE, PAISLEY PA1 1TJ • www.holidayguides.com

All weather fun - guaranteed! Unique combination of indoor/outdoor attractions. 3 Watercoasters, Toboggan Run, Arctic Gliders, boats, 15 Playzones for all ages. Biggest indoor venture zone in UK with 5 floors of play and rides. Big Fun Farm with U-drive Tractor ride, new Sea Dragon Swing Ship, Falconry Centre.	**Open:** mid-March to November open daily at 9.30am. Winter: open weekends and local school holidays. **Directions:** 5 miles from Dartmouth on A3122. Follow brown tourist signs from A38.

FHG GUIDES, ABBEY MILL BUSINESS CENTRE, PAISLEY PA1 1TJ • www.holidayguides.com

Themed exhibition, changed annually, based in a Tudor house. Collection contains items of dress for women, men and children from 17th century to 1990s, from high fashion to everyday wear.	**Open:** Open from Spring Bank Holiday to end September. 11am to 5pm Tuesday to Friday. **Directions:** centre of town, opposite Market Square. Mini bus up High Street stops outside.

FHG GUIDES, ABBEY MILL BUSINESS CENTRE, PAISLEY PA1 1TJ • www.holidayguides.com

Children's farm and petting centre with lots of farm animals and exotic animals too, including camels, otters, monkeys, meerkats and lots more. Lots of hands-on, with bottle feeding, reptile handling and bunny cuddling happening daily.	**Open:** March to Oct: 10am-5pm daily; Nov to Feb 10am to 4pm daily. Closed Christmas, Boxing Day and New Year's Day. **Directions:** A181 from A19, head towards coast; signposted from there.

FHG GUIDES, ABBEY MILL BUSINESS CENTRE, PAISLEY PA1 1TJ • www.holidayguides.com

FHG READERS' OFFER 2009

BARLEYLANDS FARM & CRAFT VILLAGE
Barleylands Road, Billericay,
Essex CM11 2UD
Tel: 01268 290229 • Fax: 01268 290222
e-mail: info@barleylands.co.uk
www.barleylands.co.uk

FREE entry for one child with each full paying adult
Valid during 2009

NOT TO BE USED IN CONJUNCTION WITH ANY OTHER OFFER

FHG READERS' OFFER 2009

AVON VALLEY RAILWAY
Bitton Station, Bath Road, Bitton,
Bristol BS30 6HD
Tel: 0117 932 5538
e-mail: info@avonvalleyrailway.org
www.avonvalleyrailway.org

One FREE child with every fare-paying adult
Valid May - Oct 2009 (not 'Day Out with Thomas' events)

NOT TO BE USED IN CONJUNCTION WITH ANY OTHER OFFER

FHG READERS' OFFER 2009

CIDER MUSEUM & KING OFFA DISTILLERY
21 Ryelands Street, Hereford,
Herefordshire HR4 0LW
Tel: 01432 354207
e-mail: enquiries@cidermuseum.co.uk
www.cidermuseum.co.uk

TWO for the price of ONE admission
Valid to end December 2009

NOT TO BE USED IN CONJUNCTION WITH ANY OTHER OFFER

FHG READERS' OFFER 2009

MUSEUM OF KENT LIFE
Lock Lane, Sandling, Maidstone,
Kent ME14 3AU
Tel: 01622 763936 • Fax: 01622 662024
e-mail: enquiries@museum-kentlife.co.uk
www.museum-kentlife.co.uk

One child FREE with one full-paying adult
Valid during 2009

NOT TO BE USED IN CONJUNCTION WITH ANY OTHER OFFER

Set in over 700 acres of unspoilt Essex countryside, this former working farm is one of the county's most popular tourist attractions. The spectacular craft village and educational farm provide the perfect setting for a great day out.

Open: 7 days a week from 10am-5pm all year except 25/26 December and 1st January

Directions: follow brown tourist signs from A127 and A12.

The Avon Valley Railway offers a whole new experience for some, and a nostalgic memory for others.

PETS MUST BE KEPT ON LEADS AND OFF TRAIN SEATS

Open: Steam trains operate every Sunday, Easter to October, plus Bank Holidays and Christmas.

Directions: on the A431 midway between Bristol and Bath at Bitton.

Learn how traditional cider and perry was made, how the fruit was harvested, milled, pressed and bottled. Walk through original champagne cider cellars, and view 18th century lead crystal cider glasses.

Open: April to October: 10am-5pm Tues-Sat. November to March 11am-3pm Tues-Sat.

Directions: off A438 Hereford to Brecon road, near Sainsbury's supermarket.

Kent's award-winning open air museum is home to a collection of historic buildings which house interactive exhibitions on life over the last 150 years.

Open: seven days a week, February to start November, 10am to 5pm.

Directions: Junction 6 off M20, follow signs to Aylesford.

FHG READERS' OFFER 2009

CHISLEHURST CAVES
Old Hill, Chislehurst,
Kent BR7 5NL
Tel: 020 8467 3264 • Fax: 020 8295 0407
e-mail: info@chislehurstcaves.co.uk
www.chislehurstcaves.co.uk

FREE child entry with full paying adult.
Valid until end 2009 (not Bank Holiday weekends)

NOT TO BE USED IN CONJUNCTION WITH ANY OTHER OFFER

FHG READERS' OFFER 2009

SKEGNESS NATURELAND SEAL SANCTUARY
North Parade, Skegness,
Lincolnshire PE25 1DB
Tel: 01754 764345
e-mail: info@skegnessnatureland.co.uk
www.skegnessnatureland.co.uk

Natureland Seal Sanctuary

Free entry for one child when accompanied by
full-paying adult. Valid during 2009.

NOT TO BE USED IN CONJUNCTION WITH ANY OTHER OFFER

FHG READERS' OFFER 2009

BRESSINGHAM STEAM & GARDENS
Low Road, Bressingham, Diss,
Norfolk IP22 2AB
Tel: 01379 686900 • Fax: 01379 686907
e-mail: info@bressingham.co.uk
www.bressingham.co.uk

One child FREE with two paying adults
Valid Easter to October 2009 (ref 8175)

NOT TO BE USED IN CONJUNCTION WITH ANY OTHER OFFER

FHG READERS' OFFER 2009

NEWARK AIR MUSEUM
The Airfield, Winthorpe, Newark,
Nottinghamshire NG24 2NY
Tel: 01636 707170
e-mail: newarkair@onetel.com
www.newarkairmuseum.org

Party rate discount for every voucher (50p per person
off normal admission). Valid during 2009.

NOT TO BE USED IN CONJUNCTION WITH ANY OTHER OFFER

Miles of mystery and history beneath your feet! Grab a lantern and get ready for an amazing underground adventure. Your whole family can travel back in time as you explore this labyrinth of dark mysterious passageways. See the caves, church, Druid altar and more.

Open: Wed to Sun from 10am; last tour 4pm. Open daily during local school and Bank holidays (except Christmas). Entrance by guided tour only.

Directions: A222 between A20 and A21; at Chislehurst Station turn into Station Approach; turn right at end, then right again into Caveside Close.

FHG GUIDES, ABBEY MILL BUSINESS CENTRE, PAISLEY PA1 1TJ • www.holidayguides.com

---

Well known for rescuing and rehabilitating orphaned and injured seal pups found washed ashore on Lincolnshire beaches. Also: penguins, aquarium, pets' corner, reptiles, Floral Palace (tropical birds and butterflies etc).

Open: daily from 10am. Closed Christmas/Boxing/New Year's Days.

Directions: at the north end of Skegness seafront.

FHG GUIDES, ABBEY MILL BUSINESS CENTRE, PAISLEY PA1 1TJ • www.holidayguides.com

---

Explore one of Europe's leading steam collections, take a ride over 5 miles of narrow gauge steam railway, wander through beautiful gardens, or visit the only official 'Dads' Army' exhibition. Two restaurants and garden centre.

Open: Easter to October 10.30am - 5pm

Directions: 2½ miles west of Diss and 14 miles east of Thetford on the A1066; follow brown tourist signs.

FHG GUIDES, ABBEY MILL BUSINESS CENTRE, PAISLEY PA1 1TJ • www.holidayguides.com

---

A collection of 70 aircraft and cockpit sections from across the history of aviation. Extensive aero engine and artefact displays.

Open: daily from 10am (closed Christmas period and New Year's Day).

Directions: follow brown and white signs from A1, A46, A17 and A1133.

FHG GUIDES, ABBEY MILL BUSINESS CENTRE, PAISLEY PA1 1TJ • www.holidayguides.com

FHG · **KUPERARD**
READERS' OFFER 2009

CITY OF CAVES
Drury Walk, Upper Level,
Broadmarsh Shopping Centre,
Nottingham NG1 7LS
Tel: 0015 952 0555
www.cityofcaves.co.uk

one FREE child with every full paying adult.
Valid until August 31st 2009

NOT TO BE USED IN CONJUNCTION WITH ANY OTHER OFFER

FHG · **KUPERARD**
READERS' OFFER 2009

GALLERIES OF JUSTICE
Shire Hall, High Pavement,
Nottingham NG1 1HN
Tel: 0115 952 05555
e-mail: info@nccl.org.uk
www.galleriesofjustice.org.uk

one FREE child for every full paying adult.
Valid until August 31 2009

NOT TO BE USED IN CONJUNCTION WITH ANY OTHER OFFER

FHG · **KUPERARD**
READERS' OFFER 2009

FERRY FARM PARK
Ferry Farm, Boat Lane, Hoveringham
Nottinghamshire NG14 7JP
Tel & Fax: 0115 966 4512
e-mail: enquiries@ferryfarm.co.uk
www.ferryfarm.co.uk

20% OFF admission price.
Valid during 2009

NOT TO BE USED IN CONJUNCTION WITH ANY OTHER OFFER

FHG · **KUPERARD**
READERS' OFFER 2009

THE TALES OF ROBIN HOOD
30 - 38 Maid Marian Way,
Nottingham NG1 6GF
Tel: 0115 9483284 • Fax: 0115 9501536
e-mail: robinhoodcentre@mail.com
www.robinhood.uk.com

One FREE child with full paying adult per voucher
Valid from January to December 2009

NOT TO BE USED IN CONJUNCTION WITH ANY OTHER OFFER

Enter and explore these ancient caves and see how the people of Nottingham have used them for over 750 years.	**Open:** daily 10.30-5pm (tours every half hour). **Directions:** in Nottingham city centre on the upper level of Broadmarsh Shopping Centre.

FHG GUIDES, ABBEY MILL BUSINESS CENTRE, PAISLEY PA1 1TJ • www.holidayguides.com

Let us welcome you to Nottingham's notorious county gaol, and once behind bars, our resident ghosts won't want you to leave!	**Open:** peak season - daily 10am-5pm; off peak Tues - Sun 10am-4pm. Tours every half hour. **Directions:** in the heart of the historic Lace Market district, just 10 minutes' walk from train station.

FHG GUIDES, ABBEY MILL BUSINESS CENTRE, PAISLEY PA1 1TJ • www.holidayguides.com

Family-run farm park set in beautiful countryside next to river. 20-acre site with animal handling, large indoor soft play area, go-karts, trampolines, pedal tractors, swings, slides, zipline and assault course. New Jumicar children's driving activity (small extra charge)	**Open:** daily 10am to 5.30pm April to end September. Closed Mondays except Bank Holidays and during Nottinghamshire school holidays. Please check for winter opening hours. **Directions:** off A612 Nottingham to Southwell road.

FHG GUIDES, ABBEY MILL BUSINESS CENTRE, PAISLEY PA1 1TJ • www.holidayguides.com

Travel back in time with Robin Hood and his merry men on an adventure-packed theme tour, exploring the intriguing and mysterious story of their legendary tales of Medieval England. Enjoy film shows, live performances, adventure rides and even try archery! Are you brave enough to join Robin on his quest for good against evil?	**Open:** 10am-5pm, last admission 4pm. **Directions:** follow the brown and white tourist information signs whilst heading towards the city centre.

FHG GUIDES, ABBEY MILL BUSINESS CENTRE, PAISLEY PA1 1TJ • www.holidayguides.com

FHG READERS' OFFER 2009

FLEET AIR ARM MUSEUM
RNAS Yeovilton, Ilchester,
Somerset BA22 8HT
Tel: 01935 840565
e-mail: enquiries@fleetairarm.com
www.fleetairarm.com

One child FREE with full paying adult
Valid during 2009 except Bank Holidays

NOT TO BE USED IN CONJUNCTION WITH ANY OTHER OFFER

FHG READERS' OFFER 2009

THE HELICOPTER MUSEUM
The Heliport, Locking Moor Road,
Weston-Super-Mare BS24 8PP
Tel: 01934 635227 • Fax: 01934 645230
e-mail: helimuseum@btconnect.com
www.helicoptermuseum.co.uk

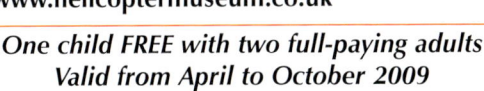

One child FREE with two full-paying adults
Valid from April to October 2009

NOT TO BE USED IN CONJUNCTION WITH ANY OTHER OFFER

FHG READERS' OFFER 2009

EXMOOR FALCONRY & ANIMAL FARM
Allerford, Near Porlock, Minehead,
Somerset TA24 8HJ
Tel: 01643 862816
e-mail: exmoor.falcon@virgin.net
www.exmoorfalconry.co.uk

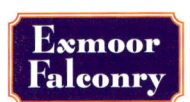

10% off entry to Falconry Centre
Valid during 2009

NOT TO BE USED IN CONJUNCTION WITH ANY OTHER OFFER

FHG READERS' OFFER 2009

EASTON FARM PARK
Pound Corner, Easton, Woodhouse,
Suffolk IP13 0EQ
Tel: 01728 746475
e-mail: info@eastonfarmpark.co.uk
www.eastonfarmpark.co.uk

One FREE child entry with a full paying adult
Only one voucher per group. Valid during 2009.

NOT TO BE USED IN CONJUNCTION WITH ANY OTHER OFFER

Europe's largest naval aviation collection with over 40 aircraft on display, including Concorde 002 and Ark Royal Aircraft Carrier Experience. Situated on an operational naval air station.

Open: open daily April to October 10am-5.30pm; November to March 10am-4.30pm (closed Mon and Tues).

Directions: just off A303/A37 on B3151 at Ilchester. Yeovil rail station 10 miles.

The world's largest helicopter collection - over 70 exhibits, includes two royal helicopters, Russian Gunship and Vietnam veterans plus many award-winning exhibits. Cafe, shop. Flights.

PETS MUST BE KEPT UNDER CONTROL

Open: Wednesday to Sunday 10am to 5.30pm. Daily during school Easter and Summer holidays and Bank Holiday Mondays. November to March: 10am to 4.30pm

Directions: Junction 21 off M5 then follow the propellor signs.

Falconry centre with animals - flying displays, animal handling, feeding and bottle feeding - in 15th century NT farmyard setting on Exmoor. Also falconry and outdoor activities, hawk walks and riding.

Open: 10.30am to 5pm daily

Directions: A39 west of Minehead, turn right at Allerford, half a mile along lane on left.

Family day out down on the farm, with activities for children every half hour (included in entry price). Indoor and outdoor play areas. Riverside cafe, gift shop. For more details visit the website.

Open: 10.30am-6pm daily March to September.

Directions: signposted from A12 in the direction of Framlingham.

FHG READERS' OFFER 2009

THE NATIONAL HORSERACING MUSEUM
99 High Street,
Newmarket,
Suffolk CB8 8JH
Tel: 01638 667333
www.nhrm.co.uk

One FREE adult or concession with on paying full price.
Valid Easter to end October 2009. Museum admission only.

NOT TO BE USED IN CONJUNCTION WITH ANY OTHER OFFER

FHG READERS' OFFER 2009

EARNLEY BUTTERFLIES & GARDENS
133 Almodington Lane, Earnley, Chichester,
West Sussex PO20 7JR
Tel: 01243 512637
e-mail: earnleygardens@msn.com
www.earnleybutterfliesandgardens.co.uk

£1 per person off normal entry prices.
Valid late March to end October 2009.

NOT TO BE USED IN CONJUNCTION WITH ANY OTHER OFFER

FHG READERS' OFFER 2009

HATTON FARM VILLAGE AT HATTON COUNTRY WORLD
Dark Lane, Hatton, Near Warwick,
Warwickshire CV35 8XA
Tel: 01926 843411
e-mail: hatton@hattonworld.com
www.hattonworld.com

Admit one child FREE with one full-paying adult day ticket. Valid during
2009 except Bank Holidays or for entrance to Santa's Grotto promotion.

NOT TO BE USED IN CONJUNCTION WITH ANY OTHER OFFER

FHG READERS' OFFER 2009

FALCONRY UK BIRDS OF PREY CENTRE
Sion Hill Hall, Kirby Wiske
Near Thirsk, North Yorkshire YO7 4GU
Tel: 01845 587522
e-mail: mail@falconrycentre.co.uk
www.falconrycentre.co.uk

TWO for ONE on admission to Centre. Cheapest ticket
free with voucher. Valid 1st March to 31st October.

NOT TO BE USED IN CONJUNCTION WITH ANY OTHER OFFER

Stories of racing, ride the horse simulator, or take a 'behind the scenes' tour of the training grounds and yards.	**Open:** Easter to end October, 7 days a week 11am to 5pm. Last admission 4pm. **Directions:** on the High Street in the centre of Newmarket.

FHG GUIDES, ABBEY MILL BUSINESS CENTRE, PAISLEY PA1 1TJ • www.holidayguides.com

3 attractions in 1. Tropical butterflies, exotic animals of many types in our Noah's Ark Rescue Centre. Theme gardens with a free competition for kids. Rejectamenta - the nostalgia museum.	**Open:** 10am - 6pm daily late March to end October. **Directions:** signposted from A27/A286 junction at Chichester.

FHG GUIDES, ABBEY MILL BUSINESS CENTRE, PAISLEY PA1 1TJ • www.holidayguides.com

Hatton Farm Village offers a wonderful mix of farmyard animals, adventure play, shows, demonstrations, and events, all set in the stunning Warwickshire countryside.	**Open:** daily 10am-5pm (4pm during winter). Closed Christmas Day and Boxing Day. **Directions:** 5 minutes from M40 (J15), A46 towards Coventry, then just off A4177 (follow brown tourist signs).

FHG GUIDES, ABBEY MILL BUSINESS CENTRE, PAISLEY PA1 1TJ • www.holidayguides.com

Birds of prey centre with over 60 birds including owls, hawks, falcons, kites, vultures and eagles. 3 flying displays daily. When possible public welcome to handle birds after each display. No dogs allowed.	**Open:** 1st March to 31st October 10.30am to 5.30pm. Flying displays 11.30am, 1.30pm and 3.30pm daily. **Directions:** on the A167 between Northallerton and the Ripon turn off. Follow brown tourist signs.

FHG GUIDES, ABBEY MILL BUSINESS CENTRE, PAISLEY PA1 1TJ • www.holidayguides.com

FHG READERS' OFFER 2009

YORKSHIRE DALES FALCONRY & WILDLIFE CONSERVATION CENTRE
Crow's Nest, Giggleswick, Near Settle LA2 8AS
Tel: 01729 822832 • Fax: 01729 825160
e-mail: info@falconryandwildlife.com
www.falconryandwildlife.com

One child FREE with two full-paying adults
Valid until end 2009

NOT TO BE USED IN CONJUNCTION WITH ANY OTHER OFFER

FHG READERS' OFFER 2009

WORLD OF JAMES HERRIOT
23 Kirkgate, Thirsk,
North Yorkshire YO7 1PL
Tel: 01845 524234
Fax: 01845 525333
www.worldofjamesherriot.org

Admit TWO for the price of ONE (one voucher per transaction only). Valid until October 2009

NOT TO BE USED IN CONJUNCTION WITH ANY OTHER OFFER

FHG READERS' OFFER 2009

MUSEUM OF RAIL TRAVEL 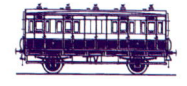
Ingrow Railway Centre, Near Keighley,
West Yorkshire BD21 5AX
Tel: 01535 680425
e-mail: admin@vintagecarriagestrust.org
www.vintagecarriagestrust.org

"ONE for ONE" free admission
Valid during 2009 except during special events (ring to check)

NOT TO BE USED IN CONJUNCTION WITH ANY OTHER OFFER

FHG READERS' OFFER 2009

EUREKA! THE MUSEUM FOR CHILDREN
Discovery Road, Halifax,
West Yorkshire HX1 2NE
Tel: 01422 330069 • Fax: 01422 398490
e-mail: info@eureka.org.uk
www.eureka.org.uk

One FREE child on purchase of full price adult ticket
Valid from 1/10/08 to 31/12/09. Excludes groups.

NOT TO BE USED IN CONJUNCTION WITH ANY OTHER OFFER

All types of birds of prey exhibited here, from owls and kestrels to eagles and vultures. Special flying displays 12 noon, 1.30pm and 3pm. Winter shows 12noon and 1.30pm. Bird handling courses arranged for either half or full days.

GUIDE DOGS ONLY

Open: 10am to 4.30pm summer 10am to 4pm winter

Directions: on main A65 trunk road outside Settle. Follow brown direction signs.

Visit James Herriot's original house recreated as it was in the 1940s. Television sets used in the series 'All Creatures Great and Small'. There is a children's interactive gallery with life-size model farm animals and three rooms dedicated to the history of veterinary medicine.

Open: daily. Easter-Oct 10am-5pm; Nov-Easter 11am to 4pm

Directions: follow signs off A1 or A19 to Thirsk, then A168, off Thirsk market place

---

A fascinating display of railway carriages and a wide range of railway items telling the story of rail travel over the years.

ALL PETS MUST BE KEPT ON LEADS

Open: daily 11am to 4.30pm

Directions: approximately one mile from Keighley on A629 Halifax road. Follow brown tourist signs

---

As the UK's National Children's Museum, Eureka! is a place where children play to learn and grown-ups learn to play.

Open: daily except 24-26 December, 10am to 5pm

Directions: leave M62 at J24 for Halifax. Take A629 to town centre, following brown tourist signs.

FHG READERS' OFFER 2009

THE GRASSIC GIBBON CENTRE
Arbuthnott, Laurencekirk,
Aberdeenshire AB30 1PB
Tel: 01561 361668
e-mail: lgginfo@grassicgibbon.com
www.grassicgibbon.com

TWO for the price of ONE entry to exhibition (based on full adult rate only). Valid during 2009 (not groups)

NOT TO BE USED IN CONJUNCTION WITH ANY OTHER OFFER

FHG READERS' OFFER 2009

SCOTTISH MARITIME MUSEUM
Harbourside, Irvine,
Ayrshire KA12 8QE
Tel: 01294 278283
Fax: 01294 313211
www.scottishmaritimemuseum.org

TWO for the price of ONE
Valid from April to October 2009

NOT TO BE USED IN CONJUNCTION WITH ANY OTHER OFFER

FHG READERS' OFFER 2009

DALSCONE FARM FUN
Dalscone Farm, Edinburgh Road,
Dumfries DG1 1SE
Tel: 01387 257546 • Shop: 01387 254445
e-mail: dalscone@btconnect.com
www.dalsconefarm.co.uk

One FREE adult (16 years+)
Valid during 2009

NOT TO BE USED IN CONJUNCTION WITH ANY OTHER OFFER

FHG READERS' OFFER 2009

GALLOWAY WILDLIFE CONSERVATION PARK
Lochfergus Plantation, Kirkcudbright,
Dumfries & Galloway DG6 4XX
Tel & Fax: 01557 331645
e-mail: info@gallowaywildlife.co.uk
www.gallowaywildlife.co.uk

One FREE child or Senior Citizen with two full paying adults.
Valid Feb - Nov 2009 (not Easter weekend and Bank Holidays)

NOT TO BE USED IN CONJUNCTION WITH ANY OTHER OFFER

Visitor Centre dedicated to the much-loved Scottish writer Lewis Grassic Gibbon. Exhibition, cafe, gift shop. Outdoor children's play area. Disabled access throughout.	**Open:** daily April to October 10am to 4.30pm. Groups by appointment including evenings. **Directions:** on the B967, accessible and signposted from both A90 and A92.

FHG GUIDES, ABBEY MILL BUSINESS CENTRE, PAISLEY PA1 1TJ • www.holidayguides.com

Scotland's seafaring heritage is among the world's richest and you can relive the heyday of Scottish shipping at the Maritime Museum.	**Open:** 1st April to 31st October - 10am-5pm **Directions:** situated on Irvine harbourside and only a 10 minute walk from Irvine train station.

FHG GUIDES, ABBEY MILL BUSINESS CENTRE, PAISLEY PA1 1TJ • www.holidayguides.com

Indoor adventure play area, farm park, toyshop and cafe. A great day out for all the family, with sledge and zip slides, mini-golf, trampolines, bumper boats, pottery painting and so much more.	**Open:** Monday to Saturday 10am-5.30pm. **Directions:** just off the A75/A701 roundabout heading for Moffat and Edinburgh.

FHG GUIDES, ABBEY MILL BUSINESS CENTRE, PAISLEY PA1 1TJ • www.holidayguides.com

The wild animal conservation centre of Southern Scotland. A varied collection of over 150 animals from all over the world can be seen within natural woodland settings. Picnic areas, cafe/gift shop, outdoor play area, woodland walks, close animal encounters.	**Open:** 10am to dusk 1st February to 30 November. **Directions:** follow brown tourist signs from A75; one mile from Kirkcudbright on the B727.

FHG GUIDES, ABBEY MILL BUSINESS CENTRE, PAISLEY PA1 1TJ • www.holidayguides.com

FHG READERS' OFFER 2009

CREETOWN GEM ROCK MUSEUM
Chain Road, Creetown, Newton Stewart
Dumfries & Galloway DG8 7HJ
Tel: 01671 820357 • Fax: 01671 820554
e-mail: enquiries@gemrock.net
www.gemrock.net

10% Discount on admission.
Valid during 2009.

NOT TO BE USED IN CONJUNCTION WITH ANY OTHER OFFER

FHG READERS' OFFER 2009

MYRETON MOTOR MUSEUM
Aberlady,
East Lothian
EH32 0PZ
Tel: 01875 870288

One child FREE with each paying adult
Valid during 2009

NOT TO BE USED IN CONJUNCTION WITH ANY OTHER OFFER

FHG READERS' OFFER 2009

BO'NESS & KINNEIL RAILWAY
Bo'ness Station, Union Street,
Bo'ness, West Lothian EH51 9AQ
Tel: 01506 822298
e-mail: enquiries.railway@srps.org.uk
www.srps.org.uk

FREE child train fare with one paying adult/concession. Valid 29th March-26th Oct 2009. Not Thomas events or Santa Steam trains

NOT TO BE USED IN CONJUNCTION WITH ANY OTHER OFFER

FHG READERS' OFFER 2009

BUTTERFLY & INSECT WORLD
Dobbies Garden World, Melville Nursery,
Lasswade, Midlothian EH18 1AZ
Tel: 0131-663 4932 • Fax: 0131-654 2774
e-mail: info@edinburgh-butterfly-world.co.uk
www.edinburgh-butterfly-world.co.uk

It's a jungle in here!

£1.50 OFF full adult admission (max. 2 adults per voucher)
Photocopies not accepted. Valid during 2009.

NOT TO BE USED IN CONJUNCTION WITH ANY OTHER OFFER

A fantastic display of gems, crystals, minerals and fossils. An experience you'll treasure forever. Gift shop, tearoom and AV display.	**Open:** Summer - 9.30am to 5.30pm daily; Winter - 10am to 4pm daily. Closed Christmas to end January. **Directions:** follow signs from A75 Dumfries/Stranraer.

FHG GUIDES, ABBEY MILL BUSINESS CENTRE, PAISLEY PA1 1TJ • www.holidayguides.com

On show is a large collection, from 1899, of cars, bicycles, motor cycles and commercials. There is also a large collection of period advertising, posters and enamel signs.	**Open:** March-November - open daily 11am to 4pm. December-February - weekends 11am to 3pm or by special appointment. **Directions:** off A198 near Aberlady. Two miles from A1.

FHG GUIDES, ABBEY MILL BUSINESS CENTRE, PAISLEY PA1 1TJ • www.holidayguides.com

Steam and heritage diesel passenger trains from Bo'ness to Birkhill for guided tours of Birkhill fireclay mines. Explore the history of Scotland's railways in the Scottish Railway Exhibition. Coffee shop and souvenir shop.	**Open:** weekends Easter to October, daily July and August. **Directions:** in the town of Bo'ness. Leave M9 at Junction 3 or 5, then follow brown tourist signs.

FHG GUIDES, ABBEY MILL BUSINESS CENTRE, PAISLEY PA1 1TJ • www.holidayguides.com

See free-flying exotic butterflies in a tropical rainforest paradise. Have close encounters of the crawly kind in the 'Bugs & Beasties' exhibition that includes arrow frogs, tarantulas, amazing leaf-cutter ants and a unique seasonal Scottish Honey Bee display.	**Open:** daily. 9.30am-5.30pm summer, 10am-5pm winter. **Directions:** located just off the Edinburgh City Bypass at the Gilmerton exit or at the Sherrifhall roundabout.

FHG GUIDES, ABBEY MILL BUSINESS CENTRE, PAISLEY PA1 1TJ • www.holidayguides.com

231

FHG
·K·U·P·E·R·A·R·D·
READERS' OFFER 2009

CLYDEBUILT SCOTTISH MARITIME MUSEUM
Braehead Shopping Centre, King's Inch Road,
Glasgow G51 4BN
Tel: 0141-886 1013 • Fax: 0141-886 1015
e-mail: clydebuilt@scotmaritime.org.uk
www.scottishmaritimemuseum.org

Clydebuilt

HALF PRICE admission for up to 4 persons.
Valid during 2009.

NOT TO BE USED IN CONJUNCTION WITH ANY OTHER OFFER

FHG
·K·U·P·E·R·A·R·D·
READERS' OFFER 2009

SPEYSIDE HEATHER GARDEN & VISITOR CENTRE
Speyside Heather Centre, Dulnain Bridge,
Inverness-shire PH26 3PA
Tel: 01479 851359 • Fax: 01479 851396
e-mail: enquiries@heathercentre.com
www.heathercentre.com

Speyside HEATHER GARDEN

FREE entry to 'Heather Story' exhibition
Valid during 2009

NOT TO BE USED IN CONJUNCTION WITH ANY OTHER OFFER

Looking for Holiday Accommodation?

FHG
·K·U·P·E·R·A·R·D·

for details of hundreds of properties throughout the UK, visit our website

www.holidayguides.com

The story of Glasgow and the River Clyde brought vividly to life using AV, hands-on and interactive techniques. You can navigate your own ship, safely load your cargo, operate an engine, and go aboard the 130-year-old coaster 'Kyles'. Ideal for kids young and old wanting an exciting day out. New - The Clyde's Navy.

Open: 10am to 5.30pm daily

Directions: Green Car Park near M&S at Braehead Shopping Centre.

FHG GUIDES, ABBEY MILL BUSINESS CENTRE, PAISLEY PA1 1TJ • www.holidayguides.com

Award-winning attraction with unique 'Heather Story' exhibition, gallery, giftshop, large garden centre selling 300 different heathers, antique shop, children's play area and famous Clootie Dumpling restaurant.

Open: all year except Christmas Day and New Year's Day.

Directions: just off A95 between Aviemore and Grantown-on-Spey.

FHG GUIDES, ABBEY MILL BUSINESS CENTRE, PAISLEY PA1 1TJ • www.holidayguides.com

Other specialised holiday guides from FHG
PETS WELCOME!
COUNTRY HOTELS OF BRITAIN
WEEKEND & SHORT BREAKS IN BRITAIN & IRELAND
THE GOLF GUIDE WHERE TO PLAY, WHERE TO STAY
500 GREAT PLACES TO STAY
SELF-CATERING HOLIDAYS IN BRITAIN
BED & BREAKFAST STOPS IN BRITAIN
CARAVAN & CAMPING HOLIDAYS IN BRITAIN
FAMILY BREAKS IN BRITAIN

Published annually: available in all good bookshops or direct from the publisher:
FHG Guides, Abbey Mill Business Centre, Seedhill, Paisley PA1 1TJ
Tel: 0141 887 0428 • Fax: 0141 889 7204
e-mail: admin@fhguides.co.uk • www.holidayguides.com

FHG
·K·U·P·E·R·A·R·D·
READERS' OFFER 2009

LLANBERIS LAKE RAILWAY
Gilfach Ddu, Llanberis,
Gwynedd LL55 4TY
Tel: 01286 870549
e-mail: info@lake-railway.co.uk
www.lake-railway.co.uk

One pet travels FREE with each full fare paying adult
Valid Easter to October 2009

NOT TO BE USED IN CONJUNCTION WITH ANY OTHER OFFER

FHG
·K·U·P·E·R·A·R·D·
READERS' OFFER 2009

NATIONAL CYCLE COLLECTION
Automobile Palace, Temple Street,
Llandrindod Wells, Powys LD1 5DL
Tel: 01597 825531
e-mail: cycle.museum@powys.org.uk
www.cyclemuseum.org.uk

TWO for the price of ONE
Valid during 2009 except Special Event days

NOT TO BE USED IN CONJUNCTION WITH ANY OTHER OFFER

FHG
·K·U·P·E·R·A·R·D·
READERS' OFFER 2009

RHONDDA HERITAGE PARK
Lewis Merthyr Colliery, Coed Cae Road,
Trehafod, Near Pontypridd CF37 2NP
Tel: 01443 682036
e-mail: info@rhonddaheritagepark.com
www.rhonddaheritagepark.com

Two adults or children for the price of one when accompanied by a full paying adult. Valid until end 2009 for full tours only. Not valid on special event days/themed tours.

NOT TO BE USED IN CONJUNCTION WITH ANY OTHER OFFER

Please note

All the information in this book is given in good faith in the belief that it is correct. However, the publishers cannot guarantee the facts given in these pages, neither are they responsible for changes in policy, ownership or terms that may take place after the date of going to press. Readers should always satisfy themselves that the facilities they require are available and that the terms, if quoted, still apply.

A 60-minute ride along the shores of beautiful Padarn Lake behind a quaint historic steam engine. Magnificent views of the mountains from lakeside picnic spots.

DOGS MUST BE KEPT ON LEAD AT ALL TIMES ON TRAIN

Open: most days Easter to October. Free timetable leaflet on request.

Directions: just off A4086 Caernarfon to Capel Curig road at Llanberis; follow 'Country Park' signs.

FHG GUIDES, ABBEY MILL BUSINESS CENTRE, PAISLEY PA1 1TJ • www.holidayguides.com

---

Journey through the lanes of cycle history and see bicycles from Boneshakers and Penny Farthings up to modern Raleigh cycles. Over 250 machines on display

PETS MUST BE KEPT ON LEADS

Open: 1st March to 1st November daily 10am onwards.

Directions: brown signs to car park. Town centre attraction.

FHG GUIDES, ABBEY MILL BUSINESS CENTRE, PAISLEY PA1 1TJ • www.holidayguides.com

---

Make a pit stop whatever the weather! Join an ex-miner on a tour of discovery, ride the cage to pit bottom and take a thrilling ride back to the surface. Multi-media presentations, period village street, children's adventure play area, restaurant and gift shop. Disabled access with assistance.

Open: Open daily 10am to 6pm (last tour 4pm). Closed Mondays Oct - Easter, also Dec 25th to early Jan.

Directions: Exit Junction 32 M4, signposted from A470 Pontypridd. Trehafod is located between Pontypridd and Porth.

FHG GUIDES, ABBEY MILL BUSINESS CENTRE, PAISLEY PA1 1TJ • www.holidayguides.com

---

Looking for holiday accommodation?

for details of hundreds of properties throughout the UK visit:

www.holidayguides.com

DIRECTORY OF WEBSITE AND E-MAIL ADDRESSES

A quick-reference guide to holiday accommodation with an e-mail address and/or website, conveniently arranged by country and county, with full contact details.

Self-Catering
Hoseasons Holidays Ltd, Lowestoft, Suffolk NR32 2LW
Tel: 01502 502628
- e-mail: louise.thacker@hoseasons.co.uk
- website: www.hoseasons.co.uk

•LONDON

Hotel
Athena Hotel, 110-114 Sussex Gardens, Hyde Park, LONDON W2 1UA
Tel: 020 7706 3866
- e-mail: athena@stavrouhotels.co.uk
- website: www.stavrouhotels.co.uk

Hotel
Gower Hotel, 129 Sussex Gardens, Hyde Park, LONDON W2 2RX
Tel: 020 7262 2262
- e-mail: gower@stavrouhotels.co.uk
- website: www.stavrouhotels.co.uk

B & B
Hanwell B & B, 110a Grove Avenue, Hanwell, LONDON W7 3ES
Tel: 020 8567 5015
- e-mail: tassanimation@ad.com
- website: www.ealing-hanwell-bed-and-breakfast.co.uk/new/index

Hotel
Queens Hotel, 33 Anson Road, Tufnell Park, LONDON N7
Tel: 020 7607 4725
- e-mail: queens@stavrouhotels.co.uk
- website: www.stavrouhotels.co.uk

B & B
S. Armanios, 67 Rannoch Road, Hammersmith, LONDON W6 9SS
Tel: 020 7385 4904
- website: www.thewaytostay.co.uk

•CAMBRIDGESHIRE

B&B
Mrs H. Marsh, The Meadow House, 2A High Street, BURWELL, Cambridgeshire CB25 0HB
Tel: 01638 741926
- e-mail: hilary@themeadowhouse.co.uk
- website: www.themeadowhouse.co.uk

B & B
Mrs Hatley, Manor Farm, Landbeach, CAMBRIDGE, Cambridgeshire CB4 8ED
Tel: 01223 860165
- e-mail: vhatley@btinternet.com
- website: www.smoothhound.co.uk/hotels/manorfarm4

•CHESHIRE

Guest House / Self-Catering
Mrs Joanne Hollins, Balterley Green Farm, Deans Lane, BALTERLEY, Near Crewe, Cheshire CW2 5QJ
Tel: 01270 820 214
- e-mail: greenfarm@balterley.fsnet.co.uk
- website: www.greenfarm.freeserve.co.uk

Country Hotel
Higher Huxley Hall, Huxley, CHESTER, Cheshire CH3 9BZ
Tel: 01829 781 484
- e-mail: info@huxleyhall.co.uk
- website: www.huxleyhall.co.uk

•CORNWALL

Self-Catering
Cornish Traditional Cottages, Blisland, BODMIN, Cornwall PL30 4HS
Tel: 01208 821666
- e-mail: info@corncott.com
- website: www.corncott.com

Self-Catering
Penrose Burden Holiday Cottages, St Breward, BODMIN, Cornwall PL30 4LZ
Tel: 01208 850277 or 01208 850617
- website: www.penroseburden.co.uk

www.holidayguides.com

236 WEBSITE DIRECTORY

Hotel
Stratton Gardens Hotel, Cot Hill, Stratton, BUDE, Cornwall EX23 9DN
Tel: 01288 352500
• e-mail: moira@stratton-gardens.co.uk
• website: www.stratton-gardens.co.uk

Hotel
Hampton Manor Country House Hotel, Alston, CALLINGTON, Cornwall PL17 8LX
Tel: 01579 370494
• e-mail: hamptonmanor@supanet.com
• website: www.hamptonmanor.co.uk

Hotel / Self-Catering
Wringford Down, Hat Lane, CAWSAND, Cornwall PL10 1LE
Tel: 01752 822287
• e-mail: accommodation@wringforddown.co.uk
• website: www.cornwallholidays.co.uk
  www.wringforddown.co.uk

Self-Catering
Mineshop Holiday Cottages, CRACKINGTON HAVEN, Bude, Cornwall EX23 0NR
Tel: 01840 230338
• e-mail: tippett@mineshop.freeserve.co.uk
• website: www.mineshop.co.uk

Self-Catering
Delamere Holiday Bungalows, DELABOLE
Contact: Mrs J. Snowden, 8 Warren Road, Ickenham, Uxbridge, Middlesex UB10 8AA
Tel: 01895 234114
• e-mail: info@delamere-bungalows.com
• website: www.delamerebungalows.com

Self-Catering
Mr P. Watson, Creekside Holiday Houses, Restronguet, FALMOUTH, Cornwall
Tel: 01326 372722
• website: www.creeksideholidayhouses.co.uk

Self-Catering
Mrs Terry, "Shasta", Carwinion Road, Mawnan Smith, FALMOUTH, Cornwall TR11 5JD
Tel: 01326 250725
• e-mail: katerry@btopenworld.com

Self-Catering
Simon & Clare Hirsh, Bamham Farm Cottages, Higher Bamham Farm, LAUNCESTON, Cornwall PL15 9LD
Tel: 01566 772141
• website: www.bamhamfarm.co.uk

Self-Catering
Mrs A. E. Moore, Hollyvagg Farm, Lewannick, LAUNCESTON, Cornwall PL15 7QH
Tel: 01566 782309
• website: www.hollyvaggfarm.co.uk

Self-Catering
Celia Hutchinson, Caradon Country Cottages, East Taphouse, LISKEARD, Cornwall PL14 4NH
Tel: 01579 320355
• e-mail: celia@caradoncottages.co.uk
• website: www.caradoncottages.co.uk

Self-Catering
Mr Lowman, Cutkive Wood Holiday Lodges, St Ive, LISKEARD, Cornwall PL14 3ND
Tel: 01579 362216
• e-mail: holidays@cutkivewood.co.uk
• website: www.cutkivewood.co.uk

Self-Catering
Mrs B. A. Higgins, Trewith Holiday Cottages, Trewith, Duloe, Liskeard, LOOE, Cornwall PL14 4PR
Tel: 01503 262184
• e-mail: info@trewith.co.uk
• website: www.trewith.co.uk

Self-Catering
Valleybrook Holidays, Peakswater, Lansallos, LOOE, Cornwall PL13 2QE
Tel: 01503 220493
• website: www.valleybrookholidays.com

Self-Catering
Tracy Dennett, Talehay Holiday Cottages, Pelynt, Near LOOE, Cornwall PL13 2LT
Tel: 01503 220252
• e-mail: infobookings@talehay.com
• website: www.talehay.co.uk

Self-catering Lodges
Blue Bay Lodge, Trenance, MAWGAN PORTH, Cornwall TR8 4DA
Tel: 01637 860324
• e-mail: hotel@bluebaycornwall.co.uk
• website: www.bluebaycornwall.co.uk

Guest House
Mrs Dewolfreys, Dewolf Guest House, 100 Henver Road, NEWQUAY, Cornwall TR7 3BL
Tel: 01637 874746
• e-mail: holidays@dewolfguesthouse.com
• website: www.dewolfguesthouse.com

Self-Catering
Raintree House Holidays, The Old Airfield, St Merryn, PADSTOW, Cornwall PL28 8PU
Tel: 01841 520228
• e-mail: gill@raintreehouse.co.uk
• website: www.raintreehouse.co.uk

FHG Guides

WEBSITE DIRECTORY 237

Hotel
Torwood Hotel, Alexandra Road, PENZANCE, Cornwall TR18 4LZ
Tel: 01736 360063
• e-mail: lyndasowerby@aol.com
• website: www.torwoodhousehotel.co.uk

Hotel / Inn
Driftwood Spars Hotel, Trevaunance Cove, ST AGNES, Cornwall TR5 0RT
Tel: 01872 552428
• website: www.driftwoodspars.com

Guest House
Mr Gardener, The Elms, 14 Penwinnick Road, ST AUSTELL, Cornwall PL25 5DW
Tel: 01726 74981
• e-mail: pete@edenbb.co.uk
• website: www.edenbb.co.uk

Self-Catering
Mr & Mrs C.W. Pestell, Hockadays, Tregenna, Near Blisland, ST TUDY, Cornwall PL30 4QJ
Tel: 01208 850146
• website: www.hockadays.co.uk

Self-Catering
Mrs R. Reeves, Polstraul, Trewalder, Delabole, ST TUDY, Cornwall PL33 9ET
Tel: 01840 213 120
• e-mail: ruth.reeves@hotmail.co.uk
• website: www.maymear.co.uk

• CUMBRIA

Self- Catering
Kirkstone Foot Apartments Ltd, Kirkstone Pass Road, AMBLESIDE, Cumbria LA22 9EH
Tel: 015394 32232
• e-mail: enquiries@kirkstonefoot.co.uk
• website: www.kirkstonefoot.co.uk

Guest House / Self- Catering
Cuckoo's Nest & Smallwood House, Compston Road, AMBLESIDE, Cumbria LA22 9DJ
Tel: 015394 32330
• e-mail: enq@cottagesambleside.co.uk
         enq@smallwoodhotel.co.uk
• website: www.cottagesambleside.co.uk
           www.smallwoodhotel.co.uk

Guest House
Mr A. Welch, The Anchorage Guest House, Rydal Road, AMBLESIDE, Cumbria LA22 9AY
Tel: 015394 32046
• e-mail: theanchorageguesthouse@hotmail.com
• website: www.theanchorageguesthouse.co.uk

Caravan Park
Greenhowe Caravan Park, Great Langdale, AMBLESIDE, Cumbria LA22 9JU
Tel: 015394 37231
• e-mail: enquiries@greenhowe.com
• website: www.greenhowe.com

Hotel / Guest House
Mrs Liana Moore, The Old Vicarage, Vicarage Road, AMBLESIDE, Cumbria LA22 9DH
Tel: 015394 33364
• e-mail: info@oldvicarageambleside.co.uk
• website: www.oldvicarageambleside.co.uk

Self-Catering
43A Quarry Rigg, BOWNESS-ON-WINDERMERE, Cumbria.
Contact: Mrs E. Jones, 45 West Oakhill Park, Liverpool L13 4BN. Tel: 0151 228 5799
• e-mail: eejay@btinternet.com

B & B
Amanda Vickers, Mosser Heights, Mosser, COCKERMOUTH, Cumbria CA13 0SS
Tel: 01900 822644
• e-mail: amandavickers1@aol.com
• website: www.stayonacumbrianfarm.co.uk

Self-Catering
Mrs Almond, Irton House Farm, Isel, COCKERMOUTH, Cumbria CA13 9ST
Tel: 017683 76380
• website: www.irtonhousefarm.com

Self-Catering
Fisherground Farm Holidays, ESKDALE
Contact: Ian & Jennifer Hall, Orchard House, Applethwaite, Keswick, Cumbria CA12 4PN
Tel: 017687 73175
• e-mail: holidays@fisherground.co.uk
• website: www.fisherground.co.uk

Farm / Self-Catering
Mr P. Brown, High Dale Park Farm, High Dale Park, Satterthwaite, Ulverston, GRIZEDALE FOREST, Cumbria LA12 8LJ
Tel: 01229 860226
• e-mail: peter@lakesweddingmusic.com
• website: www.lakesweddingmusic.com/accomm

B & B
Paul & Fran Townsend, Pepper House, Satterthwaite, Near HAWKSHEAD, Cumbria LA12 8LS. Tel: 01229 860226
• website: www.pepper-house.co.uk

Guest House
Mr Taylorson, Rickerby Grange, Portinscale, KESWICK, Cumbria CA12 5RH
Tel: 017687 72344
• e-mail: stay@rickerbygrange.co.uk
• website: www.rickerbygrange.co.uk

238 WEBSITE DIRECTORY

Self-Catering
Brook House Cottage Holidays,
Bassenthwaite Hall Farm, Bassenthwaite
Village, Near KESWICK, Cumbria CA12 4QP
Tel: 017687 76393
• e-mail: stay@amtrafford.co.uk
• website:
www.holidaycottageslakedistrict.co.uk

B & B
Greta Naysmith, Cocklake House, Mallerstang,
KIRKBY STEPHEN, Cumbria CA17 4JT
Tel: 017683 72080
• e-mail: gretamartensassociates@kencomp.net

Self-Catering
Mrs S.J. Bottom, Crossfield Cottages,
KIRKOSWALD, Penrith, Cumbria CA10 1EU
Tel: 01768 898711
• e-mail: info@crossfieldcottages.co.uk
• website: www.crossfieldcottages.co.uk

Inn
The Britannia Inn, Elterwater, LANGDALE,
Cumbria LA22 9HP. Tel: 015394 37210
• e-mail: info@britinn.co.uk
• website: www.britinn.co.uk

Self-Catering
Hartsop Hall Cottages, Hartsop,
PATTERDALE, Cumbria.
Contact: Mrs F. Townsend, Pepper House,
Satterthwaite, Cumbria LA12 8LS
Tel: 01229 860206
• website: www.hartsophallcottages.com

Self-Catering
Mr & Mrs Iredale, Carrock Cottages,
Carrock House, Hutton Roof, PENRITH,
Cumbria CA11 0XY
Tel: 01768 484111
• e-mail: info@carrockcottages.co.uk
• website: www.carrockcottages.co.uk

Guest House / Inn
The Troutbeck Inn, Troutbeck, PENRITH,
Cumbria CA11 0SJ. Tel: 01768 483635
• e-mail: info@thetroutbeckinn.co.uk
• website: www.thetroutbeckinn.co.uk

Golf Club
Seascale Golf Club, The Banks, SEASCALE,
Cumbria CA20 1QL
Tel: 01946 728202
• e-mail: seascalegolfclub@googlemail.com
• website: www.seascalegolfclub.co.uk

Caravan & Camping
Cove Caravan & Camping Park, Watermillock,
ULLSWATER, Penrith, Cumbria CA11 0LS
Tel: 017684 86549
• e-mail: info@cove-park.co.uk
• website: www.cove-park.co.uk

B & B / Self-Catering
Barbara Murphy, Land Ends Country Lodge,
Watermillock, ULLSWATER, Near Penrith,
Cumbria CA11 0NB
Tel: 01768 486438
• e-mail: infolandends@btinternet.com
• website: www.landends.co.uk

•DERBYSHIRE

Self-Catering Holiday Cottages
Mark Redfern, Paddock House Farm Holiday
Cottages, Alstonefield, ASHBOURNE,
Derbyshire DE6 2FT
Tel: 01335 310282
• e-mail: info@paddockhousefarm.co.uk
• website: www.paddockhousefarm.co.uk

Hotel
Biggin Hall, Biggin-by-Hartington, BUXTON,
Derbyshire SK17 0DH
Tel: 01298 84451
• e-mail: enquiries@bigginhall.co.uk
• website: www.bigginhall.co.uk

Self-Catering
Mrs Gillian Taylor, Priory Lea Holiday Flats,
50 White Knowle Road, BUXTON,
Derbyshire SK17 9NH
Tel: 01298 23737
• e-mail: priorylea@hotmail.co.uk
• website:
www.cressbrook.co.uk/buxton/priorylea

Inn
Devonshire Arms, Peak Forest, Near
BUXTON, Derbyshire SK17 8EJ
Tel: 01298 23875
• e-mail: enquiries@devarms.com
• website: www.devarms.com

Guest House
Ivy House Farm Guest House, STANTON-
BY-BRIDGE, Derby, Derbyshire DE73 7HT
Tel: 01332 863152
• e-mail: mary@guesthouse.fsbusiness.co.uk
• website: www.ivy-house-farm.com

•DEVON

Self-Catering
Helpful Holidays, Mill Street, Chagford,
DEVON
Tel: 01647 433593
• e-mail: help@helpfulholidays.com
• website: www.helpfulholidays.com

WEBSITE DIRECTORY 239

Self-Catering
Farm & Cottage Holidays, DEVON
Tel: 01237 479698
• website: www.holidaycottages.co.uk

B & B
Lynda Richards, Gages Mill, Buckfastleigh Road, ASHBURTON, Devon TQ13 7JW
Tel: 01364 652391
• e-mail: gagesmill@aol.com
• website: www.gagesmill.co.uk

Self-Catering
Wooder Manor, Widecombe-in-the-Moor, ASHBURTON, Devon TQ13 7TR
Tel: 01364 621391
• e-mail: angela@woodermanor.com
• website: www.woodermanor.com

Hotel
Sandy Cove Hotel, Combe Martin Bay, BERRYNARBOR, Devon EX34 9SR
Tel: 01271 882243/882888
• website: www.sandycove-hotel.co.uk

B & B / Self-Catering
Mr & Mrs Lewin, Lake House Cottages and B&B, Lake Villa, BRADWORTHY, Devon EX22 7SQ
Tel: 01409 241962
• e-mail: info@lakevilla.co.uk
• website: www.lakevilla.co.uk

Self-Catering / Organic Farm
Little Comfort Farm Cottages, Little Comfort Farm, BRAUNTON, North Devon EX33 2NJ
Tel: 01271 812414
• e-mail: info@littlecomfortfarm.co.uk
• website: www.littlecomfortfarm.co.uk

Guest House
Woodlands Guest House, Parkham Road, BRIXHAM, South Devon TQ5 9BU
Tel: 01803 852040
• e-mail: woodlandsbrixham@btinternet.com
• website: www.woodlandsdevon.co.uk

Self-Catering / B & B / Caravans
Mrs Gould, Bonehayne Farm, COLYTON, Devon EX24 6SG
Tel: 01404 871416/871296
• e-mail: gould@bonehayne.co.uk
• website: www.bonehayne.co.uk

Self-Catering / B&B
Mrs Lee, Church Approach Holidays, Farway, COLYTON, Devon EX24 6EQ
Tel: 01404 871383/871202
• e-mail: lizlee@eclipse.co.uk
• website: www.churchapproach.co.uk

Holiday Park
Manleigh Holiday Park, Rectory Road, COMBE MARTIN, North Devon EX34 0NS
Tel: 01271 883353
• e-mail: info@manleighpark.co.uk
• website: www.manleighpark.co.uk

Self-Catering
Mrs S.R. Ridalls, The Old Bakehouse, 7 Broadstone, DARTMOUTH, Devon TQ6 9NR
Tel: 01803 834585
• e-mail: oldbakehousecottages@yahoo.com
• website: www.oldbakehousedartmouth.co.uk

Self-Catering
Mr & Mrs R. Jones, Stowford Lodge, Langtree, GREAT TORRINGTON, Devon EX38 8NU
Tel: 01805 601540
• e-mail: enq@stowfordlodge.co.uk
• website: www.stowfordlodge.co.uk

Hotel
St Brannocks House, St Brannocks Road, ILFRACOMBE, Devon EX34 8EQ
Tel: 01271 863873
• e-mail: barbara@stbrannockshouse.co.uk
• website: www.stbrannockshouse.co.uk

Guest House
Maureen Corke, Varley House, Chambercombe Park, ILFRACOMBE, Devon EX34 9QW. Tel: 01271 863927
• e-mail: info@varleyhouse.co.uk
• website: www.varleyhouse.co.uk

Inn
The Blue Ball Inn, Countisbury, LYNMOUTH, Near Lynton, Devon EX35 6NE
Tel: 01598 741263
• website: www.BlueBallinn.com
    www.exmoorsandpiper.com

Self-Catering
Doone Valley Holidays
Contact: Mr C. Harman, Cloud Farm, Oare, LYNTON, Devon EX35 6NU
Tel: 01598 714234
• e-mail: doonevalleyholidays@hotmail.com
• website: www.doonevalleyholidays.co.uk

Self-Catering
Crab Cottage, NOSS MAYO, South Hams, South of Dartmoor, Devon
Tel: 01425 471 372
• e-mail: 07enquiries@crab-cottage.co.uk
• website: www.crab-cottage.co.uk

Guest House
The Commodore, 14 Esplanade Road, PAIGNTON, Devon TQ4 6EB
Tel: 01803 553107
• e-mail: info@commodorepaignton.com
• website: www.commodorepaignton.com

www.holidayguides.com

240 WEBSITE DIRECTORY

Guest House
Jane Hill, Beaumont, Castle Hill, SEATON, Devon EX12 2QW
Tel: 01297 20832
• e-mail: jane@lymebay.demon.co.uk
• website: www.smoothhound.co.uk/hotels/beaumon1.html

Hotel
Riviera Lodge Hotel, 26 Croft Road. TORQUAY, Devon TQ2 5UE
Tel: 01803 209309
• e-mail: stay@rivieralodgehotel.co.uk
• website: www.rivieralodgehotel.co.uk

Guest House
Mrs L Read, Silverlands Guest House, 27 Newton Road, TORQUAY, Devon TQ2 5DB
Tel: 01803 292013
• e-mail: enquiries@silverlandsguesthouse.co.uk
• website: www.silverlandsguesthouse.co.uk

Self-Catering
Marsdens Cottage Holidays, 2 The Square, Braunton, WOOLACOMBE, Devon EX33 2JB
Tel: 01271 813777
• e-mail: holidays@marsdens.co.uk
• website: www.marsdens.co.uk

Holiday Park
Woolacombe Bay Holiday Parks, WOOLACOMBE, North Devon EX34 7HW
Tel: 01271 870343
• e-mail: goodtimes@woolacombe.com
• website: www.woolacombe.com/fcw

Caravan & Camping
North Morte Farm Caravan & Camping Park, Mortehoe, WOOLACOMBE, Devon EX34 7EG
Tel: 01271 870381
• e-mail: info@northmortefarm.co.uk
• website: www.northmortefarm.co.uk

Self-catering
Mrs L Hunt, Sunnymeade, Dean Cross, West Down, WOOLACOMBE, North Devon EX34 8NT
Tel: 01271 863668
• e-mail: info@sunnymeade.co.uk
• website: www.sunnymeade.co.uk

• DORSET

Self-Catering
Luccombe Farm Cottages, Luccombe Farm, Milton Abbas, BLANDFORD FORUM, Dorset DT11 0BE
Tel: 01258 880558
• e-mail: mkayll@aol.com
• website: www.luccombeholidays.co.uk

Hotel
Southbourne Grove Hotel, 96 Southbourne Road, BOURNEMOUTH, Dorset BH6 3QQ
Tel: 01202 420503
• e-mail: neil@pack1462.freeserve.co.uk
• website: www.tiscover.co.uk/southbournegrovehotel

Guest House
T. Derby, Southernhay Guest House, 42 Alum Chine Road, BOURNEMOUTH, Dorset BH4 8DX
Tel: 01202 761251
• e-mail: enquiries@southernhayhotel.co.uk
• website: www.thesouthernhayhotel.co.uk

Self-Catering
C. Hammond, Stourcliffe Court, 56 Stourcliffe Avenue, Southbourne, BOURNEMOUTH, Dorset BH6 3PX
Tel: 01202 420698
• website: www.stourcliffecourt.co.uk

Self-Catering Cottage / Farmhouse B & B
Mrs S. E. Norman, Frogmore Farm, Chideock, BRIDPORT, Dorset DT6 6HT
Tel: 01308 456159
• e-mail: bookings@frogmorefarm.com
• website: www.frogmorefarm.com

Chalet Park / Caravans
Owlpen Caravans Ltd, 148 Burley Road, Bransgore, Near CHRISTCHURCH, New Forest, Dorset BH23 8DB
Tel: 01425 672875
• e-mail: owlpen@hotmail.com
• website: www.owlpen-caravans.co.uk

Guest House
Mrs Valerie Bradbeer, Nethercroft, Winterbourne Abbas, DORCHESTER, Dorset DT2 9LU
Tel: 01305 889337
• e-mail: v.bradbeer@ukonline.co.uk
• website: www.nethercroft.com

Hotel
Cromwell House Hotel, LULWORTH COVE, Dorset BH20 5RJ
Tel: 01929 400253
• e-mail: catriona@lulworthcove.co.uk
• website: www.lulworthcove.co.uk

Hotel
Fairwater Head Hotel, Hawkchurch, Near Axminster, LYME REGIS, Dorset EX13 5TX
Tel: 01297 678349
• e-mail: info@fairwaterheadhotel.co.uk
• website: www.fairwaterheadhotel.co.uk

FHG Guides

WEBSITE DIRECTORY 241

Self-Catering
Westover Farm Cottages, Wootton Fitzpaine, Near LYME REGIS, Dorset DT6 6NE
Tel: 01297 560451/561295
- e-mail: wfcottages@aol.com
- website: www.westoverfarmcottages.co.uk

Farm / Self-Catering
White Horse Farm, Middlemarsh, SHERBORNE, Dorset DT9 5QN
Tel: 01963 210222
- e-mail: enquiries@whitehorsefarm.co.uk
- website: www.whitehorsefarm.co.uk

Hotel
The Knoll House, STUDLAND BAY, Dorset BH19 3AW
Tel: 01929 450450
- e-mail: info@knollhouse.co.uk
- website: www.knollhouse.co.uk

Hotel
The Lugger Inn, 30 West Street, Chickerell, WEYMOUTH, Dorset DT3 4DY
Tel: 01305 766611
- e-mail: info@theluggerinn.co.uk
- website: www.theluggerinn.co.uk

Guest House / Self-Catering
Olivia Nurrish, Glenthorne, Castle Cove, 15 Old Castle Road, WEYMOUTH, Dorset DT4 8QB
Tel: 01305 777281
- e-mail: info@glenthorne-holidays.co.uk
- website: www.glenthorne-holidays.co.uk

•ESSEX

Farm House B&B / Self-Catering
Mrs Brenda Lord, Pond House, Earls Hall Farm, St Osyth, CLACTON ON SEA, Essex CO16 8BP Tel: 01255 820458
- e-mail: brenda_lord@farming.co.uk
- website: www.earlshallfarm.info

•GLOUCESTERSHIRE

Hotel
The Bowl Inn & Lilies Restaurant, 16 Church Road, Lower Almondsbury, BRISTOL, Gloucs BS32 4DT
Tel: 01454 612757
- e-mail: reception@thebowlinn.co.uk
- website: www.thebowlinn.co.uk

Hotel
Tudor Farmhouse Hotel, CLEARWELL, Forest of Dean, Gloucs GL16 8JS
Tel: 01594 833046
- e-mail: info@tudorfarmhousehotel.co.uk
- website: www.tudorhousehotel.co.uk

Caravan & Camping
Tudor Caravan Park, Shepherds Patch, SLIMBRIDGE, Gloucestershire GL2 7BP
Tel: 01453 890483
- e-mail: info@tudorcaravanpark.co.uk
- website: www.tudorcaravanpark.co.uk

B & B
Anthea & Bill Rhoton, Hyde Crest, Cirencester Road, MINCHINHAMPTON, Gloucs GL6 8PE
Tel: 01453 731631
- e-mail: stay@hydecrest.co.uk
- website: www.hydecrest.co.uk

•HAMPSHIRE

Hotel
Bramble Hill Hotel, Bramshaw, Near LYNDHURST, New Forest, Hants SO43 7JG
Tel: 02380 813165
- website: www.bramblehill.co.uk

•HEREFORDSHIRE

Farmhouse / B & B
Mrs M. E. Drzymalski, Thatch Close, Llangrove, ROSS-ON-WYE, Herefordshire HR9 6EL
Tel: 01989 770300
- e-mail: info@thatchclose.co.uk
- website: www.thatchclose.co.uk

•ISLE OF WIGHT

Guest House / Self-Catering
Frenchman's Cove / Coach House, Alum Bay, Old Road, TOTLAND BAY, Isle of Wight PO39 0HZ
Tel: 01983 752227
- e-mail: boatfield@frenchmanscove.co.uk
- website: www.frenchmanscove.co.uk

Farmhouse B & B / Self-Catering Cottages
Mrs F.J. Corry, Little Span Farm, Rew Lane, Wroxall, VENTNOR, Isle of Wight PO38 3AU
Tel: 01983 852419
- e-mail: info@spanfarm.co.uk
- website: www.spanfarm.co.uk

•KENT

Guest House
S. Twort, Heron Cottage, Biddenden, ASHFORD, Kent TN27 8HH
Tel: 01580 291358
- e-mail: susantwort@hotmail.com
- website: www.heroncottage.info

242 WEBSITE DIRECTORY

Hotel
Collina House Hotel, 5 East Hill, TENTERDEN, Kent TN30 6RL Tel: 01580 764852/764004
• e-mail: enquiries@collinahousehotel.co.uk
• website: www.collinahousehotel.co.uk

•LANCASHIRE

Guest House
Mrs Roslyn Holdsworth, Broadwater House, 356 Marine Road, MORECAMBE, Lancashire LA5 4AQ. Tel: 01524 411333
• e-mail: enquiries@thebroadwaterhotel.co.uk
• website: www.thebroadwaterhotel.co.uk

•LINCOLNSHIRE

Farm B & B / Self-catering cottage
Mrs C.E. Harrison, Baumber Park, Baumber, HORNCASTLE, Lincolnshire LN9 5NE
Tel: 01507 578235/07977 722776
• e-mail: mail@baumberpark.com
 mail@gathmanscottage.co.uk
• website: www.baumberpark.com
 www.gathmanscottage.co.uk

Farmhouse B & B
S Evans, Willow Farm, Thorpe Fendykes, SKEGNESS, Lincolnshire PE24 4QH
Tel: 01754 830316
• e-mail: willowfarmhols@aol.com
• website: www.willowfarmholidays.co.uk

Hotel
Petwood Hotel, Stixwould Road, WOODHALL SPA, Lincolnshire LN10 6QF
Tel: 01526 352411
• e-mail: reception@petwood.co.uk
• website: www.petwood.co.uk

•MERSEYSIDE

Guest House
Holme Leigh Guest House, 93 Woodcroft Road, Wavertree, LIVERPOOL, Merseyside L15 2HG
Tel: 0151 734 2216
• e-mail: info@holmeleigh.com
• website: www.holmeleigh.com

•NORFOLK

Self-Catering
Blue Riband Holidays, HEMSBY, Great Yarmouth, Norfolk NR29 4HA
Tel: 01493 730445
• website: www.BlueRibandHolidays.co.uk

Self-Catering
Sand Dune Cottages, Tan Lane, CAISTER-ON-SEA, Great Yarmouth, Norfolk NR30 5DT
Tel: 01493 720352
• e-mail: sand.dune.cottages@amserve.net
• website: www.eastcoastlive.co.uk/sites/sanddunecottages.php

Self-Catering
Carefree Holidays, Chapel Briars, Yarmouth Road, GREAT YARMOUTH, Norfolk NR29 4NJ
Tel: 01493 732176
• e-mail: tony@carefree-holidays.co.uk
• website: www.carefree-holidays.co.uk

Hotel
The Stuart House Hotel, 35 Goodwins Road, KING'S LYNN, Norfolk PE30 5QX
Tel: 01553 772169
• e-mail: reception@stuarthousehotel.co.uk
• website: www.stuarthousehotel.co.uk

Self-catering
Scarning Dale, Dale Road, SCARNING, Dereham, Norfolk NR1 2QN
Tel: 01362 687269
• e-mail: jean@scarningdale.co.uk
• website: www.scarningdale.co.uk

•NORTHUMBERLAND

Self-Catering
Northumberland Cottages Ltd, The Old Stable Yard, Chathill Farm, CHATHILL
Tel: 01665 589434
• e-mail: enquiries@northumberlandcottages.com
• website: www.northumberlandcottages.com

Self-Catering
Mrs S. M. Saunders, Scotchcoulthard Holiday Cottages, HALTWHISTLE, Northumberland NE49 9NH
Tel: 01434 374470
• e-mail: scotchcoulthard@hotmail.com
• website: www.scotchcoulthard.co.uk

•NOTTINGHAMSHIRE

Caravan & Camping Park
Orchard Park, Marnham Road, Tuxford, NEWARK, Nottinghamshire NG22 0PY
Tel: 01777 870228
• e-mail: info@orchardcaravanpark.co.uk
• website: www.orchardcaravanpark.co.uk

www.holidayguides.com

WEBSITE DIRECTORY

• OXFORDSHIRE

Leisure Park
Cotswold Wildlife Park, BURFORD,
Oxfordshire OX18 4JN
Tel: 01993 823006
• website: www.cotswoldwildlifepark.co.uk

Guest House
The Bungalow, Cherwell Farm, Mill Lane, Old Marston, OXFORD, Oxfordshire OX3 0QF
Tel: 01865 557171
• e-mail: ros.bungalowbb@btinternet.com
• www.cherwellfarm-oxford-accomm.co.uk

Guest House
Nanford Guest House, 137 Iffley Road, OXFORD, Oxfordshire OX4 1EJ
Tel: 01865 244743
• e-mail: b.cronin@btinternet.com
• website: www.nanfordguesthouse.com

B & B / Self-Catering
Katharine Brown, Hill Grove Farm, Crawley Dry Lane, Minster Lovell, WITNEY, Oxfordshire OX29 0NA
Tel: 01993 703120
• e-mail: katharinemcbrown@btinternet.com
• website: www.countryaccom.co.uk/hill-grove-farm

• SHROPSHIRE

Farm / B & B
Mrs M. Jones, Acton Scott Farm, Acton Scott, CHURCH STRETTON, Shropshire SY6 6QN
Tel: 01694 781260
• e-mail: fhg@actonscottfarm.co.uk
• website: www.actonscottfarm.co.uk

Hotel
Rowena Jones, Longmynd Hotel, Cunnery Rd, CHURCH STRETTON, Shropshire SY6 6AG
Tel: 01694 722244
• e-mail: info@longmynd.co.uk
• website: www.longmynd.co.uk

Self-Catering
Clive & Cynthia Prior, Mocktree Barns Holiday Cottages, Leintwardine, LUDLOW, Shropshire SY7 0LY
Tel: 01547 540441
• e-mail: mocktreebarns@care4free.net
• website: www.mocktreeholidays.co.uk

• SOMERSET

Self-Catering
Westward Rise Holiday Park, South Road, BREAN, Burnham-on-Sea, Somerset TA8 2RD
Tel: 01278 751310
• e-mail: info@westwardrise.com
• website: www.westwardrise.com

Farm / B & B
Mrs M. Hasell, The Model Farm, Norton Hawkfield, Pensford, BRISTOL, Somerset BS39 4HA
Tel: 01275 832144
• e-mail: margarethasell@hotmail.com
• website: www.themodelfarm.co.uk

Farmhouse / Self-Catering
Josephine Smart, Leigh Farm, Old Road, Pensford, Near BRISTOL, Somerset BS39 4BA
Tel: 01761 490281
• website: www.leighfarmholidays.co.uk

Farm Self-Catering
Jane Styles, Wintershead Farm, Simonsbath, EXMOOR, Somerset TA24 7LF
Tel: 01643 831222
• e-mail: info@wintershead.co.uk
• website: www.wintershead.co.uk

B & B
North Down Farm, Pyncombe Lane, Wiveliscombe, TAUNTON, Somerset TA4 2BL
Tel: 01984 623730
• e-mail: jennycope@btinternet.com
• website: www.north-down-farm.co.uk

B & B
The Old Mill, Netherclay, Bishop's Hull, TAUNTON, Somerset TA1 5AB
Tel: 01823 289732
• website: www.theoldmillbandb.co.uk

Farm / Guest House
G. Clark, Yew Tree Farm, THEALE, Near Wedmore, Somerset BS28 4SN
Tel: 01934 712475
• e-mail: enquiries@yewtreefarmbandb.co.uk
• website: www.yewtreefarmbandb.co.uk

Self-Catering
Croft Holiday Cottages, 2 The Croft, Anchor Street, WATCHET, Somerset TA23 0BY
Tel: 01984 631121
• e-mail: croftcottages@talk21.com
• website: www.cottagessomerset.com

Please mention **FHG Guides** when enquiring about accommodation featured in this publication.

• STAFFORDSHIRE

Farm B & B / Self-Catering
Mrs M. Hiscoe-James, Offley Grove Farm, Adbaston, ECCLESHALL, Staffs ST20 0QB
Tel: 01785 280205
- e-mail: enquiries@offleygrovefarm.co.uk
- website: www.offleygrovefarm.co.uk

Self-Catering
Field Head Farmhouse Holidays, Calton, WATERHOUSES, Stoke-on-Trent, Staffordshire ST10 3LB
Tel: 01538 308352
- e-mail: info@field-head.co.uk
- website: www.field-head.co.uk

• SUFFOLK

B & B
Cobbles, Nethergate Street, CLARE, Suffolk CO10 8NP
Tel: 01787 277539
- e-mail: cobbles@cobblesclare.co.uk
- website: www.cobblesclare.co.uk

Guest House
The Grafton Guest House, 13 Sea Road, FELIXSTOWE, Suffolk IP11 2BB
Tel: 01394 284881
- e-mail: info@grafton-house.com
- website: www.grafton-house.com

B & B / Self-Catering
Mrs Sarah Kindred, High House Farm, Cransford, Woodbridge, FRAMLINGHAM, Suffolk IP13 9PD
Tel: 01728 663461
- e-mail: b&b@highhousefarm.co.uk
- website: www.highhousefarm.co.uk

Self-Catering
Windmill Lodges Ltd, Redhouse Farm, Saxtead, Woodbridge, FRAMLINGHAM, Suffolk IP13 9RD
Tel: 01728 685238
- e-mail: holidays@windmilllodges.co.uk
- website: www.windmilllodges.co.uk

Self-Catering
Kessingland Cottages, Rider Haggard Lane, KESSINGLAND, Suffolk.
Contact: S. Mahmood, 156 Bromley Road, Beckenham, Kent BR3 6PG
Tel: 020 8650 0539
- e-mail: jeeptrek@kjti.co.uk
- website: www.k-cottage.co.uk

Self-Catering
Southwold/Walberswick Self-Catering Properties.
Durrants incorporating, H.A. Adnams, 98 High Street, SOUTHWOLD, Suffolk IP18 6DP
Tel: 01502 723292
- website: www.durrants.com

• EAST SUSSEX

Self-Catering
Crowhurst Park, Telham Lane, BATTLE, East Sussex TN33 0SL
Tel: 01424 773344
- e-mail: inquiries@crowhurstpark.co.uk
- website: www.crowhurstpark.co.uk

Self-Catering
"Pekes", CHIDDINGLY, East Sussex
Contact: Eva Morris, 124 Elm Park Mansions, Park Walk, London SW10 0AR
Tel: 020 7352 8088
- e-mail: pekes.afa@virgin.net
- website: www.pekesmanor.com

Guest House / Self-Catering
Longleys Farm Cottage, Harebeating Lane, HAILSHAM, East Sussex BN27 1ER
Tel: 01323 841227
- e-mail: longleysfarmcottagebb@dsl.pipex.com
- website: www.longleysfarmcottage.co.uk

Hotel
Grand Hotel, Grand Parade, St Leonards, HASTINGS, East Sussex TN38 0DD
Tel: 01424 428510
- e-mail: info@grandhotelhastings.co.uk
- website: www.grandhotelhastings.co.uk

Self-Catering Cottage
4 Beach Cottages, Claremont Road, SEAFORD, East Sussex BN25 2QQ
Contact: Julia Lewis, 47 Wandle Bank, London SW19 1DW Tel: 020 8542 5073
- e-mail: cottage@beachcottages.info
- website: www.beachcottages.info

• WEST SUSSEX

Self-Catering
Mrs M. W. Carreck, New Hall Holiday Flat and Cottage, New Hall Lane, Small Dole, HENFIELD, West Sussex BN5 9YJ
Tel: 01273 492546
- website: www.newhallcottage.co.uk

WEBSITE DIRECTORY 245

• WARWICKSHIRE

Guest House / B & B
Julia & John Downie, Holly Tree Cottage, Pathlow, STRATFORD-UPON-AVON, Warwickshire CV37 0ES
Tel: 01789 204461
- e-mail: john@hollytree-cottage.co.uk
- website: www.hollytree-cottage.co.uk

• WILTSHIRE

Guest House
Stillmeadow, 18 Bradford Road, Winsley, BRADFORD-ON-AVON, Wiltshire BA15 2HW
Tel:01722 722119
- e-mail: sue.gilby@btinternet.com
- website: www.stillmeadow.co.uk

Guest House
Alan & Dawn Curnow, Hayburn Wyke Guest House, 72 Castle Road, SALISBURY, Wiltshire SP1 3RL
Tel: 01225 412627
- e-mail: hayburn.wyke@tinyonline.co.uk
- website: www.hayburnwykeguesthouse.co.uk

• WORCESTERSHIRE

Guest House
Ann & Brian Porter, Croft Guest House, Bransford, GREAT MALVERN, Worcester, Worcestershire WR6 5JD
Tel: 01886 832227
- e-mail: hols@crofthousewr6.fsnet.co.uk
- website: www.croftguesthouse.com

Self-Catering Cottages
Rochford Park Cottages, Rochford Park, TENBURY WELLS, Worcestershire WR15 8SP
Tel: 01584 781392
- e-mail: cottages@rochfordpark.co.uk
- website: www.rochfordpark.co.uk

Guest House
Moseley Farm B & B, Moseley Road, Hallow, WORCESTER, Worcestershire WR2 6NL
Tel: 01905 641343
- e-mail: moseleyfarmbandb@aol.com
- website: www.moseleyfarmbandb.co.uk

• EAST YORKSHIRE

Guest House / Camping
Mrs Jeanne Wilson, Robeanne House, Driffield Lane, Shiptonthorpe, YORK, East Yorkshire YO43 3PW
Tel: 01430 873312
- e-mail: enquiries@robeannehouse.co.uk
- website: www.robeannehouse.co.uk

• NORTH YORKSHIRE

Farmhouse B & B
Mrs Julie Clarke, Middle Farm, Woodale, COVERDALE, Leyburn,
North Yorkshire DL8 4TY Tel: 01969 640271
- e-mail: j-a-clarke@hotmail.co.uk
- www.yorkshirenet.co.uk/stayat/middlefarm

Farm
Mrs Linda Tindall, Rowantree Farm, Fryup Road, Ainthorpe, DANBY, Whitby, North Yorkshire YO21 2LE
Tel: 01723 515155
- e-mail: krbsatindall@aol.com
- website: www.rowantreefarm.co.uk

Farmhouse B&B
Mr & Mrs Richardson, Egton Banks Farmhouse, GLAISDALE, Whitby, North Yorkshire YO21 2QP
Tel: 01947 897289
e-mail: egtonbanksfarm@agriplus.net
- website: www.egtonbanksfarm.agriplus.net

Self-Catering
Rudding Estate Cottages, Rudding Park Estate Ltd, Haggs Farm, Haggs Road, Follifoot, HARROGATE, North Yorkshire HG3 1EQ
Tel: 01423 844844
- e-mail: info@rudding.com
- website: www.rudding.com/cottages

B & B
Cocklake House, Mallerstang, Near HAWES
Contact: Greta Naysmith, Cocklake House, Mallerstang, Kirkby Stephen,
Cumbria CA17 4JT. Tel: 017683 72080
- e-mail: gretamartensassociates@kencomp.net

Guest House
The New Inn Motel, Main Street, HUBY, York, North Yorkshire YO61 1HQ
Tel: 01347 810219
- enquiries@newinnmotel.freeserve.co.uk
- website: www.newinnmotel.co.uk

Self-Catering
Allaker in Coverdale, West Scrafton, LEYBURN, North Yorkshire DL8 4RM
Contact: Mr Adrian Cave, 21 Kenilworth Road, London W5 5PA Tel: 020 856 74862
- e-mail: ac@adriancave.com
- www.adriancave.com/allaker

Self-Catering
Abbey Holiday Cottages, MIDDLESMOOR, 12 Panorama Close, Pateley Bridge, Harrogate, North Yorkshire HG3 5NY
Tel: 01423 712062
- e-mail: info@abbeyhall.cottages.co.uk
- website: www.abbeyholidaycottages.co.uk

246 WEBSITE DIRECTORY

Farmhouse B&B
Browson Bank Farmhouse, Dalton, RICHMOND, North Yorkshire DL11 7HE
Tel: 01325 718504
• website: www.browsonbank.co.nr

Self-Catering
Waterfront House, RIPON
Contact: Mrs C. Braddon, Chantry Bells, Chantry Court, Ripley, Harrogate HG3 3AD
Tel: 01423 770704
• e-mail: chris1.braddon@virgin.net
• website: www.dalesholidayripon.co.uk

Guest House / Self-Catering
Sue & Tony Hewitt, Harmony Country Lodge, 80 Limestone Road, Burniston, SCARBOROUGH, North Yorkshire YO13 0DG
Tel: 0800 2985840
• e-mail: mail@harmonylodge.net
• website: www.harmonylodge.co.uk

B & B
Beck Hall, Malham, SKIPTON, North Yorkshire BD23 4DJ. Tel: 01729 830332
• e-mail: simon@beckhallmalham.com
• website: www.beckhallmalham.com

B & B
Gamekeepers Inn, Long Ashes Park, Threshfield, Near SKIPTON, North Yorkshire BD23 5PN. Tel: 01756 752434
• e-mail: info@gamekeeperinn.co.uk
• website: www.gamekeeperinn.co.uk

Self-Catering
Mrs Jones, New Close Farm, Kirkby Malham, SKIPTON, North Yorkshire BD23 4DP
Tel: 01729 830240
• brendajones@newclosefarmyorkshire.co.uk
• website: www.newclosefarmyorkshire.co.uk

Self-Catering
Mrs J. McNeil, Swallow Holiday Cottages, Long Leas Farm, Hawsker, WHITBY, North Yorkshire YO22 4LA
Tel: 01947 603790
• website: www.swallowcottages.co.uk

Guest House
Ashford Guest House, 8 Royal Crescent, WHITBY, North Yorkshire YO21 3EJ
Tel: 01947 602138
• e-mail: info@ashfordguesthouse.co.uk
• website: www.ashfordguesthouse.co.uk

Self-Catering
Greenhouses Farm Cottages, Near WHITBY.
Contact: Mr J.N. Eddleston, Greenhouses Farm, Lealholm, Near Whitby, North Yorkshire YO21 2AD. Tel: 01947 897486
• e-mail: n_eddleston@yahoo.com
• www.greenhouses-farm-cottages.co.uk

B & B
Mr & Mrs Leedham, York House, 62 Heworth Green, YORK, North Yorkshire YO31 7TQ
Tel: 01904 427070
• e-mail: yorkhouse.bandb@tiscali.co.uk
• website: www.yorkhouseyork.co.uk

Self-Catering
York Lakeside Lodges Ltd, Moor Lane, YORK, North Yorkshire YO24 2QU
Tel: 01904 702346
• e-mail: neil@yorklakesidelodges.co.uk
• website: www.yorklakesidelodges.co.uk

•WEST YORKSHIRE

Farm B & B / Self-Catering Cottages
Currer Laithe Farm, Moss Carr Road, Long Lee, KEIGHLEY, West Yorkshire BD21 4SL
Tel: 01535 604387
• website: www.currerlaithe.co.uk

•SCOTLAND

•ABERDEEN, BANFF & MORAY

Hotel
P. A. McKechnie, Cambus O' May Hotel, BALLATER, Aberdeenshire AB35 5SE
Tel: 013397 55428
• e-mail: mckechnie@cambusomay.freeserve.co.uk
• website: www.cambusomayhotel.co.uk

B & B
Davaar B & B, Church Street, DUFFTOWN, Moray, AB55 4AR
Tel: 01340 820464
• e-mail: davaar@cluniecameron.co.uk
• website: www.davaardufftown.co.uk

•ANGUS & DUNDEE

Golf Club
Edzell Golf Club, High Street, EDZELL, Brechin, Angus DD9 7TF
Tel: 01356 648462
• e-mail: secretary@edzellgolfclub.net
• website: www.edzellgolfclub.net

WEBSITE DIRECTORY 247

•ARGYLL & BUTE

Self-Catering
Ardtur Cottages, APPIN, Argyll PA38 4DD
Tel: 01631 730223
- e-mail: pery@btinternet.com
- website: www.selfcatering-appin-scotland.com

Self-Catering
Inchmurrin Island Self-Catering Holidays,
Inchmurrin Island, LOCH LOMOND G63 0JY
Tel: 01389 850245
- e-mail: scotts@inchmurrin-lochlomond.com
- website: www.inchmurrin-lochlomond.com

Self-Catering
Airdeny Chalets, Glen Lonan, Taynuilt,
OBAN, Argyll PA35 1HY Tel: 01866 822648
- e-mail: jenifer@airdenychalets.co.uk
- website: www.airdenychalets.co.uk

Self-Catering
Linda Battison,
Cologin Country Chalets & Lodges,
Lerags Glen, OBAN, Argyll PA34 4SE
Tel: 01631 564501
- e-mail: info@cologin.co.uk
- website: www.cologin.co.uk

Self-Catering
Colin Mossman, Lagnakeil Lodges,
Lerags, OBAN, Argyll PA34 4SE
Tel: 01631 562746
- e-mail: info@lagnakeil.co.uk
- website: www.lagnakeil.co.uk

•AYRSHIRE & ARRAN

B & B
Mrs J Clark, Eglinton Guest House,
23 Eglinton Terrace, AYR, Ayrshire KA7 1JJ
Tel: 01292 264623
- e-mail: eglintonguesthouse@yahoo.co.uk
- website: www.eglinton-guesthouse-ayr.com

Farmhouse / B & B
Mrs Nancy Cuthbertson, West Tannacrieff,
Fenwick, KILMARNOCK, Ayrshire KA3 6AZ
Tel: 01560 600258
- e-mail: westtannacrieff@btopenworld.com
- website: www.smoothhound.co.uk/hotels/westtannacrieff.html

Self-Catering
1 Guildford Street, MILLPORT, Isle of Cumbrae
Contact: Mrs B. McLuckie, Muirhall Farm,
Larbert, Stirlingshire FK5 4EW
Tel: 01324 551570
- e-mail: b@1-guildford-street.co.uk
- website: www.1-guildford-street.co.uk

•BORDERS

Guest House
Hizzy's Guest House, 23B North Bridge St,
HAWICK, Roxburghshire TD9 9BD
Tel: 01450 372101
- e-mail: frankiemcfarlane@btinternet.com
- website: www.hizzys.co.uk

Self-Catering
Glebe House, Hownam, By KELSO,
Borders TD5 8AL
Tel: 07971 522040
- e-mail: enquiries@holidayhomescotland.co.uk
- website: www.holidayhomescotland.com

B & B
The Garden House, Whitmuir, SELKIRK,
Borders TD7 4PZ
Tel: 01750 721728
- e-mail: whitmuir@btconnect.com
- website: www.whitmuirfarm.co.uk

B & B
The Meadows, 4 Robinsland Drive, WEST
LINTON, Nr Edinburgh, Peeblesshire EH46 7JD
Tel: 01968 661798
- e-mail: mwthain@btinternet.com
- website: www.themeadowsbandb.co.uk

Self-Catering
Mrs C. M. Kilpatrick, Slipperfield House,
WEST LINTON, Peeblesshire EH46 7AA
Tel: 01968 660401
- e-mail: cottages@slipperfield.com
- website: www.slipperfield.com

•DUMFRIES & GALLOWAY

Self-Catering
Cloud Cuckoo Lodge, CASTLE DOUGLAS
Contact: Mrs Lesley Wykes, Cuckoostone
Cottage, St John's Town Of Dalry, Castle
Douglas DG7 3UA Tel: 01644 430375
- e-mail: enquiries@cloudcuckoolodge.co.uk
- website: www.cloudcuckoolodge.co.uk

Guest House
Celia Pickup, Craigadam, CASTLE
DOUGLAS, Kirkcudbrightshire DG7 3HU
Tel: 01556 650233
- website: www.craigadam.com

Self-Catering
Barend Holiday Village, Barend Farmhouse,
SANDYHILLS, Dalbeattie, Dumfries &
Galloway DG5 4NU
Tel: 01387 780663
- e-mail: info@barendholidayvillage.co.uk
- website: www.barendholidayvillage.co.uk

Self-Catering
Ae Farm Cottages, Gubhill Farm, Ae, DUMFRIES, Dumfriesshire DG1 1RL
Tel: 01387 860648
• e-mail: gill@gubhill.co.uk
• website: www.aefarmcottages.co.uk

Farm / Camping & Caravans / Self-Catering
Barnsoul Farm Holidays, Barnsoul Farm, Shawhead, DUMFRIES, Dumfriesshire DG2 9SQ. Tel: 01387 730249
• e-mail: barnsouldg@aol.com
• website: www.barnsoulfarm.co.uk

Self-Catering
Hope Cottage, THORNHILL, Dumfries & Galloway DG3 5BJ
Contact: Mrs S. Stannett Tel: 01848 500228
• e-mail: a.stann@btinternet.com
• website: www.hopecottage.co.uk

• EDINBURGH & LOTHIANS

Guest House
Kenvie Guest House, 16 Kilmaurs Road, EDINBURGH EH16 5DA
Tel: 0131 6601964
• e-mail: dorothy@kenvie.co.uk
• website: www.kenvie.co.uk

Guest House
International Guest House, 37 Mayfield Gardens, EDINBURGH EH9 2BX
Tel: 0131 667 2511
• e-mail: intergh1@yahoo.co.uk
• website: www.accommodation-edinburgh.com

• HIGHLANDS

Self-Catering
Cairngorm Highland Bungalows, AVIEMORE.
Contact: Linda Murray, 29 Grampian View, Aviemore, Inverness-shire PH22 1TF
Tel: 01479 810653
• e-mail: linda.murray@virgin.net
• website: www.cairngorm-bungalows.co.uk

Self Catering
Frank & Juliet Spencer-Nairn, Culligran Cottages, Struy, Near BEAULY, Inverness-shire IV4 7JX . Tel: 01463 761285
• e-mail: info@culligrancottages.co.uk
• website: www.culligrancottages.co.uk

Self-Catering
Tyndrum, BOAT OF GARTEN, Inverness-shire
Contact: Mrs Naomi C. Clark, Dochlaggie, Boat of Garten PH24 3BU
Tel: 01479 831242
• e-mail: dochlaggie99@aol.com

Self-Catering
The Treehouse, BOAT OF GARTEN, Inverness-shire
Contact: Anne Mather Tel: 0131 337 7167
• e-mail: fhg@treehouselodge.plus.com
• website: www.treehouselodge.co.uk

Guest House
Mrs Lynn Benge, The Pines Country House, Duthil, CARRBRIDGE, Inverness-shire PH23 3ND
Tel: 01479 841220
• e-mail: lynn@thepines-duthil.co.uk
• website: www.thepines-duthil.co.uk

Self-Catering
Carol Hughes, Glenurquhart Lodges, Balnain, DRUMNADROCHIT, Inverness-shire IV63 6TJ
Tel: 01456 476234
• e-mail: info@glenurquhart-lodges.co.uk
• website: www.glenurquhart-lodges.co.uk

Hotel
The Clan MacDuff Hotel, Achintore Road, FORT WILLIAM, Inverness-shire PH33 6RW
Tel: 01397 702341
• e-mail: reception@clanmacduff.co.uk
• website: www.clanmacduff.co.uk

Golf Club
Golspie Golf Club, Ferry Road, GOLSPIE, Sutherland, Highlands KW10 6SY
Tel: 01408 633 266
• e-mail: info@golspie-golf-club.co.uk
• website: www.golspie-golf-club.co.uk

Caravan & Camping
Auchnahillin Caravan & Camping Park, Daviot East, INVERNESS, Inverness-shire IV2 5XQ. Tel: 01463 772286
• e-mail: info@auchnahillin.co.uk
• website: www.auchnahillin.co.uk

Hotel
Kintail Lodge Hotel, Glenshiel, KYLE OF LOCHALSH, Ross-shire IV40 8HL
Tel: 01599 511275
• e-mail: kintaillodgehotel@btinternet.com
• website: www.kintaillodgehotel.co.uk

Hotel
Whitebridge Hotel, Whitebridge, LOCH NESS, Inverness-shire IV2 6UN
Tel: 01456 486626
• e-mail: info@whitebridgehotel.co.uk
• website: www.whitebridgehotel.co.uk

B & B / Self-Catering Chalets
Mondhuie Chalets and B&B, Mondhuie, NETHY BRIDGE, Inverness-shire PH25 3DF
Tel: 01479 821062
• e-mail: david@mondhuie.com
• website: www.mondhuie.com

WEBSITE DIRECTORY 249

Self-Catering
Innes Maree Bungalows, POOLEWE, Ross-shire IV22 2JU
Tel: 01445 781454
* e-mail: info@poolewebungalows.com
* website: www.poolewebungalows.com

Hotel / Sporting Lodge
Borgie Lodge Hotel, SKERRAY, Sutherland KW14 7TH Tel: 01641 521332
* e-mail: info@borgielodgehotel.co.uk
* website: www.borgielodgehotel.co.uk

•LANARKSHIRE

Caravan & Holiday Home Park
Mount View Caravan Park, Station Road, ABINGTON, South Lanarkshire ML12 6RW
Tel: 01864 502808
* e-mail: info@mountviewcaravanpark.co.uk
* website: www.mountviewcaravanpark.co.uk

Self-Catering
Carmichael Country Cottages, Carmichael Estate Office, Westmains, Carmichael, BIGGAR, Lanarkshire ML12 6PG
Tel: 01899 308336
* e-mail: chiefcarm@aol.com
* website: www.carmichael.co.uk/cottages

Farm B & B
Dykecroft Farm, Kirkmuirhall, LESMAHAGOW, Lanarkshire ML11 0JQ
Tel: 01555 892226
* e-mail: dykecroft.bandb@tiscali.co.uk
* website: www.dykecroftfarm.co.uk

•PERTH & KINROSS

Self-Catering
Loch Tay Lodges, Remony, Acharn, ABERFELDY, Perthshire PH15 2HS
Tel: 01887 830209
* e-mail: remony@btinternet.com
* website: www.lochtaylodges.co.uk

Self-Catering Cottages
Dalmunzie Highland Cottages, SPITTAL OF GLENSHEE, Blairgowrie, Perthshire PH10 7QE Tel: 01250 885226
* e-mail: enquiries@dalmunziecottages.com
* website: www.dalmunziecottages.com

Self-Catering
Ardoch Lodge, STRATHYRE, Near Callander, Perthshire FK18 8NF
Tel: 01877 384666
* e-mail: ardoch@btinternet.com
* website: www.ardochlodge.co.uk

•STIRLING & TROSSACHS

Hotel
Culcreuch Castle Hotel & Estate, Kippen Road, FINTRY, Stirlingshire G63 0LW
Tel: 01360 860555
* e-mail: info@culcreuch.com
* website: www.culcreuch.com

•WALES

Self-Catering
Quality Cottages, Cerbid, Solva, HAVERFORDWEST, Pembrokeshire SA62 6YE
Tel: 01348 837871
* website: www.qualitycottages.co.uk

•ANGLESEY & GWYNEDD

Self-Catering / Caravan Site
Bryn Gloch Caravan and Camping Park, Betws Garmon, CAERNARFON, Gwynedd LL54 7YY Tel: 01286 650216
* e-mail: eurig@bryngloch.co.uk
* website: www.bryngloch.co.uk

Self-Catering
Parc Wernol, Chwilog Fawr, Chwilog, Pwllheli, CRICCIETH, Gwynedd LL53 6SW
Tel: 01766 810506
* e-mail: catherine@wernol.co.uk
* website: www.wernol.co.uk

Caravan & Camping Site
Marian Rees, Dôl Einion, Tal-y-Llyn, TYWYN, Gwynedd LL36 9AJ
Tel: 01654 761312
* e-mail: marianrees@tiscali.co.uk

•CARMARTHENSHIRE

Self-Catering
The Old Stables Cottage, Wren Cottage & The Farmhouse, Sir Johns Hill Farm, Gosport Street, LAUGHARNE, Carmarthenshire SA33 4TD
Tel: 01994 427001
* website: www.sirjohnshillfarm.co.uk

www.holidayguides.com

250 WEBSITE DIRECTORY

• CEREDIGION

Hotel
Queensbridge Hotel, Victoria Terrace, ABERYSTWYTH, Ceredigion SY23 2DH
Tel: 01970 612343
• e-mail: queensbridgehotel@btinternet.com
• website: www.queensbridgehotel.com
www.queensbridgehotelaberystwyth.co.uk

• PEMBROKESHIRE

Country House
Angelica Rees, Heathfield Mansion, Letterston, Near FISHGUARD, Pembrokeshire SA62 5EG
Tel: 01348 840263
• e-mail: angelica.rees@virgin.net
• website: www.heathfieldaccommodation.co.uk

Hotel
Trewern Arms Hotel, Nevern, NEWPORT, Pembrokeshire SA42 0NB
Tel: 01239 820395
• e-mail: info@trewern-arms-pembrokeshire.co.uk
• www.trewern-arms-pembrokeshire.co.uk

Self-catering
Ffynnon Ddofn, ST DAVIDS, Pembrokeshire. Contact: Mrs B. Rees White, Brick House Farm, Burnham Road, Woodham Mortimer, Maldon, Essex CM9 6SR. Tel: 01245 224611
• e-mail: daisypops@madasafish.com
• website: www.ffynnonddofn.co.uk

Golf Club
Tenby Golf Club, The Burrows, TENBY, Pembrokeshire SA70 7NP
Tel: 01834 842978
• e-mail: tenbygolfclub@uku.co.uk
• website: www.tenbygolf.co.uk

• POWYS

Self-Catering
Mrs Jones, Penllwyn Lodges, GARTHMYL, Powys SY15 6SB
Tel: 01686 640269
• e-mail: daphne.jones@onetel.net
• website: www.penllwynlodges.co.uk

Self-Catering
Old Stables Cottage & Old Dairy, Lane Farm, Paincastle, Builth Wells, HAY-ON-WYE, Powys LD2 3JS
Tel: 01497 851 605
• e-mail: lanefarm@onetel.com
• website: www.lane-farm.co.uk

Caravan Holiday Home
Mr & Mrs P. N. Tolson, The Pines Caravan Park, Doldowlod, LLANDRINDOD WELLS, Powys LD1 6NN
Tel: 01597 810068
• e-mail: info@pinescaravanpark.co.uk
• website: www.pinescaravanpark.co.uk

• SOUTH WALES

B & B / Self-Catering Cottages
Mrs Norma James, Wyrloed Lodge, Manmoel, BLACKWOOD, Caerphilly, South Wales NP12 0RN
Tel: 01495 371198
• e-mail: norma.james@btinternet.com
• website: www.btinternet.com/~norma.james/

Self-Catering
Cwrt-y-Gaer, Wolvesnewton, USK, Monmouthshire, South Wales NP16 6PR
Tel: 01291 650700
• e-mail: info@cwrt-y-gaer.co.uk
• website: www.cwrt-y-gaer.co.uk

• IRELAND

CO. CLARE

Self-Catering
Ballyvaughan Village & Country Holiday Homes, BALLYVAUGHAN.
Contact: George Quinn, Frances Street, Kilrush, Co. Clare Tel: 00 353 65 9051977
• e-mail: vchh@iol.ie
• website: www.ballyvaughan-cottages.com

Looking for holiday accommodation?
for details of hundreds of properties
throughout the UK visit:

www.holidayguides.com

Index of Towns and Counties

Aberfeldy, Perth & Kinross	SCOTLAND
Abergavenny, South Wales	WALES
Abergele, North Wales	WALES
Aberlour, Aberdeen, Banff & Moray	SCOTLAND
Aberystwyth, Ceredigion	WALES
Abington, Lanarkshire	SCOTLAND
Alford, Lincolnshire	MIDLANDS
Alyth, Perth & Kinross	SCOTLAND
Ambleside, Cumbria	NORTH WEST
Anglesey, Anglesey & Gwynedd	WALES
Antrim, Co. Antrim	NORTHERN IRELAND
Appleby-in-Westmorland, Cumbria	NORTH WEST
Arbroath, Angus & Dundee	SCOTLAND
Arundel, West Sussex	SOUTH EAST
Ashbourne, Derbyshire	MIDLANDS
Ashill, Norfolk	EAST
Aston Cantlow, Warwickshire	MIDLANDS
Attleborough, Norfolk	EAST
Auchterarder, Perth & Kinross	SCOTLAND
Aviemore, Highlands	SCOTLAND
Ayr, Ayrshire & Arran	SCOTLAND
Bakewell, Derbyshire	MIDLANDS
Bala, Anglesey & Gwynedd	WALES
Baldock, Hertfordshire	EAST
Ballater, Aberdeen, Banff & Moray	SCOTLAND
Ballycastle, Antrim	N. IRELAND
Ballywalter, Co Down	N. IRELAND
Bamburgh, Northumberland	NORTH EAST
Banbury, Oxfordshire	SOUTH EAST
Banchory, Aberdeen, Banff & Moray	SCOTLAND
Bangor-on-Dee, North Wales	WALES
Barmouth, Anglesey & Gwynedd	WALES
Barnard Castle, Durham	NORTH EAST
Barrhill, Ayrshire & Arran	SCOTLAND
Bath, Somerset	SOUTH WEST
Battle, East Sussex	SOUTH EAST
Beauly, Highlands	SCOTLAND
Beccles, Suffolk	EAST
Benllech, Anglesey & Gwynedd	WALES
Berwick-upon-Tweed, Northumberland	NORTH EAST
Betws-y-Coed, North Wales	WALES
Bewdley, Worcestershire	MIDLANDS
Biddenden, Kent	SOUTH EAST
Birchington, Kent	SOUTH EAST
Bishop Auckland, Durham	NORTH EAST
Blackpool, Lancashire	NORTH WEST
Blackwood, South Wales	WALES
Blair Atholl, Perth & Kinross	SCOTLAND
Blair Drummond, Stirling & Trossachs	SCOTLAND
Blairgowrie, Perth & Kinross	SCOTLAND
Blandford, Dorset	SOUTH WEST
Bodiam, East Sussex	SOUTH EAST
Bodmin, Cornwall	SOUTH WEST
Bognor Regis, West Sussex	SOUTH EAST
Boston, Lincolnshire	MIDLANDS
Branscombe, Devon	SOUTH WEST
Brean, Somerset	SOUTH WEST
Brechin, Angus & Dundee	SCOTLAND
Brecon, Powys	WALES
Bridgwater, Somerset	SOUTH WEST
Bridlington, East Yorkshire	YORKSHIRE
Brixham, Devon	SOUTH WEST
Broadway, Worcestershire	MIDLANDS
Brompton-on-Swale, North Yorkshire	YORKSHIRE
Bromyard, Worcestershire	MIDLANDS
Bucklesham, Suffolk	EAST
Bude, Cornwall	SOUTH WEST
Builth Wells, Powys	WALES
Bungay, Suffolk	EAST
Burnham-on-Sea, Somerset	SOUTH WEST
Bushmills, Antrim	N. IRELAND
Buxton, Derbyshire	MIDLANDS
Caernarfon, Anglesey & Gwynedd	WALES
Caister-on-Sea, Norfolk	EAST
Calne, Wiltshire	SOUTH WEST
Carnforth, Lancashire	NORTH WEST
Carradale, Argyll & Bute	SCOTLAND
Castle Douglas, Dumfries & Galloway	SCOTLAND
Charlbury, Oxfordshire	SOUTH EAST
Chester, Cheshire	NORTH WEST
Chichester, West Sussex	SOUTH EAST
Chipping Norton, Oxfordshire	SOUTH EAST
Chudleigh, Devon	SOUTH WEST
Cirencester, Gloucestershire	SOUTH WEST
Clacton-on-Sea, Essex	EAST
Cleethorpes, Lincolnshire	MIDLANDS
Colchester, Essex	EAST
Coldingham, Borders	SCOTLAND
Coleford, Gloucestershire	SOUTH WEST
Coleraine, Londonderry	N. IRELAND
Colyton, Devon	SOUTH WEST

INDEX OF TOWNS AND COUNTIES

Combe Martin, Devon	SOUTH WEST
Comberton, Cambridgeshire	EAST
Coniston, Cumbria	NORTH WEST
Corbridge, Northumberland	NORTH EAST
Cotswolds, Gloucestershire	SOUTH WEST
Coverack, Cornwall	SOUTH WEST
Crackington Haven, Cornwall	SOUTH WEST
Crail, Fife	SCOTLAND
Crediton, Devon	SOUTH WEST
Criccieth, Anglesey & Gwynedd	WALES
Cromer, Norfolk	EAST
Cullompton, Devon	SOUTH WEST
Dalbeattie, Dumfries & Galloway	SCOTLAND
Dartmouth, Devon	SOUTH WEST
Dawlish Warren, Devon	SOUTH WEST
Dawlish, Devon	SOUTH WEST
Devizes, Wiltshire	SOUTH WEST
Dial Post, West Sussex	SOUTH EAST
Dingwall, Highlands	SCOTLAND
Diss, Norfolk	EAST
Dolgellau, Anglesey & Gwynedd	WALES
Dorchester, Dorset	SOUTH WEST
Doune, Stirling & Trossachs	SCOTLAND
Dulverton, Somerset	SOUTH WEST
Dumfries, Dumfries & Galloway	SCOTLAND
Dunbar, Edinburgh & Lothians	SCOTLAND
Duns, Borders	SCOTLAND
Easingwold, North Yorkshire	YORKSHIRE
Eastbourne, East Sussex	SOUTH EAST
Eastergate, West Sussex	SOUTH EAST
Edmonton, London, (Central & Greater)	LONDON
Elgin, Aberdeen, Banff & Moray	SCOTLAND
Ellesmere, Shropshire	MIDLANDS
Ely, Cambridgeshire	EAST
Enniskillen, Fermanagh	N IRELAND
Ettrick Valley, Borders	SCOTLAND
Evesham, Worcestershire	MIDLANDS
Exmouth, Devon	SOUTH WEST
Fakenham, Norfolk	EAST
Felixstowe, Suffolk	EAST
Filey, North Yorkshire	YORKSHIRE
Fintry, Stirling & Trossachs	SCOTLAND
Flamborough, East Yorkshire	YORKSHIRE
Fleetwood, Lancashire	NORTH WEST
Flookburgh, Cumbria	NORTH WEST
Forfar, Angus & Dundee	SCOTLAND
Fort William, Highlands	SCOTLAND
Gairloch, Highlands	SCOTLAND
Gateshead, Tyne & Wear	NORTH EAST
Girvan, Ayrshire & Arran	SCOTLAND
Glamis, Angus & Dundee	SCOTLAND
Glencoe, Argyll & Bute	SCOTLAND
Glenrothes, Fife	SCOTLAND
Glossop, Derbyshire	MIDLANDS
Gower, South Wales	WALES
Grange-over-Sands, Cumbria	NORTH WEST
Grantham, Lincolnshire	MIDLANDS
Grantown-on-Spey, Highlands	SCOTLAND
Great Shelford, Cambridgeshire	EAST
Great Yarmouth, Norfolk	EAST
Halesowen, West Midlands	MIDLANDS
Hanley Swan, Worcestershire	MIDLANDS
Harleston, Norfolk	EAST
Harrogate, North Yorkshire	YORKSHIRE
Hastings, East Sussex	SOUTH EAST
Haverfordwest, Pembrokeshire	WALES
Hawes, North Yorkshire	YORKSHIRE
Hayling Island, Hampshire	SOUTH EAST
Helmsley, North Yorkshire	YORKSHIRE
Helston, Cornwall	SOUTH WEST
Hemel Hempstead, Hertfordshire	EAST
Hereford, Herefordshire	MIDLANDS
Hertford, Hertfordshire	EAST
Hexham, Northumberland	NORTH EAST
Highcliffe-on-Sea, Dorset	SOUTH WEST
Hillsborough, Co Down	N. IRELAND
Holmes Chapel, Cheshire	NORTH WEST
Holsworthy, Devon	SOUTH WEST
Holt, Norfolk	EAST
Hope Valley, Derbyshire	MIDLANDS
Horncastle, Lincolnshire	MIDLANDS
Hunstanton, Norfolk	EAST
Huntingdon, Cambridgeshire	EAST
Hutton-le-Hole, North Yorkshire	YORKSHIRE
Ilfracombe, Devon	SOUTH WEST
Inveraray, Argyll & Bute	SCOTLAND
Inverness, Highlands	SCOTLAND
Ipswich, Suffolk	EAST
Jedburgh, Borders	SCOTLAND
John O Groats, Highlands	SCOTLAND
Kendal, Cumbria	NORTH WEST
Kesh, Fermanagh	N IRELAND
Keswick, Cumbria	NORTH WEST
Kidderminster, Worcestershire	MIDLANDS
Kilkeel, Co Down	N IRELAND
Killorglin, Co. Kerry	IRELAND
Killyleagh, Co Down	N IRELAND
Kinghorn, Fife	SCOTLAND

INDEX OF TOWNS AND COUNTIES 253

Kings Lynn, Norfolk	EAST
Kingsbridge, Devon	SOUTH WEST
Kinlochleven, Argyll & Bute	SCOTLAND
Kirkbymoorside, North Yorkshire	YORKSHIRE
Kirkwall, Orkney	SCOTLAND
Laide, Highlands	SCOTLAND
Lancaster, Lancashire	NORTH WEST
Lauragh, Co. Kerry	IRELAND
Leiston, Suffolk	EAST
Leominster, Herefordshire	MIDLANDS
Leven, Fife	SCOTLAND
Leyburn, North Yorkshire	YORKSHIRE
Linlithgow, Edinburgh & Lothians	SCOTLAND
Little Asby, Cumbria	NORTH WEST
Little Tarrington, Herefordshire	MIDLANDS
Llanarth, Ceredigion	WALES
Llandovery, Carmarthenshire	WALES
Llandysul, Ceredigion	WALES
Llangadog, Carmarthenshire	WALES
Llantwit Major, South Wales	WALES
Llanuwchllyn, Anglesey & Gwynedd	WALES
Loch Lomond, Argyll & Bute	SCOTLAND
Loch Rannoch, Perth & Kinross	SCOTLAND
Lochearnhead, Perth & Kinross	SCOTLAND
Lochinver, Highlands	SCOTLAND
London, (Central & Greater)	LONDON
Longniddry, Edinburgh & Lothians	SCOTLAND
Looe, Cornwall	SOUTH WEST
Loughton, London, (Central & Greater)	LONDON
Lower Wick, Gloucestershire	SOUTH WEST
Lowestoft, Suffolk	EAST
Lune Valley, Lancashire	NORTH WEST
Lutterworth, Leicestershire	MIDLANDS
Mablethorpe, Lincolnshire	MIDLANDS
Macclesfield, Cheshire	NORTH WEST
MacDuff, Aberdeen, Banff & Moray	SCOTLAND
Maldon, Essex	EAST
Malvern, Worcestershire	MIDLANDS
Manorbier, Pembrokeshire	WALES
Mansfield, Nottinghamshire	MIDLANDS
Market Bosworth, Warwickshire	MIDLANDS
Market Harborough, Leicestershire	MIDLANDS
Market Rasen, Lincolnshire	MIDLANDS
Marston, West Midlands	MIDLANDS
Matlock, Derbyshire	MIDLANDS
Mawgan Porth, Cornwall	SOUTH WEST
Meriden, West Midlands	MIDLANDS
Merthyr Tydfil, South Wales	WALES
Milford-on-Sea, Hampshire	SOUTH EAST
Milton Keynes, Buckinghamshire	SOUTH EAST
Minehead, Somerset	SOUTH WEST
Modbury, Devon	SOUTH WEST
Mold, North Wales	WALES
Monifieth, Angus & Dundee	SCOTLAND
Monmouth, South Wales	WALES
Moreton-in-Marsh, Gloucestershire	SOUTH WEST
Motherwell, Lanarkshire	SCOTLAND
Mundesley, Norfolk	EAST
Nairn, Highlands	SCOTLAND
New Beaconsfield, Buckinghamshire	SOUTH EAST
Newark, Nottinghamshire	MIDLANDS
Newby Bridge, Cumbria	NORTH WEST
Newcastle Emlyn, Carmarthenshire	WALES
Newcastle, Co Down	N IRELAND
Newcastle-upon-Tyne, Tyne & Wear	NORTH EAST
Newport Pagnell, Buckinghamshire	SOUTH EAST
Newquay, Cornwall	SOUTH WEST
Newton Abbot, Devon	SOUTH WEST
Newton Stewart, Dumfries & Galloway	SCOTLAND
North Walsham, Norfolk	EAST
Northallerton, North Yorkshire	YORKSHIRE
Northwich, Cheshire	NORTH WEST
Norwich, Norfolk	EAST
Oakham, Leicestershire	MIDLANDS
Oban, Argyll & Bute	SCOTLAND
Olney, Buckinghamshire	SOUTH EAST
Orcheston, Wiltshire	SOUTH WEST
Otterburn, Northumberland	NORTH EAST
Padstow, Cornwall	SOUTH WEST
Paignton, Devon	SOUTH WEST
Peebles, Borders	SCOTLAND
Penrith, Cumbria	NORTH WEST
Penzance, Cornwall	SOUTH WEST
Perranporth, Cornwall	SOUTH WEST
Peterborough, Cambridgeshire	EAST
Peterchurch, Herefordshire	MIDLANDS
Pickering, North Yorkshire	YORKSHIRE
Pidley, Cambridgeshire	EAST
Pitlochry, Perth & Kinross	SCOTLAND
Polzeath, Cornwall	SOUTH WEST
Poole, Dorset	SOUTH WEST
Porlock, Somerset	SOUTH WEST
Porthmadog, Anglesey & Gwynedd	WALES
Portstewart, Londonderry	N IRELAND
Poulton-le-Fylde, Lancashire	NORTH WEST
Prees, Shropshire	MIDLANDS

INDEX OF TOWNS AND COUNTIES

Prestatyn, North Wales	WALES
Preston, Lancashire	NORTH WEST
Pwllheli, Anglesey & Gwynedd	WALES
Radcliffe-on-Trent, Nottinghamshire	MIDLANDS
Radnage, Buckinghamshire	SOUTH EAST
Redruth, Cornwall	SOUTH WEST
Rhayader, Powys	WALES
Ringwood, Hampshire	SOUTH EAST
Ripley, Derbyshire	MIDLANDS
Rochdale, Lancashire	NORTH WEST
Romsey, Hampshire	SOUTH EAST
Ross-on-Wye, Herefordshire	MIDLANDS
Royston, Hertfordshire	EAST
Rugby, Warwickshire	MIDLANDS
St Agnes, Cornwall	SOUTH WEST
St Andrews, Fife	SCOTLAND
St Austell, Cornwall	SOUTH WEST
St Davids, Pembrokeshire	WALES
St Ives, Cornwall	SOUTH WEST
Salcombe, Devon	SOUTH WEST
Salisbury, Wiltshire	SOUTH WEST
Saltfleet, Lincolnshire	MIDLANDS
Sandringham, Norfolk	EAST
Saundersfoot, Pembrokeshire	WALES
Scarborough, North Yorkshire	YORKSHIRE
Scourie, Highlands	SCOTLAND
Seaton, Devon	SOUTH WEST
Sheringham, Norfolk	EAST
Shielbridge, Highlands	SCOTLAND
Shrewsbury, Shropshire	MIDLANDS
Silloth-on-Solway, Cumbria	NORTH WEST
Skegness, Lincolnshire	MIDLANDS
Skelmorlie, Ayrshire & Arran	SCOTLAND
Slimbridge, Gloucestershire	SOUTH WEST
Snowdonia, Anglesey & Gwynedd	WALES
South Molton, Devon	SOUTH WEST
South Shields, Tyne & Wear	NORTH EAST
Southminster, Essex	EAST
Southsea, Hampshire	SOUTH EAST
Sproatley, East Yorkshire	YORKSHIRE
Standlake, Oxfordshire	SOUTH EAST
Stanford Bishop, Herefordshire	MIDLANDS
Stepps, Lanarkshire	SCOTLAND
Stirling, Stirling & Trossachs	SCOTLAND
Stoke-on-Trent, Staffordshire	MIDLANDS
Stourport on Severn, Worcestershire	MIDLANDS
Stowmarket, Suffolk	EAST
Stranraer, Dumfries & Galloway	SCOTLAND
Stratford-upon-Avon, Warwickshire	MIDLANDS
Sutton Coldfield, West Midlands	MIDLANDS
Sutton in Ashfield, Nottinghamshire	MIDLANDS
Sutton-on-Sea, Lincolnshire	MIDLANDS
Swadlincote, Derbyshire	MIDLANDS
Swaffham, Norfolk	EAST
Tal-y-Llyn, Anglesey & Gwynedd	WALES
Tarbert, Argyll & Bute	SCOTLAND
Tattershall, Lincolnshire	MIDLANDS
Taunton, Somerset	SOUTH WEST
Tavistock, Devon	SOUTH WEST
Tayinloan, Argyll & Bute	SCOTLAND
Telford, Shropshire	MIDLANDS
Tenby, Pembrokeshire	WALES
Tewkesbury, Gloucestershire	SOUTH WEST
Thornbury, Devon	SOUTH WEST
Trearddur Bay, Anglesey & Gwynedd	WALES
Trimingham, Norfolk	EAST
Truro, Cornwall	SOUTH WEST
Tuxford, Nottinghamshire	MIDLANDS
Ullswater, Cumbria	NORTH WEST
Uttoxeter, Staffordshire	MIDLANDS
Wadebridge, Cornwall	SOUTH WEST
Waltham Cross, Hertfordshire	EAST
Walton-on-the-Naze, Essex	EAST
Wareham, Dorset	SOUTH WEST
Warwick, Warwickshire	MIDLANDS
Watchet, Somerset	SOUTH WEST
Weeley, Essex	EAST
Wells-next-the-Sea, Norfolk	EAST
Welshpool, Powys	WALES
West Bexington, Dorset	SOUTH WEST
Westbury, Wiltshire	SOUTH WEST
Weston-under-Lizard, Staffordshire	MIDLANDS
Westray, Orkney	SCOTLAND
Wetherby, North Yorkshire	YORKSHIRE
Weymouth, Dorset	SOUTH WEST
Whitby, North Yorkshire	YORKSHIRE
Wimborne, Dorset	SOUTH WEST
Windermere, Cumbria	NORTH WEST
Wirral, Cheshire	NORTH WEST
Wisbech, Cambridgeshire	EAST
Withernsea, East Yorkshire	YORKSHIRE
Wokingham, Berkshire	SOUTH EAST
Wolvey, Leicestershire & Rutland	MIDLANDS
Woodbridge, Suffolk	EAST
Wookey Hole, Somerset	SOUTH WEST
Wool, Dorset	SOUTH WEST
Woolacombe, Devon	SOUTH WEST
Worksop, Nottinghamshire	MIDLANDS
York, North Yorkshire	YORKSHIRE

Other FHG titles for 2009

255

FHG Guides Ltd have a large range of attractive holiday accommodation guides for all kinds of holiday opportunities throughout Britain. They also make useful gifts at any time of year. Our guides are available in most bookshops and larger newsagents but we will be happy to post you a copy direct if you have any difficulty. POST FREE for addresses in the UK. We will also post abroad but have to charge separately for post or freight.

FHG KUPERARD

£7.99

500 Great Places to Stay in Britain
- Coast & Country Holidays
- Full range of family accommodation

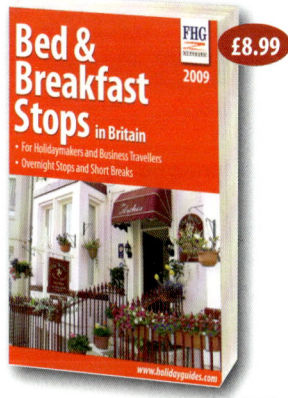

£8.99

Bed & Breakfast Stops in Britain
- For holidaymakers and business travellers
- Overnight stops and Short Breaks

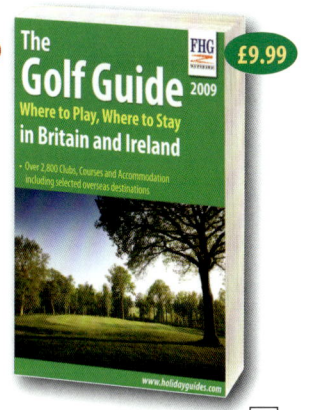

£9.99

The Golf Guide
Where to play, Where to stay.
- Over 2800 golf courses in Britain with convenient accommodation.
- Holiday Golf in France, Portugal, Spain, USA and Thailand.

£9.99

The Original Pets Welcome!
- The bestselling guide to holidays for pets and their owners

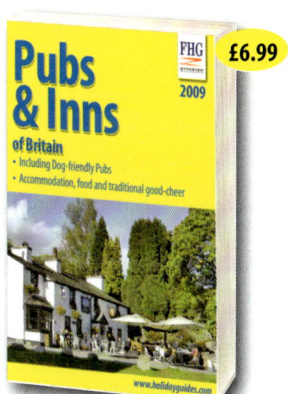

£6.99

Pubs & Inns of Britain
- Including Dog-friendly Pubs
- Accommodation, food and traditional good cheer

£7.99

Weekend & Short Breaks in Britain
- Accommodation for holidays and weekends away

Family Breaks £7.99	**Self-Catering Holidays** £8.99	**Country Hotels** £6.99
☐	☐	☐
Family Breaks in Britain • Accommodation, attractions and resorts • Suitable for those with children and babies	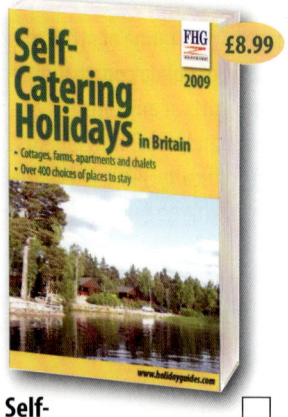 **Self-Catering Holidays** in Britain • Cottages, farms, apartments and chalets • Over 400 places to stay	**Country Hotels** of Britain • Hotels with Conference, Leisure and Wedding Facilities

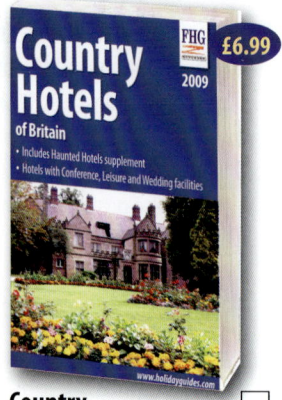

Tick your choice above and send your order and payment to

**FHG Guides Ltd. Abbey Mill Business Centre
Seedhill, Paisley, Scotland PA1 1TJ
TEL: 0141- 887 0428 • FAX: 0141- 889 7204
e-mail: admin@fhguides.co.uk**

Deduct 10% for 2/3 titles or copies; 20% for 4 or more.

Send to: NAME ....

   ADDRESS ....

   ....

   ....

   POST CODE ....

I enclose Cheque/Postal Order for £ ....

   SIGNATURE ....DATE ....

Please complete the following to help us improve the service we provide.
How did you find out about our guides?:

☐ Press   ☐ Magazines   ☐ TV/Radio   ☐ Family/Friend   ☐ Other